THE COMPLETE GUIDE TO AFFILIATE MARKETING ON THE WEB

HOW TO USE AND PROFIT FROM AFFILIATE MARKETING PROGRAMS

BY BRUCE C. BROWN

THE COMPLETE GUIDE TO AFFILIATE MARKETING ON THE WEB: HOW TO USE AND PROFIT FROM AFFILIATE MARKETING PROGRAMS

Copyright © 2009 Atlantic Publishing Group, Inc.
1405 SW 6th Avenue • Ocala, Florida 34471 • Phone 800-814-1132 • Fax 352-622-1875
Web site: www.atlantic-pub.com • E-mail: sales@atlantic-pub.com
SAN Number: 268-1250

ISBN-13: 978-1-60138-125-5   ISBN-10: 1-60138-125-5

Library of Congress Cataloging-in-Publication Data

Brown, Bruce C. (Bruce Cameron), 1965-
   The complete guide to affiliate marketing on the Web : how to use and profit from affiliate marketing programs / by Bruce C. Brown.
      p. cm.
   Includes bibliographical references and index.
   ISBN-13: 978-1-60138-125-5 (alk. paper)
   ISBN-10: 1-60138-125-5 (alk. paper)
   1. Affiliate programs (World Wide Web) 2. Internet marketing. I.
Title. II. Title: Guide to affiliate marketing on the Web. III. Title:
Affiliate marketing on the Web.

   HF5415.1265.B763 2008
   658.8'72--dc22
                              2008041330

Printed in the United States

Printed on Recycled Paper

PROJECT MANAGER: Melissa Peterson • mpeterson@atlantic-pub.com
INTERIOR DESIGN: Nicole Deck • ndeck@atlantic-pub.com

Author Dedication

This book is dedicated to my beautiful wife.

Where would I be without you in my life all these years?

Bruce C. Brown

"In war there is no substitute for victory."

— The Godfather, 1972

""Go — proclaim liberty throughout all the lands, and to all the inhabitants thereof."

— The Ten Commandments, 1956

Table of Contents

Foreword

Affiliate Marketing is a fantastic way for Internet-savvy entrepreneurs to make money on the Web. While the possibilities for making money online are endless, affiliate marketing is one of the most dynamic ways to do so. Unlike many endeavors, affiliate marketing gives *everyone* an equal opportunity to make money with their passions. Sports car enthusiasts, gardeners, and video-game connoisseurs can all try their hand at affiliate marketing, learn what works and what does not, and earn an income promoting things they enjoy. If you have the patience and dedication to build a well-constructed site, affiliate marketing can help you build a thriving part-time or full-time business doing what you love.

There are numerous ways to integrate affiliate links into your online content, such as linking a picture of a product on your blog to an online store where a user can buy that product, showing actual items for sale that are related to your content, or even just integrating a banner ad or text links. When used effectively, affiliate marketing can help you make ads feel less like advertising and more like content, improving the experience for your users. Because affiliate compensation is linked to the sales and leads that you drive for your advertisers, you also have the potential to earn more money than you could with banner or paid search ads.

If you are considering becoming an affiliate, *The Complete Guide to Affiliate Marketing on the Web* is a very good place to start. The book goes into detail about selecting programs that are right for you, the importance of generating unique and quality content, and attracting customers that will earn you a return. It includes common mistakes and interviews with successful affiliates, who offer many tips and tricks that they have learned along the way.

If you are an online retailer or are looking to drive more traffic to your own site, this book also offers step-by-step guidance for setting up an affiliate program to attract new customers. By following these guidelines, business owners can increase revenues and grow their businesses by essentially recruiting a network of marketers to help promote their products.

At eBay, for example, there are more than 100,000 affiliates that promote eBay products across the Web, driving a significant amount of traffic to eBay sites around the world. Our affiliates are a very important part of our online marketing efforts. eBay pays its affiliates a percentage of the revenue we make from that traffic in return and works closely with affiliates to ensure they are maximizing the effectiveness of their advertising space and driving quality traffic to eBay. Because these affiliates are driving traffic to eBay that the company might not have otherwise attracted, the result is a win-win for eBay and for its affiliates.

One of the things we have learned at eBay is that the most successful affiliates provide trustworthy, engaging sites for their visitors that include unique content and relevant affiliate offers. This ensures that the customers driven through the affiliate to the merchant site are interested in the products the affiliate is promoting and are, therefore, more likely to make a purchase. Engaged customers, as we call them, are much more profitable for both the affiliate and the business for which the affiliate is driving traffic. The Complete Guide will give you a very good set of basics on how to become a productive affiliate.

A few other tips to consider for driving good traffic include:

- Offer customers timely, relevant content and promote affiliate offers that will help customers solve a particular problem. This will make your site more valuable and ensure your customers come back to you.

- Know the products you are promoting and do not offer customers too many things at once. You will attract quality traffic by providing fewer, more trustworthy recommendations.

- Where possible, work closely with the merchants you are promoting to figure out what works best for them. It is likely they will have insights that will help you and your campaigns.

- It may sounds obvious, but read the terms and conditions from the merchants you want to work with. This is the Merchants' way of telling you how they want you to promote their program. They all have different rules and this may help you determine who you really want to work with. It can also help you avoid getting expired from their programs by employing tactics that are not allowed in their terms.

- Test, test, test is a mantra to live by in affiliate marketing. Try different layouts and copy, determine what works and fine-tune your campaign to maximize efficiency and profits. What works will be different for different types of affiliates, different products and merchants, so it is crucial for all affiliates to experiment and fine-tune.

Success in affiliate marketing, as with anything else, requires patience and a continued effort to learn and adapt to what works. Whether you are launching an affiliate program or an affiliate marketing campaign, *The*

Complete Guide to Affiliate Marketing on the Web is a great place to start your ongoing education. With this book and a healthy dose of entrepreneurial energy and creativity, you will be well on your way to success.

Best of luck!

Steve Hartman and Will Martin-Gill

eBay Partner Network

1 Introduction

This is the seventh book I have written, and the sixth in a series designed to help businesses and individuals increase revenue, improve advertisement and marketing programs, utilize technologies such as blogs, e-mail marketing and pay-per-click advertising to sell more products, improve communications, increase customer base, and expand their foothold on the marketplace. Affiliate marketing is the next logical topic to tackle, and in this book, I will provide you with a wealth of knowledge defining affiliate marketing, how you can use it to increase sales, generate revenue, and use the power of the Internet to increase your customer base exponentially.

When you think about affiliate marketing, there are two main ideas you need to understand. Your perspective on these ideas will drive how you deploy affiliate marketing for your Web site or business. Affiliate marketing is simply defined as: A Web-based marketing practice, often using automated systems or specialized software in which a business rewards their affiliate for each visitor, customer, or sale which is brought about as a result of the affiliate's marketing efforts. In most cases, the reward is monetary in the form of a monthly commission check. Most well-designed affiliate programs are easy to implement, require little or no setup, are free, and can instantly generate a new source of revenue for you.

Affiliate Marketing Options

Essentially, you have two affiliate marketing options.

- Host an affiliate program on your Web site so others can join your affiliate network and sell your products on their Web sites. They will earn a commission for each sale, and you will sell more products through them. This is the ultimate solution for those who have products to sell — imagine your products advertised for free on thousands of Web sites across the world.

- Join an affiliate network and sell other products on your Web site for which you will earn a commission on each sale. You do nothing and pay nothing. The setup is simple — all you do is keep the content updated with what you want to advertise on your Web site, and cash the monthly commission check.

My first real exposure to affiliate marketing was through trial and error. I placed an advertisement on my Web site and hoped that someone would click on it, make a purchase, and eventually, I would get a commission from that sale. This was not a fruitful venture, and ultimately, I removed the banner ads from my site. The reason it did not work was primarily due to a lack of marketing — effectively showcasing the products on my Web site — and the technical limitations of how the affiliate marketing program was deployed.

Establishing an affiliate marketing program of your own or joining someone else's affiliate program will, in itself, not generate substantial revenue for you unless you effectively deploy and administer it. Following this brief introduction we will get into the details of how to establish your own affiliate program or join an affiliate network and ensure that you are optimally positioned for success.

Think about the basic philosophy and principles of an affiliate marketing program: You can sell other people's products on your Web site for free, and they pay you a commission to do it. You do not ever touch the products; are not responsible for the sale, packaging, shipping, customer service, customer complaints, problem resolution, returns, or headaches; and for the simple act of allowing their products to be sold on your Web site, you get a monthly commission check.

Alternatively, if you wish to establish your own affiliate marketing campaign for your products, you are implementing a program that allows others to sell your products for you, and you pay them a commission fee. Instead of your products being sold on your Web site, they can be sold on dozens, hundreds, or thousands of other high-traffic sites. The increased sales and profits more than offset the commission fees you will pay, and you still have full control over the affiliates, can approve who is allowed to participate in your program, and still retain administrative control overs your products, pricing, inventory, sales, and record keeping.

Who Is This Book For?

This book is written for anyone who has a Web site, is considering developing a Web site, companies with an established online presence who wish to expand their marketing campaigns, small businesses, large businesses, and sole proprietors. If you are interested in making money, increasing Web site traffic, driving up revenue, and improving the financial posture of your organization by selling products on your Web site, or authorizing others to sell your products on their Web site, this book is for you. It is designed to help you improve sales of your existing product or increase revenue by implementing or joining an affiliate program. I will cover a wide array of topics to ensure that you are fully prepared and ready to start your affiliate marketing venture.

As you read this book, you will quickly discover that affiliate marketing is one of the best ways, if done properly, to increase your revenue for little or no investment. You can implement your own affiliate marketing program, letting others sell your products with minimal investment, minimal effort, and big returns. As with all my books, my immediate goal is to inform, educate, inspire, and provide you with relevant ideas you can immediately implement into your business, all at little or no cost.

This book is the ideal affiliate marketing guide for businesses or organizations with limited budgets, minimal marketing plans, and limited technical support staffs. You do not need to be Amazon.com — or have their budget — to implement an effective and highly successful affiliate marketing campaign, but you can get the same great results. An effective affiliate marketing program equals increased sales and increased revenues!

How This Book Is Organized

Throughout this book I will cover all the areas of affiliate marketing that you need to know to become successful. In particular, I will provide you with the following basics.

Affiliate 101: The Basics You Need to Know About Affiliate Marketing

To fully understand how being an affiliate for another Web site or hosting your own affiliate program can benefit your business. You need to understand the basics of how it works, the multitude of variables involved, and the finite differences between affiliate programs, affiliate networks, and affiliate marketing techniques so you can choose the method that will work best for your company or Web site and maximize your revenue potential. This chapter will provide you with all the information you need to understand affiliate programs, including the history of affiliates, how affiliate programs work, and how you can start an affiliate program to directly improve the overall marketing strategy of your business or Web site and increase your revenue's bottom line or sales volume totals.

Market Research

Market research will help you narrow down the scope of your affiliate efforts and concentrate on the products or affiliate networks which will maximize your revenue stream. Joining or hosting an affiliate program for products that do not sell, have little markup, or are not a fast-moving commodity may not be the best choice for you. Some basic market research will go a long way toward achieving your goal of affiliate marketing success. I will show you how to perform basic market research at no cost with a maximum return on your time investment resulting in increased revenue or sales.

How Do I Get Started?

You know the basics and have performed your market research. We will explore the variety of options available, the benefits and drawbacks for each, and get you started on the path to affiliate success. This chapter covers the basic options for affiliate programs and is a critical step in helping you determine whether you want to become an affiliate or host affiliates. Both offer varying degrees of complexity, responsibility, and revenue streams. I will discuss them all so you can make the most educated decision in implementing an affiliate program for your business or Web site.

Becoming an Affiliate of Others

There are two basic choices: You can be an affiliate of others by selling their products on your Web site and getting a commission or other reward for each referral or sale, or let others become your affiliate by selling your products on their Web sites. In this chapter, we will look in depth at the multitude of options available to you for becoming an affiliate of others. This is a quick and easy source of revenue, but there are pitfalls of which you need to be aware.

In addition to giving you the knowledge you need to succeed, this chapter is packed with active affiliate programs I recommend. You can implement them today on your Web site, instantly earning rewards and revenue.

Hosting and Implementing an Affiliate Program

Do you have stuff to sell or a Web site that sells your products, but is not exactly setting sales records? Instead of selling your products only on your Web site, try selling them on hundreds or thousands of other Web sites around the world. This may sound complicated, but you would be surprised at how easy and effective it is to implement a robust affiliate program. Ever heard of Amazon.com or eBay.com? Both of these companies have the finest affiliate programs around, and you can too. We will cover the costs and drawbacks of implementation options and showcase the success Atlantic Publishing Company has had with implementation of their affiliate program, showing how simple it can be for you.

Optimizing Your Web Site and Affiliate Program

This chapter is dedicated to search engine optimization, Web site design, and techniques to ensure that your Web site is optimized for your affiliate program. An affiliate program by itself is powerful, but an affiliate program combined with a refined and highly optimized Web site is even more powerful. Beyond the Web site, I will show you how you can implement a blog with your affiliate program and use organic search engine optimization to ensure your Web site is visible in all the major search engines.

Affiliate Program Software & Networks

Hosting your own affiliate program offers its own unique challenges because it does require some knowledge, maintenance, and administration. You need to track referrals, sales, commissions, and the data about each affiliate.

You will have to cut checks, manage accounts, develop and implement simple methods for affiliates to incorporate your products on their Web site, and build the loyalty of your affiliates so your program can grow and be successful. Luckily, there are several programs that can help you do this. I will discuss them in depth and take you on a tour of my favorite full-featured affiliate program, which is simple and extraordinarily powerful, not only as an affiliate management tool, but also for managing creative ads and much more.

Marketing and Promoting Your Web Site, Blog, and Affiliate Program

A Web site and a blog are great and a Web site with an affiliate program is even better, but not if no one knows it is there. You need to promote and market your Web site, blog, and affiliate program to attract others to become affiliates. I will show you the best ways to market and promote your Web site, blog, and affiliate program, ultimately expanding your affiliate network and significantly increasing revenue and sales volume.

Other Revenue-Generating Techniques to Use With Affiliate Programs

Affiliate programs should not be your entire advertising and marketing strategy to sell your product and increase sales revenues. Instead, it should be one implement in your toolbox of marketing techniques designed to achieve your overall sales or profit goals. In addition to good site design and search engine optimization to maximize search engine visibility, you should implement other revenue-generating techniques such as Google AdSense and more. I will show you how to expand your marketing options, ultimately increasing search engine visibility and sales revenue. These techniques, in combination with affiliate marketing, will propel sales and drive increased revenues.

AFFILIATE MISTAKES

Instead of making you learn the hard way, I will walk you through some of the common mistakes made by affiliates. You will begin the process armed with the knowledge of what not to do so you can avoid common mistakes that ultimately defeat the success of your affiliate program. My goal is to ensure that you achieve success in becoming an affiliate or hosting an affiliate program of your own. These tips will help you navigate the path to success.

IDEAS TO STIMULATE AND GROW YOUR AFFILIATE PROGRAM

I have gathered dozens of ideas to help you think outside the box. This will help you dramatically expand your affiliate program's success by encouraging others to join your program expanding your firm grasp on your sector of the affiliate marketing empire. One of my basic philosophies of Web site design is simple: Building it does not mean they will come. You have to promote, advertise, and market your Web site, and our affiliate program to draw in Web site traffic, increase customer loyalty, expand your market base, and inspire others to join your affiliate program.

AFFILIATE MARKETING CASE STUDIES

During my research, I contacted many affiliate marketing professionals, affiliate product manufacturers, and affiliate companies who were influential in the development of this book. I have published real-life examples in the form of case studies of how affiliate marketing has transformed organizations, increased customer base and revenue, and is one of the most powerful marketing tools available.

INTERVIEWS WITH AFFILIATE MARKETING EXPERTS

I have interviewed many affiliate marketing experts and professionals and compiled their responses to help you with your own affiliate marketing campaigns and ventures. These industry experts offer their advice, share their experiences, and offer candid suggestions and opinions on how you too can achieve the most success with your affiliate marketing goals.

EXPERT AFFILIATE ADVICE, TIPS, & SUGGESTIONS

This chapter is packed with a plethora of advice, tips, tricks, and suggestions from expert affiliate marketers. This wealth of information is straight from the masters of the trade and will help you succeed as you begin your journey into the affiliate marketing world. If you choose to skip all the other chapters in this book, this is the one you cannot afford to miss.

GLOSSARY

I have included a glossary of relevant terms and definitions related to affiliate marketing and other advertising and marketing techniques.

RECOMMENDED REFERENCE LIBRARY

This is my list of must-have reference books to help you develop your portfolio of success in your online marketing ventures to complement your affiliate marketing program.

I will provide you with the tools and knowledge to unlock the secrets of affiliate marketing and enable you to you harness the power of affiliate marketing to promote, advertise, and market your business in a cost-effective, easy-to-manage program that will yield increased sales and generate revenue. The Internet is the ultimate marketing tool giving you immediate access to billions of people worldwide. Affiliate marketing is the way to either make them work for you by selling your products or let you join their affiliate program and earn profits with no effort. After reading this book and applying the principles and techniques contained within, you will discover the power of affiliate marketing and the immediate impact it can have on your bottom line.

Every topic covered in this book can be exclusively designed, implemented, and managed by you. You do not need to be a professional Web designer or hire an expensive marketing firm to join an affiliate network and implement it on your site. Nor do you need to be a Web designer, programmer, or marketing expert to start your own affiliate program and market it to others.

Affiliate marketing provides you with a low-cost or no-cost solution to promote your products and generate revenue. With little or no investment and increased sales and revenue, why would you not want to embrace affiliate marketing? As with all my books, they are designed for companies, individuals, or organizations that do not have a large information technology or Web design staff, if any, and are limited on both technology budget and technical knowledge. If you are the owner, proprietor, or manager of a traditional brick and mortar or online business, affiliate marketing on the Web can open doors you never imagined in terms of sales volume and increased profits. Affiliate marketing can save you thousands of dollars in costs compared with traditional marketing programs, and reach markets never before possible through selling your products on other Web sites. If you are not up to the challenge of starting your own affiliate marketing program, joining an affiliate network is a quick and easy way to start generating revenue for your business. Keep in mind that you do not need to be an expert in affiliate marketing to be highly successful. This book will arm you with the essential skill sets you need to succeed. Let's begin our affiliate marketing adventure!

2 Affiliate 101 – The Basics You Need to Know

Before we delve deeply into understanding and implementing an affiliate marketing plan, we need to thoroughly comprehend exactly what affiliate marketing is, how it can benefit you, and how you can use it to generate revenue or increase overall sales. Let me say that affiliate marketing can be very powerful, lucrative, and profitable. That being said, as with many things on the Web, if it were that simple why aren't all of us making millions through affiliate marketing? The truth is that affiliate marketing takes some experience, knowledge, understanding, determination, and hard work. Another critical factor is that you need to have products someone would want to buy, or you have to join affiliate networks offering products someone would want to buy.

A few key principles you need to clearly understand before we go any further are the two basic types of affiliate marketing. You are either going to be an affiliate of someone else, which means that you sell their products on your Web site and they pay you a commission for each sale, or you offer an affiliate marketing program on your Web site, which lets others join your network and sell your products on their Web site while you pay them a commission fee for each sale. Both of them are fantastic programs, and when done properly, they can yield substantial results. We will take an in-depth look at each one later in this chapter.

To be fair, there are other types of affiliate marketing models used today. One is pay per impression, in which you earn a commission based on each 1,000 impressions that an ad on your Web site is displayed. These are in the form of banner ads on a Web site. This is not to be confused with pay-per-click, since in this case there is no actual click required on the advertisement. You are simply earning a commission based on the impressions or view of the advertisement. Other varieties of this model are similar, but they also require the click to occur, not just an impression, before you are paid a commission. I will discuss Google AdSense in later chapters of this book, and although I cover this topic in depth in other books, I will highlight it here as well. With AdSense, you can earn revenue for allowing context-related advertisements to be placed on your Web site.

Our Affiliate Marketing Case Study

We will use Atlantic Publishing Company, **www.atlantic-pub.com,** as our primary case study in affiliate marketing. As I have stated in previous books, and will reiterate in this book, my goal is not to provide you with a lecture on the pros and cons of affiliate marketing. My goal is to provide you with the knowledge, confidence, and skills to either become an effective and profitable affiliate or create your own affiliate marketing campaign on your Web site, dramatically increasing your sales volume. You do not need to be a Web designer, Internet marketer, or database administrator, or have earned your MBA to accomplish either of these goals. This book is a guide to help you achieve your affiliate marketing goals and should serve as a ready resource of information and practical advice which you can refer to as needed as you build your affiliate marketing program. Readers of my previous books also know that I promote free, low-cost, or cost-effective solutions. You can invest a ton of money into affiliate marketing, but you do not need to.

This book is published by Atlantic Publishing Company, which also has published my six previous books. Atlantic Publishing is a perfect case study for affiliate marketing because they have proven that an affiliate program effectively complements their overall marketing and communications strategy through their Web site, blog, affiliate network, use of e-mail marketing, and more. Affiliate marketing is a powerful ally that can positively and immediately impact your bottom line revenue, despite the fact that, as an affiliate owner, you are paying a commission for the sale of each of your products. Likewise, being an affiliate of someone else is lucrative because there is no cost, you do not process any sales transactions or handle the merchandise, and there is literally no effort on your part after the initial setup.

Atlantic Publishing Company has a unique and rich history, which epitomizes the American dream of entrepreneurial achievement, innovation, leadership, and determination. Doug Brown founded Atlantic Publishing Group, Inc. in 1982 in South Florida. An experienced restaurant manager, Doug worked as a manager for the Chart House Restaurant chain. In the spring of 1982 a knee injury forced him to take a 9-month hiatus from the industry. During his recovery, he wrote Atlantic's first title, *The Restaurant Manager's Handbook*. Using the experience he gleaned from working with Chart House Restaurants, Doug created a book that gave step-by-step instructions to anyone wishing to open their own restaurant. Soon after he published his book, he founded Atlantic Publishing Company as a part-time business, and worked out of his Ft. Lauderdale home for the next seven years.

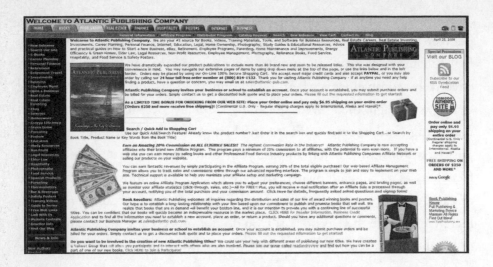

By 1989, Atlantic became a full-time business. Atlantic was a unique entity in the publishing market because they were one of the few that specialized in how-to books for the hospitality industry; as such, they faced little or no competition. In 1992, Atlantic relocated to Ocala, Florida. Tired of the fast pace and clutter of south Florida, Doug choose Ocala because of its smaller size and friendly residents. For the next four to five years, Atlantic prospered as a distributor because of its unique niche; however, by the middle to late 1990s, they faced an obstacle that almost put the company out of business.

By 1996, Atlantic was nearly devastated by its first real competition: Amazon.com. From 1996 to 1997, they experienced a 30 percent decline in sales, something that had never happened in the 15 years they had been in business. Over the next fiscal year, Atlantic experienced another 30 percent decrease in sales along with an increase in postage prices. They understood that the decline in business was due to their being a distributor of books instead of a publisher, and because they could not sell their literature as cheaply as Amazon, they ultimately were losing market strength.

By 1999, Atlantic was heavily in debt and on the verge of collapse. However, Doug knew that if Atlantic began publishing its own books and using Amazon as one of their distributors, they would no longer be in competition with the company. Discovering what was needed to rebuild Atlantic was not difficult; his main concern was having enough time and resources to do it. The next two years were difficult for Atlantic, but by 2001, they had repaid all of their debts and begun publishing their own books.

Currently, Atlantic publishes 55 to 75 books per year and uses Amazon as one of their main distributors. Branching out of the hospitality industry, they now specialize in several fields: business resources, real estate careers, real estate investing, investments, career planning, personal finance, the Internet, education, legal, home ownership, photography, study guides, educational resources, advice and practical guides on how to start a new business, eBay, retirement, employee programs, parenting, home maintenance and improvements, energy efficiency and green homes, elder law, legal resources, non-profit resources, employee management, photography, reference books, food service, hospitality, and food service and safety posters. Their goal is to maintain their reputation for finding and filling niches in the business how-to genre, and they seek to publish the highest quality books for their clients. Using a combination of research techniques, unique writing processes, and distinctive additional resources, they strive to reach this goal.

Atlantic Publishing Company also created and manages an affiliate marketing program. This robust program pays an amazing 20 percent commission for sale of their products which is one of the best you can find anywhere. You can find more information about Atlantic Publishing or their available titles by visiting **www.atlantic-pub.com**. As interesting as the story of Atlantic Publishing Company is, they boast an equally rich history in the story of their affiliate marketing strategy, which we will explain in depth throughout this book.

History of Affiliate Marketing

Believe it or not, Amazon.com was one of the first companies to embrace and launch an affiliate marketing program. Technically, the first was CDNOW.com, but Amazon.com quickly recognized the potential and was the first major online presence to promote an affiliate program. Today, Amazon.com is by far the most popular, and one of the most effective and simple ways to sell products on your Web site, earning you a commission for each sale. Launched in 1996, Associates is Amazon.com's affiliate marketing program. Associate members can join for free, adding content to their Web site quickly and easily. Considering that Amazon.com is a seller of much more than just books, they boast an enormous marketplace of products to showcase on your Web site as an affiliate. Since its inception affiliate marketing has gone through many evolutions, but the marketing principles have essentially stayed the same.

Crash Course in Affiliate Marketing

Affiliate marketing allows merchants to dramatically increase their marketplace by paying their affiliates to promote their products on a commission formula based on a sale or sales lead. Affiliate marketing, however, is not always about selling products; it also can be used simply for impressions or per action. For example, driving traffic from your Web site to the affiliate owner's site may qualify for an affiliate payment. In most cases, affiliate networks are created to sell products and expand the marketplace. In all cases, the concept is to drive traffic back to the merchant Web site. Remember, even if you are an affiliate of Atlantic Publishing Company and feature their products on your Web site, when someone clicks on the link to order or view information about the product, they are driven back to the merchant Web site to complete the sale or transaction. Typically, upon completion of the sale, you are given a commission for the sale.

In the case of Atlantic Publishing Company, for each sale that originates on your affiliate site and becomes a completed transaction or order on Atlantic's Web site, you get a 20 percent commission on the total sale. Simply put, if the visitor to your Web site clicks on something that is an affiliate item, and then goes to the merchant Web site to purchase this item, when the visitor completes the transaction on the merchant Web site, you get paid the referral or commission. As I mentioned earlier, some affiliate programs operate on a cost-per-click (CPC) basis and some are strictly sales-based. With CPC programs, the affiliates get credit based on the number of clicks on ads or banners on their Web sites. With cost-per-action (CPA) programs, affiliates only get credit when the site visitor completes a purchase or other transaction on the affiliate merchant's Web site.

There is some basic knowledge of the affiliate required before you join an affiliate program and certainly before you start your own affiliate program on your Web site. You must understand and perform some basic market research, which I will cover in the next chapter. Essentially, you must have a good understanding of the marketplace and be thoroughly familiar with the products you wish to sell or promote. If your Web site or blog is about dogs, then it would not be logical to sell products relating to automobiles, as this is not the market you are targeting.

Affiliate Marketing Networks

If you are an online retailer you have two affiliate marketing choices. You can establish your own affiliate marketing program, or you can join a well-established large affiliate network. An affiliate network has enormous reach and may get you significantly increased market presence over establishing your own affiliate program. It is not free, however, and you are restricted to the terms of service of the affiliate network. There are hundreds of affiliate networks, some are good, some are not. This book is not designed to tell you how to become an affiliate network or to join and promote hundreds of products all over your Web site. This book is designed to teach you how to establish your own in-house affiliate program, or make good choices in joining an affiliate program that targets the right marketplace which compliments your company or Web site. I said in the beginning of the book that affiliate marketing is not easy, nor is it a guaranteed money-maker. You cannot just sign up with affiliate networks, put affiliate products on your Web site, and sit back and cash the monthly commission checks. Quite frankly there will not be any commission checks coming in unless you do it right. Establishing your own affiliate program, or even joining an affiliate program, will require hard work, dedication, patience, and determination.

Affiliate Marketing Principles

Affiliate marketing has certainly grown in the past decade and has exploded in both popularity and profitability. It has expanded into every aspect of the Web and has the potential to be one of the more lucrative ways of generating both sales and revenue. The basic principles of affiliate marketing are sound and have stood the test of time: You promote my stuff on your Web site and I will pay you a commission for each sale, or I will promote your stuff on my Web site and you pay me a commission for each sale. Any commercial link on any Web site is tied to affiliate or pay-per-click (PCP) marketing in some form or another.

There is no product for sale anywhere that is not part of an affiliate network. If you want to buy golf equipment, automotive parts, running shoes, books, movies, CDs, electronic equipment, computers, you name it, someone has an affiliate program you can join. If implemented properly there is no reason for affiliate marketing not to be a tremendous success. I will give you one final caution, though: I do not subscribe to or believe the claims that, "I joined a zillion affiliate programs, put a bunch of advertisements on my Web sites, and now all I do is sit back drinking my iced tea on the beach in front of my million-dollar ocean-view house in Florida watching the mail carrier deliver fists full of commission checks to me." If it were this lucrative we would all be on the beach counting our profits. The point is that it can be very profitable, and if you implement your own affiliate program, you can dramatically increase your product sales volume.

Hopefully you now have a good understanding of affiliate marketing. The following is a recap of the two primary affiliate marketing methods that I will cover in this book.

- **Joining an Affiliate Program or Network:** This means that you have your own Web site and that you join an affiliate program or network selling other products. For example, you have a Web site or blog about running. To increase your revenue you join the affiliate network of a large running shoe merchant. This is free to you, and after joining, they provide you with the information to add their products to your Web site. They will provide you with special URLs which uniquely identify the sales that originated from your Web site. You can encourage your site visitors to buy the running shoes by following the image and other information you placed on your Web site. When they click on the image, they are taken to the merchant's site — typically directly to the product they want to buy — where they can place the order. Once the order is processed and completed, you are notified of the sale and of your commission amount. You have access to an online account to monitor your statistics, revenue, and other vital information. You can change products as often as you want to keep your Web site ever-changing and interesting. You do not process the sale, handle or ship the merchandise, provide customer service, or anything else. Once the transaction is completed, you have earned your commission. The merchant must do the rest!

- **Create or Manage Your Own In-House Affiliate Program:**
This means you have your own Web site and products to sell. You
want to expand your marketplace beyond your Web site and use
the power of thousands of other sites to promote and sell your
products for you. Those who promote these products for you on
their Web sites are your affiliates, and they fall into the category
above. They place your products and materials on their Web site.
If someone visits their site and clicks on your products, a unique
affiliate link takes them to your Web site where you complete the
transaction. You now have the luxury of featuring and promoting
your products on Web sites all over the world at no cost to you;
reaching millions of people you could not have previously reached
and who may not have known about you or your products. As each
sale is completed, the affiliate earns a commission. At the end of
each month, you pay your affiliates a commission on the sales. You
may wonder if this means you will earn less profit because you are
paying 10 percent or more per sale to someone else. That is true,
but theoretically, you are selling significantly more products than
you would have before; now, you are promoting your products on
hundreds or thousands of relevant Web sites. You must maintain
your affiliate account status, generate monthly checks, and
administer your affiliates approvals, account maintenance, and so
on; so there is some overhead and work on your part, but typically,
it is minimal. As you add new products to your inventory, you add
them to your affiliate program, and your affiliates instantly begin
promoting them. You then process the sale, handle and ship the
merchandise, provide customer service, handle the transactions, and
any other necessary details.

There are several choices of affiliate marketing software available to you if
you wish to build your own affiliate network or install an affiliate program
on your Web site. We will cover these in detail in later chapters, but here
are your general options:

- **Affiliate Network:** In this case the software is provided and hosted by the affiliate network provider. You simply join the existing network and offer your products for sale to other members of the affiliate network. They handle the program administration, reporting, commission payments, and more.

- **Hosted Affiliate Network Software:** The software is not provided to you or installed on your Web server. The software provider hosts it on their servers, and you pay a fee, usually monthly, for support and maintenance. All you have on your Web site is a small piece of tracking code; your work is minimal. Because they own and host the software you instantly benefit from software upgrades, patches, and enhancements; plus, they are responsible for all the servers, backups, and reliability. Additionally, technical support is included with the package.

- **Affiliate Network Software (Stand-Alone):** You buy the software package and own the license to use it as you see fit. This is a one-time fee and it can be expensive. You install the software on your Web server and integrate it with your shopping cart or inventory management system; sometimes installation is included for free or for a small fee. This software is packed with features, and there are no recurring fees unless you want to sign up for upgrades and patches, or other support which is typically limited or not included.

The simplest and most foolproof way of attracting traffic to your Web site would be to print the Web site's name and URL on your T-shirt, knock on every door in your neighborhood, and offer to pay each person a dollar to enter your site. This is not realistic, of course, although the concept of affiliate marketing is not much different. First, this technique is labor-intensive. Second, you would become your neighborhood's worst nightmare. And third, you can only reach so many houses in a single day. Ultimately, you would find little if any increase in Web site traffic.

This hypothetical scenario does teach us, however, about the basics of generating traffic through an affiliate network. Simple is not always going to be easy or effective, and you only have a limited amount of time and money at your disposal to accomplish this task. The amount of traffic received per unit of time or money expended should be as high as possible and traffic-generating techniques should be residual. Residual traffic means that it will continue to generate traffic without further investment of time or money long after the mechanism has been set into place. Its opposite is what I call flashflood traffic techniques; these techniques generate traffic increases for a very short period of time, typically, only while you are investing money into it, with no real promise of recurring traffic.

Let me give you two examples which will clearly show you how the two types of traffic differ.

- Imagine that you just bought a permanent link on a blogroll; the collection of links usually found on the right side of a blog. The amount of traffic you receive depends on the popularity of the blog, of course, but the traffic will continue for months, if not years, and the link will attract attention from search engines. This is an example of a residual traffic technique.

- A different scenario is that you post a topical article on your blog, and before you know it, your servers can barely keep up; the story made it across the blogosphere. A week later, however, the traffic from the blog has come to a grinding halt. This is an extreme example of flashflood traffic. Paying for traffic through Google AdWords is another flashflood traffic technique. When you stop paying, the traffic stops.

The following list highlights factors involved with traffic management.

- What is the amount of time or money required?

- What amount of traffic will you obtain per unit of time or money?

- What type of traffic, residual or flashflood, does the technique generate?

- Are there any hidden benefits or problems?

It is important to recognize that driving traffic to your Web site is critical to the success of an affiliate program. An affiliate program lets you extend your Web site and/or product visibility throughout other Web sites promoting your products and driving that customer traffic to your site. In return for this traffic and resulting sale/conversion, you pay a commission to the referrer/affiliates.

The world of affiliate traffic is full of misconceptions. Here are some facts and realities of affiliate marketing.

- Setting up an effective affiliate traffic program is not necessarily easy and will take an investment of time and money, but it can return large dividends.

- Affiliate marketing does not automatically mean a huge increase in Web site traffic. Setting up or joining an affiliate program or network alone will not necessarily bring you any noticeable increase in traffic. You still will have to promote your program through other means in order to make it effective.

- You must avoid hype and build credibility in your Web site and your products.

- Some Web surfers are reluctant to click an affiliate link or banner; but many affiliate programs have built-in methods to help combat this. It all goes back to credibility; if they trust you, this is a non-issue.

- There are no shortcuts. Affiliate traffic is one of the most labor-intensive techniques available, but also is potentially one of the most effective.

It is important to realize that affiliate marketing is perhaps one of the most effective tools you have at your disposal to generate traffic and sales; but again, only when used in conjunction with other traffic generation methods. In traditional affiliate marketing, the traffic generated is only a side issue and the main focus is on the sales figure; the traffic might be relatively low, but the conversion to sales can be fantastic.

Programs that encourage users to only subscribe to a newsletter or sign up for a community or forum are not intended to immediately generate sales. These actions are not considered a part of affiliate marketing, but part of a pay-per-action (PPA) campaign. Attempting to capture e-mails or sign-ups for future sales, however, is a technique widely used in conjunction with affiliate marketing.

Affiliate traffic is suited to those cases who seek a direct conversion of traffic to sales. There are two sides to this story. You might be interested in either becoming an affiliate or selling your product through an affiliate program. The first case does not really concern traffic generation, but it is definitely an issue you must be familiar with in order to make your affiliate program actually work; or, if you are interested in becoming an affiliate, the issue becomes maximizing the cash flow of your traffic.

When you approach affiliate marketing, you must ask yourself if you would buy the product you are promoting. This is a key question because the answer is often no. Why would you not buy the product? Is it of low quality? Is the language used to promote it too full of hype? Do you have an aversion toward the format in which the offer is available? Would you have a problem buying a product from a middleman and not the manufacturer of the product? These questions hold the key to a more effective type of affiliate marketing. Examine each issue one at a time.

Picking the Right Product

The best affiliate product to sell is the one you are most familiar with. Anything can be sold if it fits a niche, and although the niche itself might be small, the competition also will be smaller. If you have expertise in a certain field, and you pick a product related to that field, you will have a huge advantage over your competition because you will be able to understand your customers. You also will be able to instantly differentiate a quality product from a low-quality product, and quality counts. As time goes on and you attract more traffic, you build up a portfolio of affiliate products to sell to your existing customers. The basic idea is to find a customer niche you understand and know how to cater to and concentrate on marketing those products through your affiliate program.

Effective Product Web Copy or Sales Material

There are many approaches available to sell products on the Web. Why are people browsing the Web? A consistent percentage are indeed out there looking for a solution to a problem or simply looking for a product to purchase, but most of them are only looking for general information or human interaction. You should cater to those looking for a solution to a problem or a product to purchase. Catering to a small community with a high likelihood of purchase with products you know very well is a key to affiliate success. Trying to cater to everyone without specialization is much less successful. Target your Web copy to your products and provide detailed information, advantages, and reviews to generate interest. Generic banner ads plastered all over your Web site without anything else to support them will not generate conversions.

The Sales Letter Style of Web Copy

The sales letter has both advantages and disadvantages. Its use is most effective when selling products that target a niche audience. Long sales letters tend to be more effective with people 23-25 years or older and less effective with the younger ones. The sales letter format is a very old advertising and marketing approach, and its transition to the online format carries with it the advertising culture that created it. Younger people are less accustomed to the direct mail type of advertising culture and will be less likely to react to it.

Advantages of the Sales Letter Web Copy Approach:

- Less distraction to the Web reader. The sales pitch is all there is, and as the reader progresses through it, no immediate exit points can be found on the page. If someone actually reads it, the only choice faced will be whether or not to buy, which greatly increases the conversion ratio.

- The SEO effort is only directed at a single page.

- It takes relatively little time to develop.

Disadvantages of the Sale Letter Web Copy Approach:

- Many people really don't want to read a sales pitch.

- You can only target the keywords in the copy for Search Engine Optimization purposes; although, this is actually an advantage for Organic Search Engine Optimization.

- The format limits further development, because your site is essentially a sales pitch for one product.

GENERALIZED WEB COPY SALES APPROACH

The generalized Web copy sales approach is either a static site containing some articles or reviews about a product, or with Web 2.0, it can be a variety of formats for which you can choose the content. At the core of all this design is the desire to generate a more interactive experience. Through the use of blogs, forums, interactive flash Web designs, or social networking, the ultimate purpose is the same. Here are some tips:

- Make sure your Web site has loads of content. Not all pages need to have affiliate links in them, but all should have interesting and relevant content.

- Put in a variety of content to include industry news, Web site features, product reviews, cover stories, how to guides, new product releases, and more.

- Conduct polls, add a blog, open up Web forums, or use an open source social networking platform such as Pligg, **www.pligg.com,** to allow users to vote for their favorite stories or submit their own or run contests. Interactivity makes your Web site fun and interesting and keeps them coming back.

This sounds like a lot of work for selling only one product. You can sell a whole array of products on your site through your affiliate program, but I do recommend you start out small and make sure the products are somehow linked to each other and to your area of expertise; computer monitors and makeup do not really don't belong together.

The total number of pages is another advantage to successful Web sites compared to sales letter Web sites. This is an extremely important factor when it comes to search engine optimization. What you need to keep in mind now is that the more pages in a Web site the better. You cannot achieve that with a traditional sales letter.

USE HONESTY AND TRUST TO BUILD RELATIONSHIPS

This reminds me of infomercials on television featuring incredible knives that can cut through a brick, then effortlessly slice your tomatoes. This sort of high-pressure sales tactic, with misleading claims and over-the-top hype, tends to devour the world of affiliate marketing and is very ineffective.

Look at this Web copy example. Pretend you are selling a new style of pliers. Here are two text approaches.

> *These pliers will change your life!!! They are the best of the best. You will never need other pliers again, ever. Such an amazing product, designed by NASA for use on the space shuttle! Buy it now! It used to cost nearly $800, but now you can buy it for only $9.95. Order now, and I'll double your order for free!!!*

And the second approach:

> *These pliers are made of titanium-steel alloy and come with a lifetime guarantee, based on space-age technology designed by NASA. It has an adjustable head which allows it to be used for nearly any job. The pliers come at a reasonable price tag of only $4.95. Click here to order. The price does not include shipping.*

While the first example is a typical bad infomercial, it is also a very common approach in Web sales copy and in my opinion is very ineffective. If you take the time to review a product thoroughly and write honestly about it, you will convert sales. That will only happen, however, if you choose a quality product that sells for a fair price. Honesty and straightforward speech work better than hype.

Here is an example of straightforward sales copy from my first book listing from **Atlantic-pub.com**. It is not a sale pitch, and does not promise to make you a millionaire overnight, unlike what you will find on many affiliate marketing Web sites.

HOW TO USE THE INTERNET TO ADVERTISE, PROMOTE AND MARKET YOUR BUSINESS OR WEB SITE — WITH LITTLE OR NO MONEY

Interested in promoting your business and/or Web site, but don't have the big budget for traditional advertising? This new book will show you how to build, promote, and make money off your Web site or brick-and-mortar store using the Internet, with minimal costs. Let us arm you with the knowledge you need to make your business a success! Learn how to generate more traffic for your site or store with hundreds of Internet marketing methods, including many free and low-cost promotions.

This new book presents a comprehensive, hands-on, step-by-step guide for increasing Web site traffic and traditional store traffic by using hundreds of proven tips, tools, and techniques. Learn how to target more customers to your business and optimize your Web site from a marketing perspective. You will learn to target your campaign, use keywords, generate free advertising, try search-engine strategies, learn the inside secrets of e-mail marketing, and build Web communities, as well as learn about co-branding, auto-responders, Google advertising, banner advertising, eBay storefronts, Web-design information, search-engine registration, directories, and real-world examples of which strategies are succeeding and failing.

ISBN-13: 978-0-910627-57-3 • $24.95

Book Review

"It's easy to be confused about Internet marketing opportunities with a blend of fast-paced changes and tech terminology complicating the picture, but any small business owner seeking enlightenment need look no further than *How to Use the Internet to Advertise, Promote, and Market Your Business Web Site with Little Or No Money*. It pairs tried-and-tested marketing applications with easy explanations of Internet choices, pros and cons, and it covers everything from automating a Web site to optimizing a search engine result. An essential guide any business needs for making a powerful Web presence."

Affiliate Links and How to Deal With Them

A major problem you will face when dealing with affiliate links is people's reluctance to follow an affiliate link. I bring this up now because whether you want to start an affiliate program on your Web site as an advertiser or join other affiliate programs or networks as a publisher, you need to realize that there is reluctance to click on affiliate links and banner advertisements. One of the reasons I love ROIA, **www.affiliatetracking.net,** is that they use clean links, meaning there is no affiliate code in the affiliate links.

In a traditional tracking solution, links provided to the affiliate program contain code where the requisite tracking data is captured before the visitor is forwarded on to your domain. The visitor is instantaneously redirected to your site, but the link may point to the affiliate host. This is a functional, standard solution for affiliate marketing programs. In this case, you should be straightforward and acknowledge that the link presented is of the affiliate type. The rule of thumb is that if your visitors are familiar with what affiliate marketing is, and are actually okay with it, there is nothing wrong with this option; although, there is a price to pay in regard to SEO. For those who want to reinforce brand name recognition and increase search engine optimization, Direct Linking offers a very cost-effective solution.

In a Direct Linking model traffic flows uninterrupted from a partner's Web site to your domain by clicking a link to your Web site with tracking information appended at the end. Once the visitor arrives, a special, invisible code captures the tracking information and forwards it to the affiliate host, while the visitor remains at your site the entire time. This eliminates the issue of people not wanting to click a link because it directs them to a third-party Web site, your affiliate host, with whom they are not familiar.

Clean linking technology allows publishers to promote your site with a basic link to your Web site with no tracking parameters in the link and still be appropriately tracked. In a clean linking scenario, your publisher registers the domain or domains where they will place your tracking links, for example, AffiliateSite.com. Once you approve them, the ROIA system will track any click originating from that site as a publisher referral to YourSite.com, again using an invisible piece of code installed on your page, which forwards tracking information to the ROIA server.

The major benefits to clean linking are:

- No tracking parameters

- No redirect links

- Ease of use

- Added branding for YourSite.com

- Increased visitor confidence in the link.

Clean links do have limitations, the main one being that clean links must originate from a registered domain. While certainly a powerful and useful utility, they will not function in an e-mail marketing scenario, in this case consider direct linking, or if the special page tracking code is not present on the target page.

Google and other major search engines use complex algorithms to determine the order in which sites appear when a given term is searched for. One of the major factors in this algorithm is how many other sites link to yours. In traditional tracking those links point to the affiliate marketing server, which, while very effective, do not help your search engine rankings.

In direct linking you have affiliate links pointing at your domain which counts toward this search engine's popularity. There are still tracking parameters present in the links which many believe still prevents you from receiving full credit for the incoming link.

Clean linking maximizes the benefit your partnership program brings to your business. Not only do your affiliates refer your traffic, which increases your sales, but you also gain the full advantage of all those additional links from sites with related content pointing directly to your site; this increases your search engine ranking and drives even more traffic to your site. For more detailed information I recommend you visit **www. affiliatetracking.net** or **www.trackingsoft.com** for more information on ROIA and all its features. As you will read later, this is the affiliate program I use, and if you want to use a hosted affiliate program, it is the one I recommend.

Promoting Your Affiliate Program

Starting up a new Web site is like opening a store in the middle of the Sahara Desert. Land is plentiful and cheap, but no one is shopping there.

My other favorite theory is: Build it and they will come. You can build it, but do not expect instant Web site traffic. This is true for any new Web site, not just affiliate ones. This means your quest for traffic should never end. You should also employ a diverse array of traffic-gathering techniques, some of which I cover in this and my previous books.

Affiliate Program Payment Methods

Affiliate programs use different ways to determine the payment method. Each can be successful in its own way, but there are slight differences between each. The three most common methods of payment are as follows:

- **Pay-per-click.** If you enter into this type of method, you'll be paying your affiliates a total price that is determined by the number of Web visitors who click on a link on the affiliate Web page to arrive at your business Web site. These Web visitors aren't required to buy anything; all they have to do is visit your Web site through the affiliate link.

- **Pay-per-lead.** If you're using this method, you'll be paying your affiliates an amount determined by the number of Web visitors who leave information at your Web site. All the Web visitor needs to do is fill out a form on your Web site which then can be used as a lead for further sales and communication with the potential customer. Your goal is to make a sale, and obtain the Web visitor as a repeat customer so that you can increase your client database and overall sales performance.

- **Pay-per-sale.** If you're using this type of method with your affiliates, you pay a total that is determined by the number of sales you make from the Web visitors sent to your Web site from the affiliate Web site or blog, or those who click on the affiliate links and make a purchase. The amount you pay is based on either a predetermined amount that is fixed ahead of time for each sale, a flat rate, or percentage of each sale.

Essentially, by using an affiliate program you are replicating your Web site and/or products to hundreds or thousands of other Web sites throughout the world, dramatically increasing the exposure and potential sales for your profits — all at little or no cost.

The Challenges of Managing Affiliate Marketing

As I have already discussed, once you decide to use affiliate marketing, you have some choices:

- Develop your own in-house affiliate program

- Use a third party affiliate platform such as ClickBank at **www. clickbank.com** or Commission Junction at **www.cj.com.**

If you decide to develop your own in-house affiliate program, your first choice is to decide what software to use. I hope to make this easy for you by recommending ROIA, **www.trackingsoft.net**, but let's go through the process so you can make your own choices. Building the affiliate program from the ground up is a very challenging task. It requires a great deal of effort and promotion, but it also has some important benefits that are unique to managing your own program, namely, total control over all aspects of the operation.

The first hurdle you will encounter is the affiliate platform development. Here you have several choices which we have discussed previously.

- **Develop the software program yourself.** This requires good software development skills and a great deal of time. My recommendation: Do not reinvent the wheel, and do not choose this option.

- **Outsource the development process.** If you truly cannot find a software solution on the commercial market and wish to develop your own, but lack the time or skills to do so, you can contract out this work. It will be expensive and time-consuming as you test the development work, fix bugs, deploy and manage the process. My recommendation: Don't choose this option.

- **Use a free/open source affiliate software.** Free affiliate scripts can be found all over the Web. The problem is that they are typically incomplete, have no support, are bug-filled, and usually need to be customized. The advantage is that they are free to use. The best place to find free/open source scripts is at Hot Scripts, **www.hotscripts. com**. They have hundreds of free PHP affiliate scripts available. My recommendation: You'll probably regret this decision.

- **Buy affiliate software.** Yes, this is the most expensive option, but it is also the most reliable since they include support and thoroughly tested applications. In addition they are always having upgrades, which are typically free; this is a great bonus. Most software includes free installation and setup. You can use the software with in-house hosting or the affiliate company Web site, of the affiliate piece such as ROIA, **www.trackingsoft.com**, which means there is very little customization to your site other than some code placed on your Web site.

Tiered Affiliate Marketing

I prefer straight, non-tiered affiliate marketing, but there are many effective multi-tiered affiliate marketing campaigns. If you choose to use multi-level tiers, do not go beyond two-tier approaches. The basic affiliate structure falls in one of two categories.

- **Single-tier affiliate structure:** The simplest approach of the two meaning you pay a commission for every sale or lead your affiliates generate. Your affiliates only promote and sell your product.

- **Two-tier affiliate structure:** This can be expanded to multiple tiers and is a more complex model. This structure separates your affiliates into two categories: those who actually sell and those who attract other affiliates. The first tier, those who attract affiliates, receive a percentage of what the affiliates signed under them sell, while the second tier are those doing the grunt work and selling, also earning an additional commission.

Each of the approaches presented above is equally valid. The first one works best if you have access to a large pool of potential affiliates and you want to keep it simple. The second works best if you have access only to a few very active affiliate marketers and you do not mind some extra complexity. I will cover this later in more detail, but my recommendation for any new affiliates is to start out with single-tier marketing to keep it simple.

Cross-Selling and Up-Selling

Some basic common sense applies here. A higher commission percentage means you will have more affiliates while a smaller one brings more profit per sale. You will find that this is a careful balancing act between offering the maximum commission while ensuring that you are profitable when paying out that commission.

You need to think outside the box on this one to increase your overall sales volume. One great way to do this is through up-selling and cross-selling. Up-selling simply means that at the moment you convert a sale you capture details from the customer such as their e-mail address, with their permission, so you can use this in your e-mail marketing campaigns to sell more products. Cross-selling means at the time of a purchase you obtain various details from the customer such as past purchases, or you offer them similar products to purchase based on the type of products they are buying. Amazon.com does a great job of this by offering information based on past purchases, and offering you additional items you might like to consider at the time of a purchase. The PDG Shopping Cart, **www. pdgsoft.com**, has a very nice feature to manage cross-selling at the time of a customer purchase, and it definitely works to increase total sales volume.

How to Attract Affiliates

At this point, let's assume you have a fully functional affiliate program and are ready to start adding affiliates to your network. This chapter is an introduction to the entire affiliate marketing process; in later chapters I will give you much more detailed information each step of the way. The challenge for anyone starting an affiliate program is how to convince online entrepreneurs to join your network and become an affiliate of yours to promote and sell your products. Here are some options for how to do this:

Hiring an Affiliate Manager

The easy choice, and also the most expensive, is to hire an affiliate manager. An affiliate manager is someone with significant experience who can propel your program to its maximum potential. One major caveat with affiliate managers is that they are not cheap. In most cases, for the target audience of this book, you will not be hiring an affiliate manager due to the prohibitive cost. This book is designed to give you the basic skills, understanding, and knowledge to manage your own affiliate program. An affiliate manager, however, is a great option if money is not an issue. Affiliate managers possess the know-how and the contacts to get your affiliate program producing profit in a much shorter period than you could possibly achieve on your own.

The best place to hire affiliate managers is through forums dedicated to the affiliate world or through sites that specialize in intermediating freelance work. Always ask for proof of their previous performance and clearly establish goals and responsibilities.

Promoting Your Affiliate Program on Your Own

No matter what, you must promote your affiliate program and you can promote it yourself. First, you need to get to know your market. Identify where potential affiliates may congregate: forums, online groups, and so on. This is critical as you spread the word of your affiliate program. Do not discount the use of blogs; they are very powerful, and because they ping the search engines after each new posting, they are very search-engine-friendly. Your affiliate program has to be enticing to a potential affiliate. It needs to be easy-to-understand, easy to sign up for, and easy to manage. The registration process should be quick, and the marketing materials at their disposal should be diverse and effective. Use this checklist to make sure you meet the minimum requirements for an effective promotion.

- The affiliate link to join the program should be very visible.

- The registration process should be quick and painless, capturing minimum required information — affiliates can add more later — with a solid affiliate agreement and e-mail confirmation.

- The marketing materials you use should be wide-ranging, from banner ads to articles and sales copy. Atlantic Publishing Company has had success with allowing authors of books to sign up as an affiliate, earning up to 40 percent commission while promoting their own books. In this case, the book cover and copy is readily available to them to use in the affiliate program. The easier it is for an affiliate to integrate your content into their Web site, the more consistent the click-through rate will be, and you will also attract more affiliates because you have substantially decreased the workload on them to join and manage the program.

I will cover a variety of options for how to promote your new affiliate program and increase the number of affiliates in later chapters of this book. In the meantime, here are some other promotion ideas you can consider.

- Ask your friends and online neighbors to start a topic and ask questions in a forum thread that you can interject your affiliate program into. Because you are trying to draw in potential affiliates by engaging in a planted online discussion, this definitely needs to read as a natural conversation, not a canned sales pitch to promote your affiliate program. This is not one of the methods I use, however, others have had success with it.

- Offer promotional incentives to new affiliates, such as: "The first 50 affiliates will receive a 50 percent commission for the first six months."

- Buy endorsements or listings in blogs, forums, and Web sites promoting your affiliate program. Of course, you can also list your affiliate program with affiliate directories for free. There will be more on this in later chapters.

The goal with any promotional program is to ensure that your affiliate program grows and prospers.

How to Make Your Affiliates More Effective

As a general rule of thumb, do not count on your affiliates being Internet or technically savvy or experienced with affiliate marketing concepts. Expect them to ask for help and be ready to deliver it. Even software applications which appear to be very simple to you may be challenging to others. In many cases, your affiliates will need help integrating your products into their Web site. Often, if this is too challenging for them, they may sign on as an affiliate and never complete the integration.

Arm your affiliates with the information they need to succeed. Providing them with affiliate marketing articles or a resource center is a great way to inspire ideas. Giving them a copy of this book or other marketing guides may pay dividends many times over in return. Communicate with your affiliates often through e-mail, such as weekly newsletters, hints and tips, and other mechanisms to promote two-way communication.

Growing Your Affiliate Numbers

Promoting and growing your affiliate program never stops. It should be a constant process that you use to expand your affiliate network, draw in new affiliates, and promote sales conversion. It is critical that you earn credibility and gain exposure through forums, blogs, and Web sites.

Once you establish your affiliate program, be on the constant lookout for new products. In the case of Atlantic Publishing, this is easy, as they produce 75 or more new books each year; but for others, it is not so simple. If you are not adding products, you might be surprised how short a time a certain product can last on the market before it becomes obsolete. Also, once you establish a solid, reputable affiliate program and wish to start another on a new Web site, you have a significant advantage you did not have earlier. Here are some of those advantages.

- You already have a list of potential affiliates who trust you and will likely join your program.

- You already have a list of potential customers who may be interested in your new products.

Cookies and Affiliates

It is very important that you understand the concept of cookies and know how they affect your affiliate commissions. A cookie is a text file that a Web site puts on your computer to remember something about you for a predetermined period of time. This is very important to you as an affiliate because the cookie remembers your affiliate ID. If a customer visits your Web site, your cookie is served to him or her, containing your affiliate ID information, ensuring you get credit for future sales conversions. If the customer browses your Web site, clicks through to the Web site you are an affiliate of and buys something, you get the conversion and commission.

Perhaps the customer is comparison shopping and decides to wait until next week to make the purchase. When the customer comes back, he or she may bypass your Web site and go directly to the affiliate host Web site to make the purchase. Because the customer has your cookie on his or her computer, your affiliate ID is remembered, and even though the customer did not click through your Web site for this purchase, you are given credit for the conversion. Once a cookie expires the memory of your affiliate information also expires. So, if a cookie is set to 30 days, and the customer makes a purchase on day 35, you will not get credit for the conversion. It is important when joining an affiliate program to check how long a cookie is valid; a good rule of thumb is 60 days minimum.

One of the features I love about ROIA, **www.trackingsoft.com** or **www. affiliatetracking.com,** is their cookieless technology. Cookieless tracking from ROIA lets you track sales and leads without the need to place a cookie in the visitor's browser. As people become more conscious of their surfing habits, and regularly delete cookies, cookieless tracking provides another tracking solution. Here is some summary information about ROIA:

"Affiliatetracking.com, a seven-year-old respected affiliate software firm, has improved its cookieless tracking technology to allow integration with any site regardless of e-commerce cookie handling capabilities or site structure. Since the release of the Jupiter Cookie Deletion Study and subsequent studies and publications, Affiliatetracking.com has experienced a slight increase in requests for cookieless tracking capability. Unfortunately, many of these inquiries were from online businesses whose e-commerce solutions or site structures, static rather than dynamic, did not accommodate the implementation of this feature.

"As a result, Affiliatetracking.com developed a new method for integrating their cookieless tracking feature with any site regardless of their e-commerce solutions cookie handling capabilities or their site's structure. Craig Belcher, CEO of TrackingSoft LLC, states that this feature is a very important milestone for TrackingSoft LLC's existing clientele and potential clients interested in utilizing this technology. When used in conjunction with cookie-based tracking and our other strategic features, such as direct linking, our affiliate software, at its price and reliability, cannot be matched." (source: **affiliatetracking.com**)

Multi-Tier Marketing and Commissions

It is important to understand the basic principles of multi-tier marketing. It simply means that you get a publisher to sign up, and he earns a percent of commission for each sale he refers and converts. If he signs up other affiliates under him, the new second-tier affiliate earns a percentage of the commission, as does the first-level affiliate. The concept is very similar to pyramid marketing schemes. If you can get enough second-tier affiliates under you, they all generate revenue with no work on your part. As the affiliate program owner, multi-tier systems are harder to manage and cost more money in commissions. Typically, they are not effective and, in fact, will deter many potential affiliates from joining. My recommendation is that you do not engage in multi-tier marketing.

You now have a basic understanding of affiliate marketing and exactly what we will concentrate on throughout this book. Let's move on to market research.

3 Market Research

An essential step, before you begin an in-house affiliate program or become an affiliate and insert products onto your Web site, is to perform market research and craft a well-thought-out marketing plan for your business. If you think your business is too small to require an online marketing plan, think again. If you are simply looking to increase revenue as an affiliate, market research and development of a marketing plan is important also. A marketing plan is critical for you to map out your future marketing goals, and your market research will help you in preparing an effective and realistic marketing plan. Writing a marketing plan is a fairly straightforward process that requires you to set clear objectives and define how you will achieve them.

A marketing plan must be achievable, realistic, cost-effective, measurable, and flexible. Because we are concentrating only on your marketing plan and market research for your affiliate venture, this is a simple process. However, you may wish to consider taking a holistic approach, and consider all your marketing and advertising goals: pay-per-click, e-mail marketing, AdSense, Google Base, and more.

One of the main objectives in developing a marketing plan is to establish your budget. Your marketing plan may consist of:

- Market analysis

- Business objectives

- Marketing strategies

- Steps to achieving business objectives

- Realistic budget

- Realistic schedule.

Performing a Market Analysis and Market Research

A marketing plan is a living document. You must be flexible based on budget, competition, business objectives, and internal and external influences. Essentially, your market analysis helps you determine if there is a need or demand for your product or for the products you want to sell as an affiliate on your Web site. Understanding the marketplace, the desire for your products, and the competition helps you determine the key information which will be essential to establishing a successful business in a competitive environment. If there is no need for your products, you will likely fail unless you establish your presence in the marketplace. Likewise, if there is a high level of competition, you must develop a marketing plan which allows you to compete with significant competition in product, quality, availability, or price.

Knowing the marketplace's needs, and how it is currently served provides you with essential information for developing your product or service and marketing plan. In a competitive market you must separate yourself from your competition by price, service, quality, or other characteristics that make you desirable in a highly competitive market. This is a fairly obvious fact, but one that is often overlooked, even in affiliate marketing. You must have a product on your Web site that someone would want to buy. Even more than that, you must have a product on your Web site that someone would want to buy, and, you must have a Web site that convinces them to buy that product from you.

Statistics prove that up to 50 percent of a product's price is spent on marketing. With affiliate marketing, you cut that cost because others will be marketing your products for you, or you will be marketing other companies' products on your Web site for free.

The following questions will help you to perform a basic market analysis.

- What market am I trying to enter?

- What is my current competition?

- What is the market size? Is there room to grow?

- What is the market share of my competition?

- Is the market saturated or open?

- How successful is my competition?

- Is there stability in the market, or is it volatile?

- How are my competitors marketing their goods?

- What do customers seek in regard to my products, and what is most valuable to them?

- What are customers willing to pay for my products?

- What do I offer that my competition does not?

You should analyze current or previous marketing strategies, as well as those of your competition, both successful and unsuccessful. Understanding failure is as important as understanding success factors. These questions may help you analyze your potential for success in a competitive marketplace:

- Am I offering a new product line or unique product?

- What marketing strategies have I, or my competition, used successfully? What was unsuccessful? Have I used online marketing in the past? What was the success rate or return on investment?

- Have I evaluated the results of previous marketing plans: print advertising, pay-per-click, e-mail marketing, and so on? What was the impact on sales?

- How much money is allotted in my current budget? How much am I currently spending? How much was my marketing budget in the past?

- What strategies are my competitors using currently?

- Are we using any strategies currently?

- Can I afford to run an in-house affiliate marketing program?

- By becoming an affiliate, are there products out there which will complement my Web site?

- Why would someone choose our product over our competition, and why would they want to buy from our Web site?

- How do we distinguish ourselves from our competition?

- Why would someone trust us more than our competition?

- Who are our customers?

- Where do our customers come from?

You must perform what is known as primary and secondary research. Primary research includes phone interviews, surveys, Web-based surveys, focus groups, and other information-gathering techniques you will perform based on the marketplace. Primary research is the most current information available. Secondary research is data that has already been collected for other purposes, but may assist you with your market research. Examples of secondary research may be libraries, blogs, or other online resources.

Because we are concentrating on affiliate marketing, which is an online marketing venture, it is logical that your market analysis would be performed by using the Internet. The Internet contains a wealth of analytical information and may prove to be your greatest ally in performing market analysis.

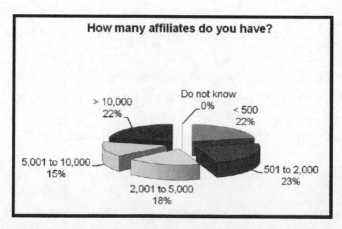

Reprinted with Permission Copyright 2008 Shawn Collins
http://blog.affiliatetip.com

Establishing Marketing Strategies

You should establish a clearly defined written strategy and marketing plan for your online business. You should consider all marketing strategies implementing those that are most relevant to your business operations and offer the most potential for increased customer base and return on investment. Your marketing strategy must be realistic and measurable. If you do not measure the results of your marketing campaign or the success rate of your affiliate marketing venture, you cannot evaluate its effectiveness or be ready to implement a shift in strategy. At a minimum your marketing strategy should include:

- Profile of the target consumer

- Competitive market analysis

- Distribution plans for your products

- Product price strategy

- Advertising budget

- Advertising and marketing strategy analysis to evaluate potential methods

- Your corporate vision and business objectives

- Brand uniqueness or image for your products

- Evaluation of your products and services

- Distinction of your company/products from competitors.

Implement and evaluate your marketing strategy as it relates to achieving your corporate business objectives. Keep in mind that some marketing plans may take significant time and investment. Think long-term, and do not be quick to change your objectives because you are not realizing the goals in your specified time. Be flexible, but allow your marketing strategies time to grow and mature. Affiliate marketing is proven to be effective, so if you are not achieving your goals, you may need to modify your affiliate marketing approach or implementation plan.

Be flexible with your affiliate marketing plans. You will find that a very small percentage of your affiliates account for most of your sales. These are known as super-affiliates. Network with your super-affiliates while trying to motivate all your affiliates to achieve success.

Keep in mind that you cannot sell everything on your Web site, and you cannot expect everyone to buy what you are selling. In fact, many people are still afraid to buy online and will avoid online purchases. If you can find a product or niche that is lucrative, stick with it. One of the secrets to affiliate marketing success is having a product people want and not everyone else has.

If you are starting up your own affiliate program, look for other similar Web sites and companies that have products which would be complementary, but not directly competitive, to yours. In other words, if you sell a book you wrote on Boston terriers, you should seek out all Web sites related to Boston terriers and then expand to general dog Web sites. I have discovered that regardless of how much market research you do, if you are going to be an affiliate of someone else, you should try multiple affiliates while searching for the ones that are truly effective for you. If an affiliate program is not working for you, dump it and consider another.

Here are two resources to consider when performing market research or identifying niches which you may consider for your marketing plan.

- **Google Trends** — With Google Trends you can compare the world's interest in your favorite topics. Enter up to five topics to see how often they have been searched on Google over time. Google Trends also shows how frequently your topics have appeared in Google News stories and in which geographic regions people have searched for them most. **www.google.com/trends**

- **TrendWatching.com** — TrendWatching.com is an independent and opinionated trend firm, scanning the globe for the most promising consumer trends, insights, and related hands-on business ideas. **www.trendwatching.com**

4

How Do I Get Started?

We have covered the basic concepts of affiliate marketing and provided guidance on how to perform market research to determine what products or markets you think will be profitable for you in your affiliate marketing campaign. Now, you are at the point where you need to make a pivotal decision. Essentially you must decide if you :

- Want to sign up to become an affiliate of others, and feature their products on your Web site

- Want to start an affiliate program allowing others to join your program to showcase and promote your products on their Web site.

While this may seem like a tough question, the answer is usually self-evident based on what type of products you offer and what type of Web site you operate. Let's discuss some examples of each so you can make an informed decision. Before we delve into each of the above options, I would like to discuss the option of joining an affiliate network.

Affiliate Networks

An affiliate network is defined as a network that consists of a group of merchants and affiliates. Merchants will join this network so that affiliates will join and promote their products. The advantage for merchants is that their products are advertised across the network of affiliates and also through a variety of means potentially including Web site advertisement, rich media, e-mail marketing, and more, ultimately lowering their overall advertising budget. With a traditional affiliate marketing program, the affiliate is paid based on a commission from the merchants they feature. Typically, the commission is based on the aggregate total of merchants that affiliates participate with, not on individual merchant performance by each affiliate.

In other words, if you join the network as an affiliate and sign up with ten merchants, your overall performance and commissions are typically based on the performance of all of the merchants as a whole, not on an individual merchant basis; this is the method to get you to put more and more affiliate links on your Web site. As a merchant, you are provided with an administrative control panel, reporting tools, tracking, and payment processing; the biggest benefit is that you have access to a large pool of potential affiliates. As an affiliate you get one control panel with integrated reports, simplified integration, and one-stop shopping.

As an affiliate, the networks are free to join because they want you to join. As a merchant, you have to pay a monthly recurring fee which is why affiliate networks are profitable to a provider. In most cases, there is a sign-up or setup fee, following by monthly recurring maintenance or support fees to maintain active membership as a merchant in an affiliate network. In many cases, instead of a flat fee, your monthly costs are based on a total percentage of your affiliate sales; therefore, if you are highly successful with your affiliate marketing, your costs can grow. This is a factor you need to consider when setting your affiliate payout percentages.

A 10 percent commission payout is the industry standard, although this percentage will vary widely. Atlantic Publishing boasts an impressive 20 percent commission, one of the highest available anywhere.

If you are willing to have advertisements on your site, then affiliate networks provide a simple and convenient means to raise revenue for your Web site. Another way of looking at it is that an affiliate network acts as the broker between the merchant and the affiliates. In this model, you can be either the merchant or the affiliate. If you have products to sell, but do not want to invest the money, time, and overhead in starting your own affiliate program on your Web site, joining an affiliate network is a great option; but keep in mind it is not free.

As an affiliate, if you wish to offer products from multiple companies and like the single control/administrative panel concept, then an affiliate network may be the best choice for you. If you know of companies that have the product you want, and you are confident in their quality, service, and reputation, you may find that higher commission percentages can be achieved by joining their affiliate program directly rather than through an affiliate network. Typically, companies who have their own affiliate programs are not part of a larger affiliate network, so if there are particular companies you wish to become an affiliate of, that may help you determine whether or not to join an affiliate network.

As a merchant, I highly recommend you consider establishing your own affiliate program on your Web site. Although the cost to establish one is typically a few hundred dollars and potentially some monthly recurring maintenance fee, you have full control of the program. An affiliate network is a great option if you do not want to commit to the support and administration of an affiliate program. There are many outstanding affiliate programs you can install on your Web site; we will discuss several of them later in the book. Designing and developing/coding a program from the ground up is not cost-effective given the variety of great programs available on the market today.

Let's take a look at some of the existing affiliate networks you may wish to consider:

Affiliate Networks

- 15 Days Cash (**www.15dayscash.com**)

- Ad Communal (**www.adcommunal.com**)

- Google AdSense (**www.google.com/adsense**)

- AffiliateWindow (**www.affiliatewindow.com**)

- TradeDoubler (**www.tradedoubler.com/pan/cms**)

- Commission Junction(**www.cj.com**)

- Clash Media (**www.clash-media.com**)

- ClickBank (**www.clickbank.com**)

- Clickbooth (**www.clickbooth.com**)

- COPEAC (**www.copeac.com**)

- CPA Storm (**www.cpastorm.com**)

- ClixGalore (**www.clixgalore.com**)

- IncentReward (**www.incentreward.com**)

- Motive Interactive (**www.motiveinteractive.com**)

- pepperjamNETWORK (**www.pepperjamnetwork.com**)

- StellarAds (**www.stellarads.com**)

- Incentaclick (**www.incentaclick.com**)

- Profitistic (**www.profitistic.co.uk**)

There are dozens, probably hundreds, of other affiliate networks to choose from, but this list provides you with a great starting point.

Become an Affiliate of Others

If you are not selling products and only offer services through your Web site, or do not feel that your products would be profitable through an affiliate program, you will want to consider becoming an affiliate of others. This option is free, easy to implement, requires minimal Web HTML coding on your Web site, and runs itself once established. You monitor your performance, and wait for the check in mail.

At this point you have two basic options: You can join an affiliate network or sign up with an individual company's affiliate program through their Web site. An affiliate network has some advantages in that there is typically no cost, but you are offered through one portal the ability to select multiple vendors of which you can become an affiliate. Additionally, you have only one control panel to monitor performance and results; whereas if you sign up with individual companies and join multiple affiliate programs, you will have separate control and administrative panels for each one. Another advantage of an affiliate network is that you usually get one check per month versus many checks per month. The choice is yours, but for now, we are going to concentrate on joining as an affiliate of a merchant Web site.

Some words of caution with affiliate networks: They are very easy to use, and you can add a wide variety of affiliate products to your site effortlessly — but do not get carried away. Adding products to your site does not necessarily mean sales or profits. Do not overdo it and flood your Web site with page after page of links, banner ads, and so on; this advice of course applies to all of your affiliate marketing goals. Find your market niche and concentrate on it, drive customers to your affiliate links, but keep it focused and relevant to your Web site. As in the previous example, if your Web site is about Boston terriers, there is little likelihood of success by adding computers and automotive supplies to your Web site because they are not related to your main content. On the other hand, custom grooming items, dog collars, shampoos, etc., may be highly profitable for you.

The next chapter has a detailed walkthrough of the process you can expect when becoming an affiliate through a merchant Web site. I have provided you with a detailed overview of the process, so we will move on to establishing your own affiliate program.

Establishing Your Own Affiliate Program

If you have products to sell, particularly if they are considered niche or highly desired items, you may consider starting your own affiliate program on your Web site. This provides you with the greatest flexibility, control, and administration over your program, affiliates, and products. One word of caution: Do not attempt to design and develop your own affiliate software — it is not worth the effort, cost, or time. In a later chapter, I will review many great products you can consider for your affiliate program.

Let's consider Atlantic Publishing Company. They develop, write, and publish books, like this book, and they do their own editing, layout, graphics, art, marketing, production, and sales. They own the copyright of their works, and because they have titles that cover a wide variety of topics, many of which are considered to be niche marketing, they are a perfect case study for establishing an affiliate program. Atlantic has an affiliate program which has been very successful for them.

One of the concepts businesses often struggle with is why should they start an affiliate program when they already sell their products on their Web site, and why should they pay a commission that is money out of their pocket. The reason is that through an affiliate you have market growth. The more Web sites on which your products are sold, the easier it is to find them. More people become aware of them, and viral marketing can take over as your products show up on Web sites, blogs, e-mails, and more.

I am an affiliate of Atlantic Publishing because they pay me 20 percent for each book I sell through my Web site or blog. I earn this by placing the links on my Web site and blog. That is the end of my work to earn the 20 percent commission. Why would Atlantic Publishing want to do this? As an author, I can direct people to my Web site and blog, and if they are interested in my books, they can click on the link on my Web site and buy them through Atlantic. I get a commission and Atlantic gets a sale they may not have gotten otherwise. Paying 20 percent on a total sale is better than no sale, which means no income. Multiply this formula times the number of affiliates and the increased marketplace presence, and you start to see the big picture.

If you have 500 affiliates, and each affiliate makes one sale per day, then that is 500 books you have sold which you would not have sold otherwise. Even with the additional 20 percent commission fee you pay, you still have a net income significantly higher than you would have with zero sales. You do need to ensure that you can absorb the commission rate and remain profitable. The 20 percent that Atlantic Publishing offers is very high; typically it is in the 7 to 12 percent range. By offering a very high commission, Atlantic attracts affiliates to join their program.

Think of the advantage of starting an affiliate program. You have full control over every aspect of the program, you can save on other marketing and advertisement costs, you can advertise your program through your blog, e-mail marketing, and more. Once established, businesses and individuals will seek you out wanting to join your program. Here are some of the basic benefits to establishing an affiliate program:

- Other businesses, Web sites, and blogs are advertising your products for you

- Your products, banner advertisement, text, and other promotional materials are on other Web sites and blogs throughout the world, driving traffic to your Web site

- You establish your presence in a very unstable Internet and earn brand-name recognition, appeal, and customer satisfaction

- You dramatically increase sales volume.

One of the challenges businesses have to overcome is the fear of the unknown, and affiliate marketing is no exception. **Amazon.com** and **eBay.com** have the finest affiliate programs around, but you do not need to be either of these companies or have their budgets, technical staffs, or power to succeed. I will walk you through this simple process in later chapters.

You do need to decide what your overall objectives and goals are before you make your decision to establish an affiliate marketing program on your Web site. Here are some basic questions to answer when trying to determine if an affiliate program is right for your business:

- **Do you want to automate the process as much as possible, allow self-registration into your affiliate program, and have your affiliate program track sales, commission and all other administrative functions?** The answer should be yes unless you want to develop and implement a manual system. There are some manual options, but these are not recommended. Do it right; give your affiliates reporting capability and let the system work for you, not the other way around.

- **What model do you want to use?** Pay for clicks, impressions, leads, or actual sales? I recommend actual sales; clicks and impressions are great, but they do not necessarily mean sales. Pay for actual sales if that is your goal or leads if your goal is to collect business leads.

- **Are you interested in multi-level marketing or two-tier marketing?** A one-tier system is straightforward: You have affiliates, and you pay them a commission for each sale or lead. In the two-tier system your affiliates can establish affiliates under them, at a lesser commission rate, meaning that for each sale from the second tier you pay them a commission, plus your first-tier rate. My advice is to keep a one-tier system and pay the maximum commission you can afford. In the long run, it is more effective and appealing to affiliates.

- **Do you want your affiliates to sell all of your products or just select products?** Similarly, do all or only some of your products qualify for a commission?

- **Do you want affiliates in your country, or do you want to expand internationally?** Do you ship internationally? International affiliates may draw in international sales.

- **Are you interested in paying a commission based on a percentage basis of the total sales or a flat fee per sale?** For example, 10 percent of the total pre-tax sales or $10 commission per sale regardless of the sale amount.

Most feature-rich affiliate programs have the essentials you need to be successful, such as online monitoring and reporting for your affiliate, e-mail notification after each sale, a variety of options for banner, text and other links, and the ability to maintain and track account status.

You now have a thorough understanding of how an affiliate program works. In the next chapter, we will dive into affiliate programs and analyze and provide examples of how to become an affiliate and how to set up and manage your own affiliate program.

AFFILIATE MARKETING SURVIVAL STRATEGIES

By Michael Bloch

Affiliate marketing can be an exciting and often frustrating experience. For those of you who want to make a living from promoting other companies' products and services, unless you are very fortunate, the road will be long and hard; fraught with traps for the unsuspecting.

How do I know this? I've been there. This article is not about how to generate massive revenue in a short space of time. It's about working through problems with honest merchants, and also strategies for catching dishonest ones. You'd be surprised at the number of affiliates who generate sales, yet never see a dime for their efforts. At the end of this article are a number of links to other strategies and tutorials I've published on affiliate marketing that may be of value to you.

Joined a Great Affiliate Program — But No Commissions?

So, you have signed up with what appears to be a great affiliate program that really suits your target audience. You have developed strategies, selected banners and other marketing materials, and published them on your site. Perhaps you have gone one step further and published reviews, articles, and tutorials on subjects related to your merchants to lead people to examine their services.

You know that the pages and ads are generating views and click-throughs. Yet for all this effort, after a couple of months, you have yet to see a return for your investment of time in developing marketing strategies and the use of your valuable Web site space. What could be wrong?

The following are some of the most common issues affecting leads and sales commissions.

Soggy Cookies

Many merchants use cookies to track your referrals. In relation to affiliate programs, a cookie is a small text file sent to the visitor's computer and stored, containing information, such as which site referred them.

Since most people do not purchase on their first visit to a site, a cookie allows for potential referrals to be tagged with your affiliate ID, so that if they should purchase on a future visit, you will still be credited for the lead or sale.

Cookie durations vary from merchant to merchant. Some last as little as a single session, while others last for years. Of course, the longer the cookie duration, the better.

Where cookie tracking methods are employed, several things can go wrong.

- The person your refer flushes out their cookies on a regular basis. There is nothing much you can do about that.

- The person you refer has cookie-blocking software operating or has browser security levels set so high that cookies are rejected. Again, there's not much you can do in this situation.

- The affiliate program software used by the merchant is not functioning correctly and is not setting cookies at all, which is the real killer.

- Some merchants who really understand the affiliate game will use more than just cookies. IP and session tracking can be added also as additional fail-safes.

The last scenario happens more regularly than you may think. Bear in mind that it is usually not an intentional problem. Many merchants do not have the technical skills to spot this kind of thing. They employ programmers or buy out-of-the-box solutions for their affiliate programs, and trust that they function correctly.

It is very important that you test to see if the cookie setting function is working correctly and that the expiration date is correct before you invest any serious time and energy into promoting a merchant program.

This is a simple task. Click on one of the affiliate links supplied to you and then check your browser cache folder. Look for this:

Cookie:yourcomputername@merchantsite.com, or

Cookie:yourcomputername@www.merchantsite.com

Be sure to examine the expiration date as well. If you cannot find the cookie, it would be a good idea to contact the merchant and ask for assistance. When approaching merchants, be polite and respectful. Take an innocent until proven guilty approach; they may not be aware of the situation. If you notify them, you not only will be saving your own sales commissions, but also those of many other affiliates.

Multiple Payment Methods

If you have joined an affiliate program through a network that also processes payments of products on behalf of merchants, it is not uncommon for merchants to offer customers multiple payment methods. It is great for customers, but not for affiliates. Here's an example:

Merchant X uses software distribution company Y as one of their distributors. You join company Y as an affiliate because they have a wide range of products/services from various merchants to choose from. You are not aware that Merchant X also uses software distribution companies A, B, and C for the same product, each processing payments for the merchant. The person you refer via the company Y affiliate network purchases a product from Merchant X, but uses the company B payment method. The end result is no commission for you. Worse still, I have seen some merchants advertise their products on some affiliate networks, but they do not even offer payment options for that network.

Before you begin advertising any products or services as an affiliate of a network that also processes orders, check the merchant site carefully. If in doubt, contact the merchant before expending any further energy, no matter how good the commission rate is. Fifty percent of $0.00 is still zero.

Be aware that many merchants offer telephone sales. How will your commission be tracked if the transaction occurs over the phone?

PHONE PAYMENTS

Increasing numbers of merchants offer pre-sales phone lines which is a great idea. The problem, however, occurs if the sales staff also takes orders over the phone. If the customer hasn't gone through the online checkout process, the sale is not tracked. If you see sales phone numbers posted on a merchant's site ask the merchant how ordering is handled. In some cases the sales staff will just coach the customer through the online checkout process which is fine — the sale will be tracked.

SOME PEOPLE DON'T LIKE AFFILIATE LINKS

Affiliate links can be very easy to spot, especially if they link directly to the merchant: e.g., **www.xyz12345.com/affiliate.htm?aid=65544w.**

A link target can be viewed by moving your mouse over a link and viewing your browser status bar. Some of your site visitors will refuse to click on affiliate links, or they will just type the merchant site address directly into their browser address bar. Affiliate links should be cloaked with JavaScript to remove the affiliate ID from view. Any merchant who really cares about his affiliates will happily introduce this function to his program — it is a relatively simple task depending on the software they are using to control their program. If they are not able to do so you can do it yourself.

Just another quick point on affiliate links: Make sure they always open in a new window. That way, your visitors will not be totally lost from your site.

DECOY PRODUCTS AND SERVICES

This strategy used by some merchants really stinks. Some affiliate programs are offered only on particular items that act as decoys. When your referred visitors arrive on the site, they are immediately distracted by other offerings. This is not always apparent on your first visit to the merchant's site.

STEALWARE

Stealware overwrites affiliate tracking codes, replaces affiliate cookies on a user's computer, or overlays links on a Web site with another affiliate's tracking link, which results in payments going to another party. The problem is quite rampant and is discussed further in this article. When reviewing a merchant's program check for clauses in the terms relating to these sorts of activities; most good merchants will explicitly state they do not allow affiliates to use these methods. If nothing is mentioned, contact the merchant for clarifications.

POOR SITE STRUCTURE

A merchant can have the best products around, but if the site and ordering process are difficult to navigate it will have a negative impact on sales. Take a look around the site and offer the merchant suggestions on how to improve the sales process. A good merchant will be glad to receive this information; it is a free consultation.

LACK OF AFFILIATE ACCOUNT INTERFACE

Affiliate software is so cheap these days that no merchant offering a program has any excuse for not having an interface available for affiliates so they can monitor their traffic and sales performance. In the many years, I have been involved in affiliate marketing, I have never had any success with a merchant who says, "We don't have an affiliate interface, but we track everything at our end and send you a monthly report." That is simply not good enough. As an affiliate, you want to be able to check your own progress because it helps you tweak your copy and sales approach. Affiliate arrangements without an account interface should be avoided.

Monitor Your Affiliate Arrangements

As the years go by, I find myself spending more time monitoring the merchants I work with. I would like to believe that the vast majority of merchants are honest, but there are some sharp operators who are unscrupulous, and I try to weed out those companies as soon as possible. They view affiliates as annoyances rather than important business partners. You will identify these people very quickly because they are slow to respond and usually quite rude.

Even the most honest merchant has problems with their affiliate software from time to time, so it is important to be vigilant and regularly check cookies and merchant sites for changes that may affect your commissions. If ever in doubt, ask — but ask nicely. Never make accusations until you have all the information.

You can make a decent living as an affiliate, and you may even generate substantial income very quickly. But the reality is that in the start-up stages, it can be very hard work. I hope these strategies and the following resources assist you in achieving your online goals.

*Michael Bloch has been working the Web as a successful marketing and development consultant since the late 1990s. Michael owns and operates **TamingTheBeast.net**, a popular Internet marketing and e-commerce resources site providing online business owners and affiliate marketers with valuable free advice, articles, tutorials, and tools.*

5 Becoming an Affiliate of Others

I have covered the basic concepts of affiliate marketing, provided guidance on how to perform market research to determine what products or markets you think will be profitable for you in your affiliate marketing campaign, and discussed in detail the essential decisions you need to make. Now, you have decided you want to sign up and become an affiliate of others, featuring their products on your Web site and earning a commission for each sale. You will be very surprised at how simple this is. Keep in mind that there are many different affiliate programs and their function and performance is similar to what I am showing you. Another option is a replicated store. You join an affiliate program and are provided with an exact copy of their Web store, which you install on your domain. This simplifies the process and makes it a turn-key solution with all your unique affiliate IDs already embedded.

Continuing to use Atlantic Publishing for our case study, we will sign up as an affiliate of Atlantic Publishing. Our new affiliate will be Casa Dos, a vacation rental situated in beautiful Crystal River, Florida. Casa Dos features beautiful waterfront accommodations in a romantic setting and is only minutes from diving with the manatees or fishing in the Gulf of Mexico for redfish, grouper, or other seafood delicacies. Crystal River is famous for its manatee-watching, diving, fishing trips, world-class golfing, and other activities. Crystal River is approximately 30-45 minutes from Cedar Key or an hour and a half to Disney World in Orlando or Busch Gardens in Tampa. You can visit Casa Dos on the Web at **www.crystalriverhouse. com**, or e-mail info@crystalriverhouse.com.

Because the owners of the luxurious house cater to retirees, and those seeking the tranquility and peace of a waterfront vacation away from the hustle and bustle of the beach, they have a unique market niche. Casa Dos is luxuriously furnished and marvelously decorated, so the owners would like to generate additional income on their Web site by adding books that their guests may enjoy reading during their stay. The owners would like the books added to their Web site as well as integrated within their reservation notification system; essentially using e-mail marketing in combination with their affiliate account.

They take it one step further by allowing guests to order books at the time of reservation. Upon arrival at Casa Dos, these new books are waiting for them with a complimentary bottle of wine. The wine is not part of the affiliate program, but they have always offered this little token of affection, and by tying it to affiliate sales, they give the visitor an extra incentive to buy the books for their visit. They could just as easily sign up with any other affiliate program, but we are going to have them join the Atlantic Publishing Affiliate Program.

If you are not selling products, or you only offer services through your Web site, you will want to consider becoming an affiliate of others, which is exactly what we are doing in this chapter. This option is free, easy to implement, requires minimal web HTML coding on your Web site, and once established, runs itself. As I stated, I will walk you through the entire process for setting up your account, setting up products on your Web page, testing your affiliate links, and monitoring your account.

Signing Up as an Affiliate

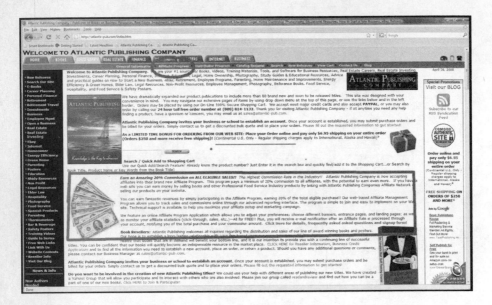

As you can see in the image above, which is a screen shot of Atlantic Publishing Company's Web site home page, their affiliate program is featured prominently with a bold tag line: "Earn an amazing 20 percent commission on all eligible sales." You also will notice in the circled section that there is another link to the affiliate program. This link is featured on every page of their Web site, so no matter which site page visitors are on, there is navigation to the affiliate sign-up page.

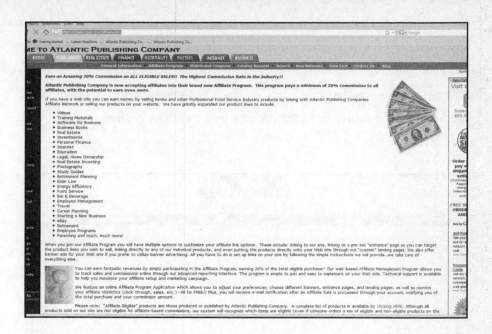

When you click the link to become an affiliate, you are navigated to the affiliate home page, which has basic requirements and a general overview of the Atlantic Publishing Company Affiliate Program. As with any affiliate program, it is important to read the information, ensure that the program will meet your needs, and review the summary of features to ensure it is robust enough to satisfy your requirements. Next, we will actually sign up as an affiliate through the Atlantic Publishing Affiliate Program.

You will notice that they instruct you to click on the link to "Read Our Agreement Terms" and then join the program. Most affiliates have terms you must agree to. Typically, these are to protect the merchant from claims arising about generated sales, but you are not given proper credit for the sale because of a faulty or incorrect link you have established on your Web site.

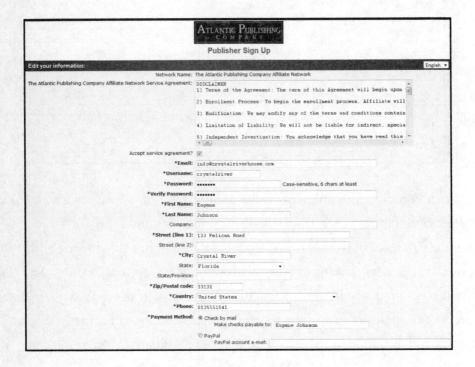

You simply fill out the form and check the "Accept service agreement" block to agree to the terms and conditions. I highly encourage you to read the Affiliate Network Service Agreement. Atlantic Publishing Company lets you accept payment via PayPal or check. Many individuals and companies like the security of receiving payments electronically via PayPal.

E-mail managed programs require you to opt-in; Atlantic requires you to opt-in and confirm your account. This also protects you from a fraudulent affiliate agreement sign-up in your name.

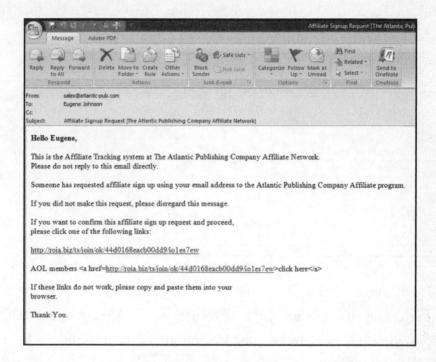

You will receive an e-mail confirmation from Atlantic Publishing, in which you must confirm the affiliate sign-up request. Upon confirmation, you will receive the notification below.

You will notice that the confirmation states that the application is being reviewed. This means that Atlantic has chosen to review and manually approve all applications instead of automatically approving all new applications. This review process typically takes 24 hours or less. In addition, Atlantic will send you an e-mail confirmation and notification that your application is being reviewed, which is shown below.

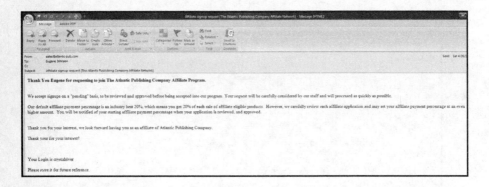

You will notice that this e-mail contains the log-on ID, but does not contain a link to the affiliate administrative control panel. After your account is approved, you will receive an e-mail notification similar to the one below, which contains your access information.

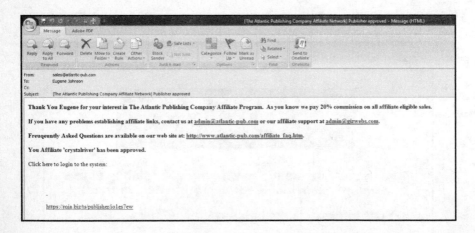

At this point, you are ready to sign in to your affiliate account and add products to your Web site. You will notice that Atlantic provided a link to their frequently asked questions for affiliates. Before we log into the control panel for our account, let's navigate to the frequently asked questions and see what information they are providing to assist us with establishing our affiliate account. You will notice they also provide e-mail links for technical support. If you are in doubt when setting up an account, take advantage of the support so you can ensure that you get all the credit for your affiliate sales.

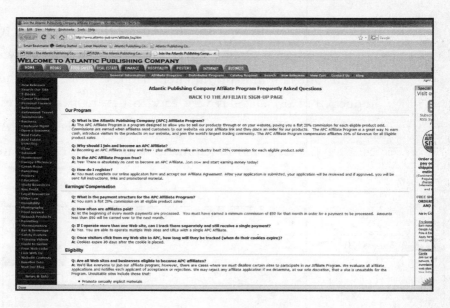

I am excited to see that, in addition to live technical support, Atlantic offers you a wealth of information about their program. You should note that this information also was available from the affiliate sign-up page to assist you with your sign-up and decision process. Let's log in to the control panel and check out our account.

Logging Into Your Affiliate Account

Atlantic Publishing Company utilizes affiliate software from TrackingSoft, LLC, called ROI Advantage® Online Advertising Tracking System. We will go through this program in depth in later chapters as we review this and other products, but overall, it is very easy to use, rich in features, cost-effective, and flexible. While these screenshots are all unique to ROIA, you can expect similar screens and functionality with most other affiliate software applications.

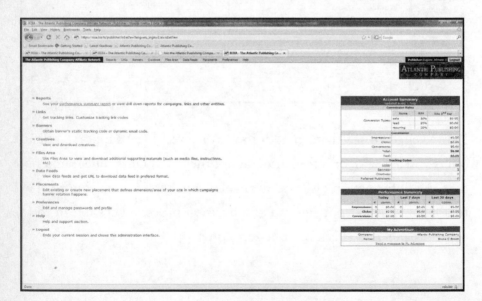

Upon logging in, you are taken to the main control panel. On the right-hand side is the account summary screen which shows you the overview of your account performance, such as conversion statistics, commission, available predefined tracking codes, performance summary, and advertiser information. The advertiser is the merchant, and you are the affiliate, or also known as the publisher. You have a variety of links to view reports, get links and custom tracking codes, grab banners, creative elements, and data feed placements, and edit your preferences and profile.

The first step for any new affiliate is to spend some time navigating the menus and becoming familiar with the interface. In general navigating is easy. There are instructions to walk you through the process. Take a close look at the summary screen; once you set up your links, this will likely be the main screen you look at on a regular basis to view and monitor your performance. As you can see in the image below, your commission percentage is set at 20 percent, and there is no second-tier commission. Because your account is new, you show no impression clicks or conversions. Since you only get paid for conversions or sales, this is the only category you should track.

Account Summary
updated every 1 hour

Commission Rates

Conversion Types:	Name	RPA	RPA 2nd tier
	sale	20%	$0.00
	lead	20%	$0.00
	recurring	20%	$0.00

Commission

Impressions:	$0.00
Clicks:	$0.00
Conversions:	$0.00
Total:	$0.00
Paid:	$0.00

Tracking Codes

Links:	38
Banners:	5
Creatives:	0
Referred Publishers:	0

Performance Summary

	Today		Last 7 days		Last 30 days	
	#	comm.	#	comm.	#	comm.
Impressions:	0	$0.00	0	$0.00	0	$0.00
Clicks:	0	$0.00	0	$0.00	0	$0.00
Conversions:	0	$0.00	0	$0.00	0	$0.00

My Advertiser

Company:	Atlantic Publishing Company
Name:	Bruce C Brown

Send a message to My Advertiser

The tracking code shows you predefined links which are pre-configured with your unique account ID. You can simply cut and paste them into your site to start your affiliate marketing campaign. You have the ability to create custom links to any product on Atlantic's Web site. Navigate to the links and banners to see what is available.

Atlantic Publishing provides many links to each of their main product lines. For example, on the left-hand side is Business Resources, EBay, Employee Management, Internet Marketing, and Career Planning. These product lines have predefined links you can use, so if you want to link to the category on Atlantic's site containing books about Homeowner Reference, you can click on that link and navigate to that directory of affiliate links. Note that every product is contained in the database as a predefined link. If you wish to link to a particular title, you can create a custom link, which I will show you later.

The screen above shows you default tracking codes, as well as the categories. Click a category on the left to drill down to that section.

Navigate to the Homeowner Reference section. You will see the list of titles, descriptions, tracking links, date, and description. Because not all items are predefined in the application, you can quickly add them. Additionally, you will notice that the help menu is available for you on each screen of the application. Under the help menu, you will see a menu option for contacting your advertiser. No matter what affiliate program you join, do not hesitate to ask for help. It is in their best interest to keep you happy and educated on how to set up your affiliate links.

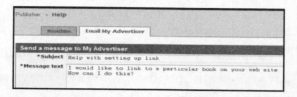

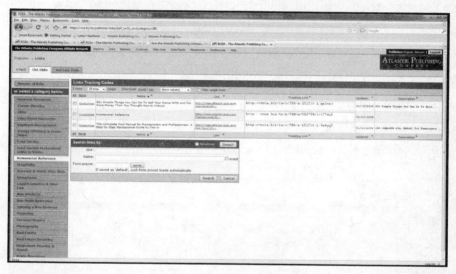

You will notice tabs to list links. In this case, they show the Homeowner Reference category and an affiliate link to that page on the Atlantic Web site, as well as two books which have been set up previously for direct links. Click on the Get Link Code tab to create custom links to any book on the Web site. As you see below you have two options.

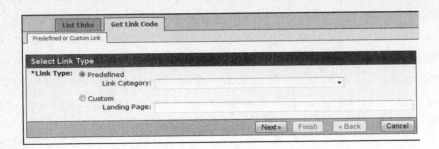

You can choose a predefined Link-by-Link Category or create a custom landing page. A landing page is the Web page where your link will point. This can be any page on the merchant Web site, but typically it is used to link directly to a product. First, let's click the predefined radio button, and then choose the Internet & World Wide Web Books from the Link Category drop-down menu. In this next screen, you will see the Internet books product line, as well as individual books in this category. You can choose the book you want and click next, or you can simply cut and paste the link from the link column for your Web site or blog. This link has your unique affiliate ID embedded in it, so when someone clicks on it, you are credited for the affiliate sale.

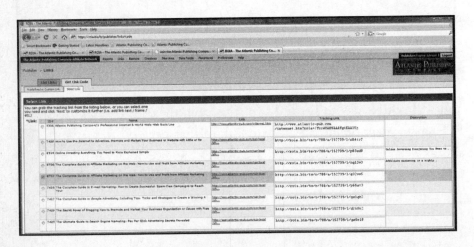

Using the radio button, choose the item you wish to use as an affiliate link and click the next button. In the screen shot below, you can see the end result which shows you the link name and the landing page and provides you with the tracking code which is your affiliate link URL. We would use this link on our Web site to link to the product. When this link is clicked on and the sale is completed, the system knows it came from your Web site, and you are given credit for the sale in the form of a commission.

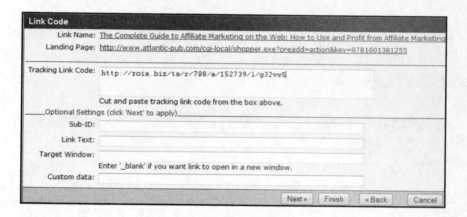

To create a custom link to a particular product you simply need to choose custom and enter the landing page, URL of the product you want.

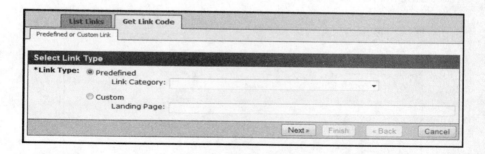

For the Casa Dos Web site, they would like to have a link to the book, *Your First Cruise: A Complete Guide to Planning and Attaining the Perfect Cruise Vacation*. Because Florida is a major cruise port origination point, they feel this would be a great addition to their Web site. Copy and paste the URL from this product on Atlantic Publishing Company's Web site into the Landing Page box and click the next button:

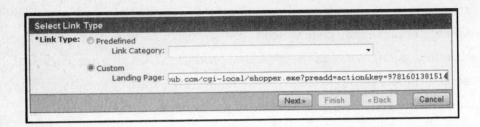

After clicking next, your custom URL is provided which is uniquely coded to your affiliate ID in the Tracking Link Code box. This link is now ready to be used on your Web site:

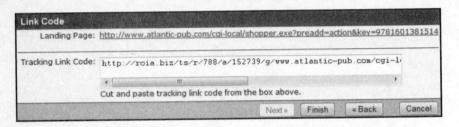

Before we start to integrate the affiliate links into our Web site take a look at the available banners which Atlantic offers us.

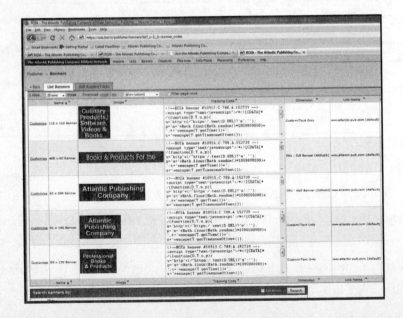

As you can see, a wide variety of banners are available. Most merchants update the banners often and are usually willing to create custom banners as well. In the case of Casa Dos, I do not intend to use banner ads; instead I want to place several books on our Web site and link directly to them. Let's go ahead and edit our Web site, add a couple of books to it, and then test them out. One major word of caution when testing your links: You can test them out by clicking on them and in the performance summary you can view the clicks. Do not test out your affiliate links by placing orders. In fact — all affiliate programs ban you from ordering through your own affiliate links; placing orders for yourself in which you get a commission for the sale is not allowed.

Integrating Affiliate Links Into Your Web Site

To edit our Web site, I am going to use Microsoft Expression Web. Since we have already integrated and provided links to the books in the reservation system and in the e-mail confirmation, we must build a page with our affiliate products. It is not uncommon to put affiliate products on most pages of a Web site. Place them strategically so they make logical sense; a Web page article about LCD monitors would be an appropriate place for affiliate LCD monitors. Place them tactfully so your site encourages the purchase and does not turn someone away from considering the purchase.

Because Atlantic's affiliate agreement allows me to copy product description and product images from their Web site onto ours, I am simply going to copy that information from their Web page into mine using Microsoft Expression Web.

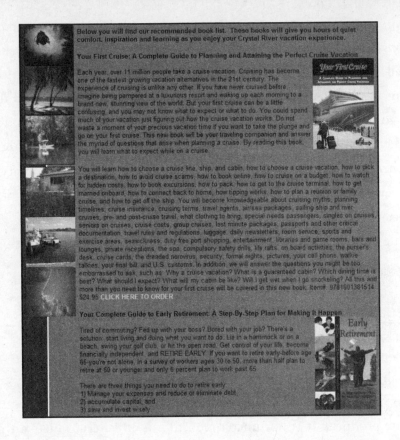

Now that our page is created and our two books are on it, we need to integrate the page with the affiliate program so that when someone clicks on the CLICK HERE TO ORDER link, we can track not only that click, but also the resulting sale and commission. To do this we go back into our affiliate control panel, create the two custom links, and, in Expression Web or another HTML editor, add a URL to each book using the unique provided customer URL embedded with your affiliate ID code.

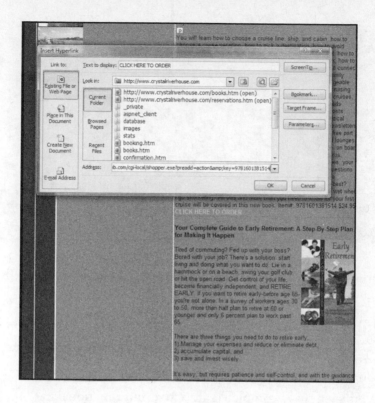

The above screenshot depicts the integration of the affiliate link for the cruise book into the Web page code. Once saved, this link is active. I will add the affiliate link to the second book now and our program is active on our Web site. Now, we can start monitoring performance. Once you place your links and save your Web page, you should open it in the browser and move the cursor over the banner ad, link, or image to ensure that your link is properly formatted, active, and working.

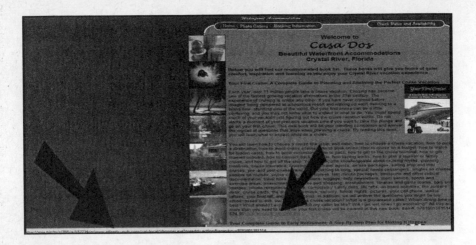

The arrows in the screen shot above point to the CLICK HERE TO ORDER link which contains the embedded affiliate URL. The link is displayed in the bottom left-hand corner where the other arrow is pointing. At this point, you are finished setting up your Web site. Of course, if you wanted to add more products on other pages, you would continue to do so, but the ones you have completed are active and functional.

Monitoring Affiliate Performance and Tracking Sales

Now that your affiliate links are established on your Web site, you can start promoting your affiliate links. We will cover promoting your links in a later chapter of this book; so for now, let's see what happens when a visitor to our site clicks on our links. One important factor to remember is that when an affiliate clicks on your link and links to one product, a cookie is placed on their computer; although, there are cookieless solutions as well. This cookie tracks you throughout the entire transaction, so if the potential customer decided to order the product you linked to, and for example buys five more books, you get the commission for the entire sale, not just the product or Web page you linked to.

It is important to understand and expect that many people may click on your links, and a much smaller percentage may actually convert the sale. Do not be alarmed if your click-through rate is high, but your actual conversions are much lower in number. For example, an order was just placed by someone visiting our Crystal River Web site, clicking on the affiliate links, and placing an order with Atlantic Publishing Company. As an affiliate, I will of course not see the order, but I will be informed that the order was placed. In the case of Atlantic Publishing Company, I will receive an e-mail notification for each item ordered; so if ten different items are ordered I will get ten different e-mails.

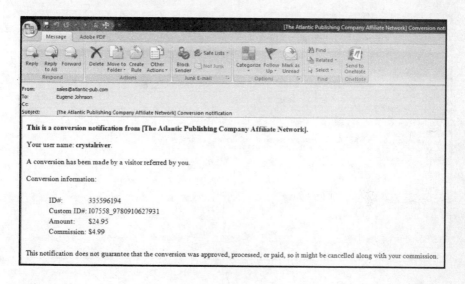

The e-mail above shows me that invoice #IO7558 was placed through my affiliate link with Atlantic Publishing Company and a sale or conversion was completed. In this case, it shows my user name for the affiliate program, tells me the ID of the product ordered, the amount of the product and my commission percentage of the sale, $4.99; 20 percent of the total. In the example below, the invoice number is identical, #IO7558; so we know that this was another line item on the same order. Remember that an e-mail notification is sent for each line item sale. In this case, the total for the line item was $249.50 and my commission total is $49.90. For the total of 30 minutes it took me to sign up with the affiliate program, place the content on my Web site, and establish the affiliate links, I have already earned nearly $55.

One thing to note on the e-mail notification is the disclaimer. This notification does not guarantee that the conversion was approved, processed, or paid, so it might be cancelled along with your commission. In the case of a cancelled order, refund, returns, or other exception, Atlantic has the right to remove this commission from your account.

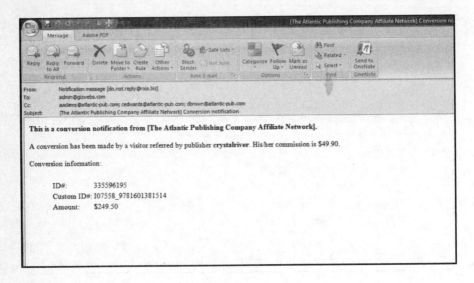

Once a month Atlantic will total your commission in compliance with their terms and agreement and pay your total commission for that period via PayPal or check. It is that simple. Go back to the control panel, and look at your performance summary.

Commission		
Impressions:	0.00%	$0.00
Clicks:	0.00%	$0.00
Conversions:	100.00%	$98.00
Total:		$98.00
Average Daily:		$3.77

Impressions	
Total:	0
Unique:	0
Commission:	$0.00

Clicks		
Total:		8
Average Daily:		0
Unique:	0.00%	0
Commission:		$0.00

Conversions	
Conversions:	11
Average Daily:	0
Total Amount:	$490.00
Average Conversion Amount:	$44.55
Average Daily Amount:	$18.85
Commission:	$98.00
Average Conversion Commission:	$8.91
Average Daily Commission:	$3.77

As you can see, we show that there were eight clicks, resulting in 11 conversions. A conversion is a sale and each line item in a sale counts as a conversion, meaning that from the eight clicks on the Web site, 11 product line items were purchased. We can see that a total of $490 in orders was processed, the average conversion amount was $44.55, the average daily amount was $18.55, and the commission was $98. Below that are commission averages, including the average daily commission. Because the affiliate is fairly new, it will take some time to build reliable averages. In less than one day, $98 was earned by joining one affiliate program. One nice feature of ROIA is the vast reports available. If you want to see how your commission is calculated, you can generate reports such as the one below, which shows details for each conversion:

Conversions

11 rows 25 rows /page Download excel | csv (show column) Filter page rows

ID#	Date created ▲	Type	Custom ID#	Amount	Commission	Custom Information
335596194	04/26/2008 02:51:36 PM	sale	I07558_9780910627931	$24.95	$4.99	
335596195	04/26/2008 02:51:37 PM	sale	I07558_9781601381514	$249.50	$49.90	
335596200	04/26/2008 02:54:00 PM	sale	I07559_9781601380494	$24.95	$4.99	
335596204	04/26/2008 02:54:01 PM	sale	I07559_9781601382047	$21.95	$4.39	
335596203	04/26/2008 02:54:01 PM	sale	I07559_9781601381514	$24.95	$4.99	
335596202	04/26/2008 02:54:01 PM	sale	I07559_9780910627931	$24.95	$4.99	
335596201	04/26/2008 02:54:01 PM	sale	I07559_9780910627726	$21.95	$4.39	
335596206	04/26/2008 02:54:02 PM	sale	I07559_9781601382108	$24.95	$4.99	
335596205	04/26/2008 02:54:02 PM	sale	I07559_9781601382351	$21.95	$4.39	
335596218	04/26/2008 02:58:46 PM	sale	I07560_9781601381514	$24.95	$4.99	
335596219	04/26/2008 02:58:46 PM	sale	I07560_9780910627931	$24.95	$4.99	
			Grand Total			
				$490.00	$98.00	
ID#	Date created ▲	Type	Custom ID#	Amount	Commission	Custom Information

Here are some general rules of thumb to follow when choosing which affiliate to join.

- They must be a solid company that has been in business for two or more years.

- Commissions are paid on time.

- Their affiliate program should be well-established.

- They use feature-rich affiliate software.

- You know someone, if possible, who recommends their program.

- They have minimal product returns or disputes.

- They provide customer and technical support.

As you know, each affiliate operates on different terms and uses a wide variety of software, but essentially the process is nearly identical. You can monitor your progress, tracking how much you are owed and when checks are issued to you. I can assure you, there is no feeling like the one you get when your first commission check arrives. Now, take a look at the process from the other side of the house. If you have products to sell, you may consider implementing an affiliate program on your Web site. In the next chapter, we will look at how Atlantic implemented and manages their affiliate program on their Web site, **www.atlantic-pub.com.**

Hosting and Implementing an Affiliate Program

You have a Web site and you have products to sell. These are the two key ingredients for establishing your own affiliate marketing program. As discussed previously, you can join an affiliate network; however, in this chapter, we will look at the process and advantages of your own affiliate program. You will be surprised at how simple and effective it is to create your own affiliate program.

With your own affiliate program you have full control over every aspect of the program and you can save on other marketing and advertising costs. Plus you can use many marketing and advertising methods to promote not only your affiliate program, but your blog as well.

How to Get Started With an Affiliate Program

Atlantic Publishing Company utilizes affiliate software from TrackingSoft, LLC, called ROI Advantage® Online Advertising Tracking System. While this chapter uses ROIA as the guide, it is certainly not the only software application available; we will provide you with information about others later in this book. ROIAdvantage is "TrackingSoft's state-of-the-art tracking solution for affiliate program and advertising campaign management. ROIA represents the culmination of seven-plus years of experience in the affiliate tracking and Web advertising market by incorporating technological advances, client feedback, and innovation. The result is a comprehensive solution, which provides not only tracking of traffic and conversions, but also an advanced interface, multi-level drill-down reporting, publisher management, support for multiple ad campaigns, advanced Web site analytics, and much more."

In Atlantic's case TrackingSoft did the complete installation on their Web site, customized the basic control panel, and provided administrative control within a couple of hours. Atlantic customized the preferences and commission percentages, established terms and agreement, and started adding products to the affiliate application. Within half a day, Atlantic was up and running with their affiliate program. Atlantic uses the PDG Shopping Cart, which most affiliate programs are compatible with, but you need to make sure your cart works with your desired software solution. Atlantic uses a hosted Web server presence, meaning they do not own and maintain their own Web servers and technical support staff for the Web servers. This saves them thousands of dollars per year; an unnecessary expense since all TrackingSoft needed for configuration was FTP access to the Web server to add the files and a few minor bits of code to the shopping cart checkout pages to ensure that the shopping cart talked with the ROIA software. For minimal cost and time investment, you can have a full-featured affiliate program running on your Web site.

Affiliate Network Service Agreement

It is important to establish your ground rules in advance. You must determine how you will run your affiliate program. Also you must determine the terms and conditions for your customer agreement. ROIA is great because it integrates the sign-up process and notification process, allowing you to customize all the notifications including the terms and conditions. As an example to follow, here is Atlantic Publishing Company's Affiliate Network Service Agreement:

DISCLAIMER

1) **Terms of the Agreement:** The term of this Agreement will begin upon our acceptance of your Affiliate application, and will end when terminated by either party. Either you or we may terminate this Agreement at any time, with or without cause, by giving the other party written notice of termination. You are only eligible to earn referral fees on sales occurring during the term.

2) **Enrollment Process:** To begin the enrollment process, Affiliate will submit an application at **www.atlantic-pub.com** who will evaluate Affiliate's application and will notify Affiliate of Affiliate's acceptance or rejection. Atlantic Publishing Company may reject Affiliate's application if Atlantic Publishing Company determines that Affiliate's site is unsuitable for the Affiliate Program. Reasons for rejection can include but are not limited to the Affiliate's site promoting violence, discrimination based on race, sex, religion, nationality, disability, sexual orientation, or age, or the Affiliate's site promoting illegal activities and/or violating intellectual property rights.

3) **Modification:** We may modify any of the terms and conditions contained in this Agreement, at any time and in our sole discretion, by posting a change notice or a new agreement on this site. Modifications may include, for example, changes in the scope of available referral fees, fee schedules, payment procedures and Program rules. IF ANY MODIFICATION IS UNACCEPTABLE TO YOU, YOUR ONLY RECOURSE IS TO TERMINATE THIS AGREEMENT. YOUR CONTINUED PARTICIPATION IN THE PROGRAM FOLLOWING OUR POSTING OF A CHANGE NOTICE OR NEW AGREEMENT ON OUR SITE WILL CONSTITUTE BINDING ACCEPTANCE OF THE CHANGE.

DISCLAIMER

4) **Limitation of Liability:** We will not be liable for indirect, special or consequential damages, or any loss of revenue, profits or data, arising in connection with this Agreement or the Program, even if we have been advised of the possibility of such damages. Further, our aggregate liability arising with respect to this Agreement and the Program will not exceed the total referral fees paid or payable to you under to this Agreement.

5) **Independent Investigation:** You acknowledge that you have read this agreement and agree to all its terms and conditions. You understand that we may at any time (directly or indirectly) solicit customer referrals on terms that may differ from those contained in this agreement or operate Web sites that are similar to or compete with your Web site. You have independently evaluated the desirability of participating in the program and are not relying on any representation, guarantee or statement other than as set forth in this agreement.

6) **Spam:** Atlantic Publishing Company has a zero tolerance policy for Spam. Any Affiliate accused of Spamming will be immediately removed from our affiliate program. The only recourse you will have to maintain your affiliate relationship is proof of "opt-in" that will undermine the validity of the Spam complaint. Valid Spam complaints will result in the immediate termination of your account and forfeiture of any commissions owed you.

7) **Miscellaneous:** This Agreement will be governed by the laws of the home state of Florida. Any action relating to this Agreement must be brought in the federal or state courts located in the home state of Florida, and you irrevocably consent to the jurisdiction of such courts. You may not assign this Agreement, by operation of law or otherwise, without our prior written consent. Subject to that restriction, this Agreement will be binding on, inure to the benefit of and be enforceable against the parties and their respective successors and assigns. Our failure to enforce your

DISCLAIMER

strict performance of any provision of this Agreement will not constitute a waiver of our right to subsequently enforce such provision or any other provision of this Agreement.

8) Linking: We will provide you with textual and graphical links (link materials) with which you may link your Web site to our Web site. These link materials are available in your affiliate log-in panel in the "Instructions" area. If you are an approved Affiliate, we grant you a non-exclusive limited license solely to reproduce and use these link materials, including our trademarks to the extent they are incorporated into these link materials, only while you are an Affiliate and only in accordance with the terms and conditions of this Agreement. You many include link materials in mailings to your opted-in lists (see section 6 regarding Spam) and in other advertisements at your discretion. You agree to display the link materials appropriately on your Web site and in advertisements, and to respect our trademarks, service marks, and other rights in the link materials. You will use only these link materials to link to **www.atlantic-pub.com**, and you will not alter the look or feel of these link materials or of our Web site in any way. You will use reasonable efforts to update to new versions of link materials as we make them available.

9) **Tracking:** Atlantic Publishing Company will be solely responsible for tracking sales using special software that communicates with the specially encoded URLs assigned to affiliates. Atlantic Publishing Company will endeavor to do its best to ensure accurate tracking of referrals made by affiliates. Affiliates will themselves be solely responsible for ensuring that these special URLs are formatted properly, a necessary prerequisite to accurate tracking of referral sales. Notwithstanding the above statement of responsibility by Atlantic Publishing Company to track sales, Affiliates hereby acknowledge and accept that the tracking system employed by Atlantic Publishing Company is not 100% fail-safe and that there may on occasion be instances of referral sales made that are not credited to an affiliate for any of the following possible reasons:

DISCLAIMER

- Failure by the affiliate to use the proper format of the specially assigned URL in promotions, Web page links, banner ads, and so on; deliberate or accidental actions by customers to circumvent an affiliate's special URL so that our software is unable to accurately track that sale.

- Bugs, glitches, or crashes of the tracking software that render it unable to accurately track sales for a period of time; acts of nature that cause irretrievable data loss on the computers and back-up disk media.

10) **Relationships and Responsibilities:** You will be solely responsible for the development, operation, and maintenance of your site and for all materials that appear on your site. For example, you will be solely responsible for:

- The technical operation of your site and all related equipment

- The accuracy and appropriateness of materials posted on your site (including, among other things, all product-related materials)

- Ensuring that materials posted on your site do not violate or infringe upon the rights of any third party (including, for example, copyrights, trademarks, privacy, or other personal or proprietary rights)

- Ensuring that materials posted on your site are not libelous or otherwise illegal.

We disclaim all liability for these matters. Further, you will indemnify and hold us harmless from all claims, damages, and expenses (including, without limitation, attorneys' fees) relating to the development, operation, maintenance, and contents of your site.

11) **Relationship of Parties:** Atlantic Publishing Company and your company are independent contractors, and nothing in this

DISCLAIMER

Agreement will create any partnership, joint venture, agency, franchise, sales representative, or employment relationship between the parties. You will have no authority to make or accept any offers or representations on our behalf. You will not make any statement, whether on your site or otherwise, that reasonably would contradict anything in this agreement.

12) You will receive 20 percent of the revenue as a commission from orders placed through your Affiliate Site for products which are designated as "affiliate-eligible" products. Affiliate-eligible products are those products produced and published by Atlantic Publishing Company.

For a sale to generate a commission to an Affiliate, the customer must complete the order form and remit full payment for the service ordered. Currently the Atlantic Publishing Company does not support Second Tier Affiliates. Affiliate commissions will only be paid on sales which are made through qualified Affiliates. Affiliates MUST have an active link on their Web site.

13) The Atlantic Publishing Company Affiliate Program will be solely responsible for processing every order placed by a customer on the Affiliate sites. Customers who purchase products and services through The Atlantic Publishing Company Affiliate Program will be deemed to be customers of The Atlantic Publishing Company Affiliate Program. Prices and availability of our products and services may vary from time to time. The Atlantic Publishing Company Affiliate Program policies will always determine the price paid by the customer. We reserve the right to reject any order that does not comply with our rules, operating procedures, and policies.

14) We make no express or implied warranties or representations with respect to the Affiliate Program or your potential to earn income from the Atlantic Publishing Company Affiliate Program. In addition, we make no representation that the

DISCLAIMER

operation of our site or the Affiliate Sites will be uninterrupted Publishing Company Affiliate Program. In other words you cannot buy from yourself or be your first purchase for the sole purpose of discounting your own purchases. You cannot buy products for yourself through your affiliate links for the sole purpose of discounting your own purchases.

This Agreement will be governed by the laws of the United States and the State of Florida, without reference to rules governing choice of laws. Any action relating to this Agreement must be brought in the Federal or State courts located in Ocala, Florida, and you irrevocably consent to the jurisdiction of such courts. You may not assign this Agreement, by operation of law or otherwise, without our prior written consent. Subject to that restriction, this Agreement will be binding on, inure to the benefit of, and enforceable against the parties and their respective successors and assigns. Our failure to enforce your strict performance of any provision of this Agreement will not constitute a waiver of our right to subsequently enforce such provision or any other provision of this Agreement.

By submitting this Affiliate Agreement form, you acknowledge that you have read this agreement and agree to all its terms and conditions. You have independently evaluated this program, and are not relying on any representation, guarantee, or statement other than as set forth in this agreement.

This is a great agreement, and I encourage you to utilize it as the baseline for your agreement. Do not establish an affiliate program without first having agreed terms and conditions.

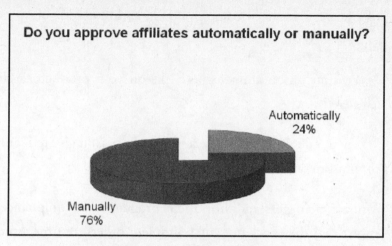

Do you approve affiliates automatically or manually?

Automatically
24%

Manually
76%

Reprinted with Permission Copyright 2008 Shawn Collins
http://blog.affiliatetip.com

Managing Your Affiliate Program

It is easier than you think. ROIA and other software applications are crammed full of reports, templates, and features and contain a variety of options to highly customize your affiliate program. The basic essentials still apply regardless of what program you use.

- You install and configure the affiliate software.

- You customize your application, establish terms and conditions, and customize the e-mail notifications.

- You put your products in your affiliate application, including banner ads and also add the ability for affiliates to create custom links.

- Create a sign-up page and advertise your affiliate program.

- As affiliates sign up, you approve them and they add your products to their Web site.

- As a visitor on an affiliate site clicks on your products, a click is registered.

- When a sale is completed, a conversion is registered and the commission amount is automatically calculated.

- Affiliate managers monitor their program for compliance and ensure that they back out any fraudulent orders, returns, cancelled orders, and so on.

- At the end of the month, using the integrated reports, you pay the affiliates for their commission.

Once you are up and running and have your sign-up page, you need to promote this page and your program benefits to encourage affiliates to join. Your sign-up page should point to your actual software application where your sign-up process is entirely automated. When an affiliate submits an application to your affiliate program, you are notified via e-mail.

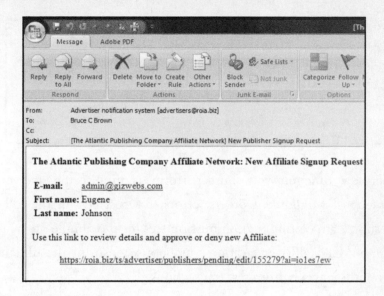

When you approve an application, unless it is set to automatically approve, you will be notified again via e-mail regarding the approval. You are also provided a link to review the affiliate.

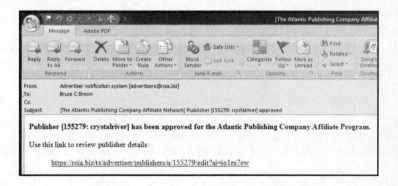

As orders are processed through your shopping cart, they are registered with the affiliate software as well, and you are provided with an e-mail notification so you can track them throughout the day.

Another key function you must perform is monitoring and making adjustments for fraudulent orders, errors, returns, etc. In the following screen shot, I am editing the commission fees for the sample orders placed through our Crystal River vacation rental house, ensuring the affiliate does not benefit financially from test transactions.

That is the entire process for managing your program. At most, it can take a couple hours per week, particularly at the end of the month when processing the payments. You should check performance reports daily. Performance reports can show you detailed breakdown by affiliate, product, time period, and much more. Below is an example of an affiliate program performance report in ROIA:

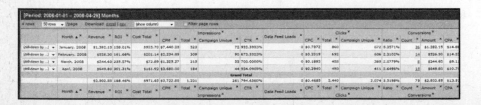

Let's take a look at some of the features in ROIA which should be in any affiliate software application. You must have the ability to customize your affiliate commission percentages and establish multi-tier marketing if you wish to enable it. Additionally, you must have the ability to set unique commission rates among your affiliates.

Edit commission rates:

RPM (rate per thousand impressions):	0	$ [USD] ▼	
RPM 2nd tier:	0	$ [USD] ▼	
Pay for total impressions?	☐	If checked, commissions will be based on total impressions instead of unique.	
RPC (rate per click):	0	$ [USD] ▼	
RPC 2nd tier:	0	$ [USD] ▼	
Pay for total clicks?	☐	If checked, commissions will be based on total clicks instead of unique.	

Rate per action (RPA) — commission paid for conversions

Sale RPA:	○ fixed rate:	0	$ [USD] ▼
	● % of conversion amount:	20	%
Lead RPA:	○ fixed rate:	0	$ [USD] ▼
	● % of conversion amount:	20	%
Recurring RPA:	○ fixed rate:	0	$ [USD] ▼
	● % of conversion amount:	20	%

2nd tier rate per action (RPA) — commission paid for conversions

Sale RPA 2nd tier:	● fixed rate:	0	$ [USD] ▼
	○ % of conversion amount:	0	%
Lead RPA 2nd tier:	● fixed rate:	0	$ [USD] ▼
	○ % of conversion amount:	0	%
Recurring RPA 2nd tier:	● fixed rate:	0	$ [USD] ▼
	○ % of conversion amount:	0	%

Do not save changes?	☐ If checked, changes will not be saved but you may apply them to past commissions on the next screen.

Next »   Finish   « Back   Cancel

You must have the ability to add custom banners as well as product links. Many affiliate applications, such as ROIA, also allow you to create customized creatives. Creatives through your affiliate program provide ready-made templates for e-mail marketing campaigns which can be further utilized and distributed by your affiliates; remember, they all agreed to no spam.

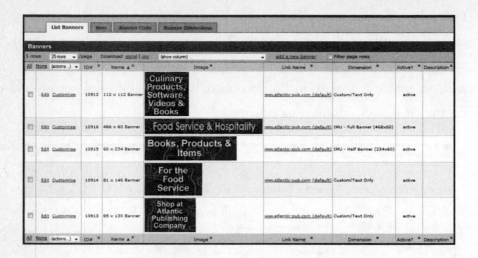

You must have the ability to approve, deny, and edit affiliate applications and accounts. Furthermore, you must be able to prepare, list, and create commission payments. You must have the ability to edit payment or commission amounts and create adjustments, and you must have a wealth of detailed reports. Last, you need to communicate with your affiliates. An integrated e-mail application simplifies this process by letting you send out text- or HTML-based e-mails to some or all of your affiliates simultaneously.

Data Feeds

Many affiliate networks or large affiliate programs offer data feeds as a method of providing their affiliates with all the information about a product in a data file, including description, pricing, reviews, and more in a spreadsheet or other format, which lets them easily manipulate and import it into their Web site. They also typically include links to images and products so they are instantly integrated into an affiliate Web site. Additionally, some affiliate programs offer dynamically generated data feeds which constantly update the content on their affiliates' Web site, ensuring that product data is always the most current available, without requiring significant manual intervention on the part of the affiliate to update their Web site.

The main advantage of an affiliate data feed is that you can add thousands of products instantly instead of manually adding them to your Web site. Because most data feeds are free, this is something you may wish to consider looking for when considering which affiliate to join. You should be aware that integration with your Web site may require some advanced programming, database, or Web design skills. Some recommended sites you can visit to read more about, and subscribe to, affiliate feeds are **www.feedshare.com** or **www.goldencan.com**. FeedProcessor, **www.feedprocessor.com,** lets you convert data feeds into dynamically generated Web sites for free.

Customer Returns

Running your own Web store and affiliate programs means you still have to deal with all the same customer service issues, except now you have to add service to your affiliates. One issue which constantly causes angst among affiliates is customer returns. When an affiliate sees a sales conversion, they do not want to see the commission being reversed out of their account as this creates mistrust and you may lose them as an affiliate. The key is to set your terms up front and communicate with your affiliates. If a customer returns a product which they ordered through an affiliate's link, that commission should be reversed when the sale is credited back to the purchaser, thus there is no commission on returns. As I discussed in the affiliate agreement, you should spell out very clear terms of service to avoid fraudulent charges, orders placed by your affiliate through their affiliate link, test orders, duplicate orders, or orders which are returned or not processed due to credit card authorization problems.

The biggest challenge when deploying your affiliate program is learning the actual software application, which can be overwhelming due to the number of features and customizations you can incorporate. This chapter was designed to show you how simple it is to set up and implement an affiliate program on your Web site. It is impossible, due to the variations of Web host providers, shopping carts, and other variables, for me to provide step-by-step installation instructions. However, every software provider listed in this book provides either free installation or a low one-time fee for initial setup and installation. Do not attempt to buy and install software yourself; it is not worth the headache. Let the professionals do it as part of the purchase or user agreement for their software. They will be more than happy to do this for you, and they can have you up and running in little more than an hour.

Each affiliate software program is different, but the process is essentially the same. I will cover the features and functionality of several affiliate programs in later chapters of this book. At this point, let's assume you have your affiliate program running, are actively looking for new affiliates to join your network, and are ready to start realizing the benefit in terms of increased sale and revenue. In the next chapter, we will look at how to optimize your Web site to maximize the potential of your affiliate marketing campaign.

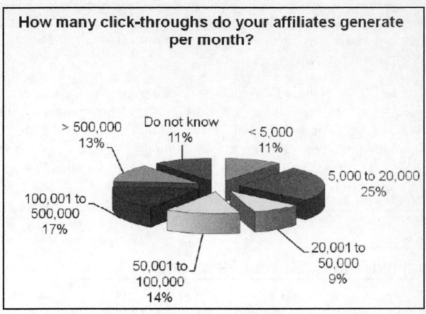

Reprinted with Permission Copyright 2008 Shawn Collins
http://blog.affiliatetip.com

AFFILIATE MARKETING: WORKING WITH MERCHANTS

By Michael Bloch

"Sign up today! Here are your banners — now paste the code into your Web pages and start making money!" How many times have you seen that blurb on a company affiliate program sign-up page?

For a few lucky Webmasters with a visitor rate of hundreds of thousands a month, this may be the case. For even fewer it may mean overnight financial success, but for most of us involved in affiliate and Web marketing, nothing could be further from the truth. Being an affiliate is hard work, but it is also very rewarding when you team up with the right merchants.

If you are not already familiar with affiliate programs, you may want to visit the pages linked throughout this article. These tutorials will

AFFILIATE MARKETING: WORKING WITH MERCHANTS

give you a basic overview about making money from Internet-based affiliate programs.

If you have located a company offering revenue-sharing opportunities for products and services that complement your Web site genre, it isn't enough just to put up banners and buttons. As mentioned in my other articles, writing up a review page of the product or service will definitely help boost sales, especially if you are recognized as being knowledgeable in your field.

Communicate With Your Merchants

But take it one step further. This step could not only increase your sales, but save you a heartache in the long run. It is really simple: Contact the merchant, let him know what you are doing to promote his product, and ask his advice about how you could improve your marketing, after all, the merchant knows his product best, or at least we hope so. The merchant should have a very good idea of the strategies used by other affiliates to boost sales. An affiliate tips page, provided by many companies, usually will not give you vital and current "insider" information, so it is important to approach merchants directly.

By contacting the merchant you are showing your enthusiasm for marketing their products and services, aiming to be what is known as a power- or super-affiliate. Any merchant who understands affiliate marketing knows that more than 90 percent of sales are generated by less than five percent of their affiliates. A good merchant will recognizeyour efforts, provide you with further information and resources and may even boost your commission rates!

Dealing With Merchants

If you go to the trouble to e-mail a merchant and he does not respond the first time, try again. If he still fails to respond, think twice about continuing promotion. A lack of communication can be indicative of other problems, including payment. Also bear in mind that some merchants work on the shotgun principle. They make big promises and set a high payout threshold knowing that few affiliates will ever reach, then they get as many affiliates to promote their products and services as possible, maximum exposure for minimal cost and effort on their part. It is not a good business model for them to utilize in the long-term, and after a while, affiliates drop away, but not before the company has raked in thousands of dollars. Many MLM (multi-level marketing) programs also work on this principle — only the people at the top generate any serious revenue. A good way to protect your payments is to sign up for affiliate programs of well-established ad networks such as Offers Quest or FastClick.

Working with a major ad network means that even if you only make a few dollars from each program, those dollars all feed a common account and accumulate rapidly, which allows you to reach the payout threshold in a shorter length of time. Most ad networks work with merchants on a money up front or monthly pay-as-you-go basis, minimizing the risk of unscrupulous merchants suddenly disappearing with your hard-earned commissions.

Demonstrate Your Web Marketing Prowess

Unless you have a very high-traffic Web site, do not ask the merchant for higher commissions in the first communication. So many affiliates do this and end up being totally ignored, as the vast majority of affiliates probably cannot deliver on their forecasts, which are usually just dreams. If you do not have a solid sales record for the product or service you are promoting, you will need to prove yourself first. Put some thought into your promotion and rack up a few sales before attempting to secure higher payout rates.

Be Professional in Your Communications

When communicating with merchants, ensure that you maintain a professional manner. If you have suggestions of how merchants could improve an offer that would convert into more sales, let them know, but be very polite and constructive in your feedback. "Your banners suck" just doesn't cut it. Remember that the Internet as a trading place is still very new in comparison to the business platforms of the past few millennia. Some of the quality companies offering an affiliate program may be just breaking into this side of marketing, and will appreciate any feedback you can give them.

A wise merchant understands that good affiliates aren't a dime a dozen and treats them with respect, assists with resources, and provides prompt payments. A wise affiliate understands that a merchant wants quality promotion and sales performance for minimum outlay. Successful merchant-affiliate partnerships are struck when both parties understand these points and work together, resulting in profits for both parties.

Michael Bloch has been working the Web as a successful marketing and development consultant since the late '90s. Michael owns and operates TamingTheBeast.net, a popular Internet marketing and e-commerce resources site providing online business owners and affiliate marketers with valuable free advice, articles, tutorials, and tools.

7 Optimizing Your Web Site, Blog and Affiliate Program

At this point, you have an established Web site, and/or blog, with a functional affiliate program. Let's spend some time optimizing your Web site and blog for search engines and increased Web site traffic. This is a vital step to be performed in concert with Chapter Nine, marketing your affiliate program. One of the main purposes of your Web site or blog, aside from marketing and communications, is to increase visibility in search engines and draw more potential customers and site visitors to your Web site. You might be asking yourself why you need to do this, when the purpose of an affiliate program is to let others promote your products for you and drive customers to your site. The fact is, you pay a commission for each affiliate sale, and you do not pay for any direct sales. Do not forget your primary purpose for a Web presence is to promote and market your products and services, and if you are selling those products online, you want customers to be able to find you quickly and easily. The affiliate program supplements your optimized Web site or blog and provides you an additional revenue stream or source of increased orders volume. Effectively designed Web sites and blogs can work for you by significantly raising your visibility in search engine rankings, resulting in increased Web site traffic.

We will cover how to promote your affiliate program in Chapter Nine, but a quick test you can perform is to search for your company online. When you search by keywords, is your affiliate program visible in the results?

Join the **Atlantic Publishing** Company **Affiliate** Program
Atlantic Publishing Company is now accepting **affiliates** into their brand new **Affiliate** Program. This program pays a minimum of 20% commission to all ...
www.atlantic-pub.com/**affiliate**.htm - 35k - Cached - Similar pages

Organic Search Engine Optimization (SEO)

Organic Search Engine Optimization will drive more targeted traffic to your Web site. Organic SEO is the process of optimizing a site so that it naturally ranks high in the major search engines. In other words, these search results are those which are natural, in response to a search on the Web versus one that is a result of paid advertisement. Organic SEO is not new; however, the pay-for-Web-ranking approach quickly beat out the organic search results which resulted in ever-increasing advertising budgets to maintain the top rankings. The advent of pay-per-click advertising compounded the situation as well. Bidding wars for top ranking took its toll on budgets, and the progression back to naturally achieving top search engine results grew in popularity. With Organic SEO your search engine ranking is maintained as a result of a combination of factors, which I have outlined in this chapter, instead of as a result of your over-extended advertising budget.

Organically Optimizing Your Web Site and Blog

Search engine optimization is a critical component to any successful Web site marketing plan. When you deploy your Web site, it needs to be optimized so potential customers can find you. There are more than two billion Web pages on the Internet which means there are many Web sites directly competing with yours for potential customers. Often, your competitors are selling identical products to yours. You need to take realistic, time-proven measures to ensure that your online business gets noticed and obtains the rankings within search engines that will deliver potential customers to you.

Google offers a variety of tools, techniques, and advice to help you with your Web site optimization. First, visit Google's Webmaster Central at **www.google.com/webmasters**. This Web page is your portal to Google's tools and advice on how to optimize your Web site for Google's search engine.

Google Webmaster Guidelines

Understanding how Google works is critical to ensure that your Web site is as successful as possible. Google makes it easy for you by publishing their Google Webmaster Guidelines to assist you in achieving the best possible results. You can read Google's Webmaster Guidelines here: **www.google. com/support/webmasters/bin/answer.py?hl=en&answer=35769**.

Google Webmaster Central

Google's Webmaster Central is an excellent starting point for developing a comprehensive SEO plan. Let's walk through each tool available to you on this site.

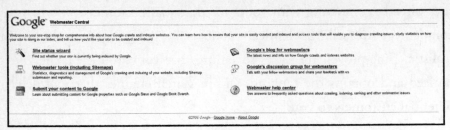

Screenshots (C) Google Inc. and are reproduced with permission.

Site Status Wizard

The Google Site Status Wizard is a tool that lets you determine if your Web site is already indexed by Google. Indexing by Google is critical if you want to have visibility in the Google Search Engine to customers. If your site is not indexed, potential customers will not find you on Google.

The tool is simple to use. Enter your URL and click the next button:

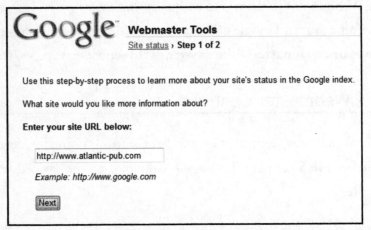

Screenshots (C) Google Inc. and are reproduced with permission

Results are presented that notify you if the site has been indexed and on what date, and gives you potential indexing problems.

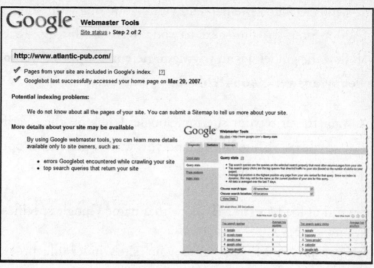

Screenshots (C) Google Inc. and are reproduced with permission.

Google Webmaster Tools

Google Webmaster Tools provide you with statistics, diagnostics, and management of Google's crawling and indexing of your Web site including sitemap submission and reporting. These tools are critical to ensuring that your site is optimized and ranked in the Google Search Engine. You can list all of your Web sites in the Google Webmaster Tools.

Screenshots (C) Google Inc. and are reproduced with permission

Your next step is to add a sitemap and verify your site with Google. Click on the "Add a Sitemap" link next to your Web site listing. To create a sitemap, follow the guidelines at: **www.google.com/support/webmasters/ bin/answer.py?answer=34654&hl=en.**

Now you want to verify your site for Google. Click on the "Verify" link to the right of your Web site listing, and you will be given two options to verify that you are the site owner:

• You can upload an HTML file with a name Google specifies.

• You can add a META tag to your site's index file provided by Google.

I recommend you choose the META tag option. You will see a screen similar to this one:

Screenshots (C) Google Inc. and are reproduced with permission.

Open your Web site in an Editor and add the provided HTML Meta Tag to the "Head" section of your Web site's home page:

```
<meta name="contactcity" content="Ocala">
<meta name="contactstate" content="FL">
<meta name="contactzipcode" content="34474">
<meta name="contactphonenumber" content="800-814-1132">
<meta name="contactfaxnumber" content="352-622-6220">
<link rel="stylesheet" href="apcnew/organized.css" type="text/css">
<meta name="verify-v1" content="UX8M795a+vT+ziH5QDOMVw+L8qkNu5vrHtVGXFxmmF8=" />
<style>
<!--
DIV.Section1 {
    page: Section1
}
-->
</style>
</head>
```

Screenshots (C) Google Inc. and are reproduced with permission.

After you add the Google Meta tag to your home page, save your home page and click the "Verify" button on the Google Web site, and your site will be verified.

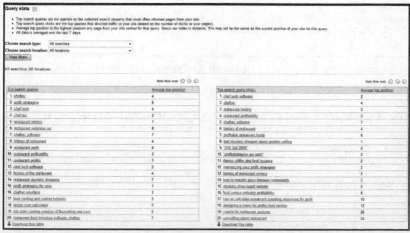

Screenshots (C) Google Inc. and are reproduced with permission.

You can now click on any of your sites to view detailed statistics. Let's take a look at one of our Web sites above. You can view detailed page ranking information as well as a variety of other detailed analyses:

Screenshots (C) Google Inc. and are reproduced with permission.

Adding Your Web Site or Blog to Google

If you completed the steps above and verified your site, it has been added to the Google Index. You may also manually submit your site at **www.google. com/addurl/?continue=/addurl**

Enter your URL, and your site will be indexed in the Google Search Engine. Note that Google states, "We add and update new sites to our index each time we crawl the Web, and we invite you to submit your URL here. We do not add all submitted URLs to our index, and we cannot make any predictions or guarantees about when or if they will appear."

Source: **google.com**

Share your place on the net with us.

We add and update new sites to our index each time we crawl the web, and we invite you to submit your URL here. We do not add all submitted URLs to our index, and we cannot make any predictions or guarantees about when or if they will appear.

Please enter your full URL, including the http:// prefix. For example: http://www.google.com/. You may also add comments or keywords that describe the content of your page. These are used only for our information and do not affect how your page is indexed or used by Google.

Please note: Only the top-level page from a host is necessary; you do not need to submit each individual page. Our crawler, Googlebot, will be able to find the rest. Google updates its index on a regular basis, so updated or outdated link submissions are not necessary. Dead links will 'fade out' of our index on our next crawl when we update our entire index.

URL: http:www.apcdist.com

Screenshots (C) Google Inc. and are reproduced with permission.

Thank you

Your site URL has been successfully added to our list of URLs to crawl. Please note that we do not add all submitted URLs to our index, and we cannot make any predictions or guarantees about when or if they will appear.

You may also be interested in Google webmaster tools, which shows you Google's view of your site, helps you diagnose problems, and lets you share information with us to help improve your site's visibility in our search results.

Want to do more?

Reach more prospects	Earn more from your website	Showcase your products for free
Google AdWords advertising allows you to create your own targeted ads. With cost-per-click pricing you decide how much to spend and you only pay when people click on your ad.	Google AdSense delivers Google ads that are relevant to the content on your pages. Earn advertising revenue with minimal effort and no additional cost.	Froogle is Google's shopping search engine. Learn more about Froogle, and how you can take advantage of free product listings.
Start reaching more prospects with Google AdWords	Earn money from your website with Google AdSense	Attract online shoppers with Froogle

Screenshots (C) Google Inc. and are reproduced with permission.

Other Google Search Engine Optimization Resources

Google provides you with content-rich resources to assist you with SEO for Google. You will want to bookmark and frequent the following:

- Official Google Webmaster Central Blog: **http://googlewebmastercentral.blogspot.com**

- Google Discussion Group for Webmasters: **http://groups.google.com/group/Google_Webmaster_Help**

- Webmaster Help Center: **www.google.com/support/webmasters**

Search Engine Optimization Techniques

Let's concentrate on Search Engine Optimization (SEO) techniques, which can be easily implemented on your Web sites:

- Basic SEO

- Proper meta tag formatting and inclusion

- Proper use of ALT tags

- Copyright pages

- Search engine services

- Privacy policies

- About and feedback pages to improve search engine visibility

- Search engine registration and submission

- Other proven Web site marketing techniques.

SEO consists of a variety of proven techniques you can use to increase the ranking of your Web site within your target market on the Internet by using keywords that are relevant and appropriate to the product or services you are selling on your Web site.

When you implement a SEO plan, you use a methodology that allows you to make sure that your Web site is visible in search engines and is subsequently found by potential customers. SEO accomplishes this by taking the keywords that people may use to search for your products or services on the Internet using a search engine and placing these keywords in title pages, meta tags, and into the content of your Web site.

When you properly use SEO and optimize your Web site based on sound Web site design principles, you know that your Web site is ready to be submitted to search engines; that you will significantly increase the visibility and ranking within the search engines, driving potential customers to your Web site; and obtain the hits you need to increase your profits and the success of your business. Focus on the content on each Web page and be sure to strive to include at least 200 or more content-related words on the pages of your site. Integrate your keywords into the content you place on each page, but be cautious of keyword stuffing. Overloading the pages with keywords may result in your being blacklisted from major search engines.

Successful Search Engine Optimization

Understanding the concepts and actions necessary for successful SEO can sometimes be confusing and hard to grasp when you are first starting out using SEO techniques. There are several steps you need to make sure to follow so that you ensure you are getting the most out of your SEO. Some of these steps include:

- Making sure that your Web site is designed correctly and set up for optimal SEO

- Choosing the right keywords that will bring the most hits to your Web site

- Using the right title tags to identify you within search engines

- Ensuring appropriate content-writing on your Web site

- Using properly formatted meta tags on your Web site

- Choosing the right search engines to which you submit your Web site

- Understanding the free and paid listing service options available.

Once you know which areas to focus on when it comes to successful SEO, you will discover that your ranking in search engines will increase dramatically.

The main problem with SEO and the number one reason most site builders fail to properly ensure that a site is optimized is that it requires patience and significant time investment to obtain high rankings in search engines. SEO will not get you immediate visibility in search engines, whereas pay-per-click advertising will. You need to be realistic in your expectations and expect it to take months to see tangible results.

Meta Tag Definition and Implementation

Meta tags are a key part of the overall SEO program that you need to implement for your Web site. There is some controversy surrounding the use of meta tags and whether or not their inclusion on Web sites truly impacts your search engine rankings. I am convinced, however, that they can be an integral part of a sound SEO plan and some search engines do utilize these tags in their indexing process. You do need to be aware that you are competing against potentially thousands of other Web sites often promoting similar products, using similar keywords, and employing other SEO techniques to achieve a top search engine ranking. Meta tags have never guaranteed top rankings on crawler-based search engines; however, they do offer a degree of control and the ability for you, as the Web site or business owner, to impact how your Web pages are indexed within the search engines.

When it comes to using keywords and key phrases in your meta keywords tag, you want to use only those keywords and phrases that you have actually included within the Web content on each of your Web pages. It is also important that you use the plural form of keywords so that both the singular and the plural will end up in any search using specific keywords and key phrases. Other keywords you should include in your meta keyword tags are any words that are the common misspelling of your keywords and phrases, as many people habitually misspell certain words. You want to make sure that search engines can still find you despite these misspellings.

Do not repeat your most important keywords and key phrases more than four to five times in a meta keyword tag. Another thing to keep in mind is that if your product or service is specific to a certain geographic location, you should mention this location in your meta keyword tag: Washington D.C., District of Columbia.

Meta tags comprise of formatted information that is inserted into the head section of each page on your Web site. To view the head of a Web page, you must view it in HTML mode rather than in the browser view. In Internet Explorer, you can click on the Toolbar on the VIEW menu and then click on SOURCE to view the source of any individual Web page. If you are using a design tool such as Microsoft Frontpage, Adobe Dreamweaver, Microsoft SharePoint Designer 2007, or Microsoft Expression Web Designer, you will need to use the HTML view to edit the source code of your Web pages. You can also use Notepad to edit your HTML source code.

This is a simple basic layout of a standard HTML Web page:

```
<!DOCTYPE HTML PUBLIC "-//W3C//DTD HTML 4.01//EN"
<HTML>
<HEAD>
<TITLE>This is the Title of My Web Page</TITLE>
</HEAD>
<BODY>
<P>This is my Web page!
</BODY>
</HTML>
```

Every Web page conforms to this basic page layout and all contain the opening <HEAD> and closing </HEAD> tags. Meta tags will be inserted between the opening and closing head tags. Other than the page title tag, which is shown above, no other information in the head section of your Web pages is viewed by Web site visitors as they browse your Web pages. The title tag is displayed across the top of the browser window and is used to provide a description of the contents of the Web paged displayed. I will explain in depth each meta tag that may be contained within the head tags.

The Title Tag

Whatever text you place in the title tag (between the <TITLE> and </TITLE>) will appear in the reverse bar of an individual's browser when they view your Web page. In the example above, the title of the Web page would read as "This is the Title of My Web Page" to the page visitor.

The title tag is used as the words to describe your page when someone adds it to their "Favorites" list or "Bookmarks" list in popular browsers such as Microsoft Internet Explorer or Mozilla Firefox. The title tag is the single most important tag in regard to search engine rankings. The title tag should be limited to 40 – 60 characters of text between the opening and closing HTML tags. All major Web crawlers will use the text of your title tag as the text they use for the title of your page in your listings as displayed in search engine results. Because the title and description tags typically appear in the search results page after completing a keyword search in the Web browser, it is critical that they be clearly and concisely written to attract the attention of site visitors. Not all search engines are alike; some will display the title and description tags in search results, but use page content alone for ranking.

The Description Tag

The description tag enables you to control the description of your individual Web pages when the search engine crawlers, which support the description tag, index, and spider the Web site. The description tag should be no more than 250 characters.

Take a look at the "Head" tag from our case study Web site **www. crystalriverhouse.com**. The tag that says "name=description" is the description tag. The text you want to be shown as your description goes between the quotation marks after the "content=" portion of the tag. Typically up to 250 characters are allowed for search engine indexing; however, the full description tag may not be displayed in search results.

```
<head>

<meta http-equiv="Content-Type" content="text/html; charset=windows-1252">

<title>Beautiful Crystal River Florida Vacation Rental Home</title>

<meta name="keywords" content="Crystal River rental, Florida, Citrus County, Grouper, Fishing, vacation home, Gulf Coast rental, Florida vacation, Florida gulf coast">

<meta name="description" content="Casa Dos Crystal River vacation rental house & resort paradise. Located on beautiful canal off Crystal River. Crystal River, Florida is famous for its manatee watching, diving, grouper and other world class fishing trips, world class golfing and many more activities.">

<meta name="language" content="en-us">

<meta name="robots" content="ALL">

<meta name="rating" content="SAFE FOR KIDS">

<meta name="distribution" content="GLOBAL">

<meta name="copyright" content="(c) 2007 APC Group, Inc.">

<meta name="revisit-after" content="30 Days">

<meta http-equiv="reply-to" content="info@crystalriverhouse.com">

<style>

<!--

.sitecredits { color: #FFFFFF}

-->

</style>

</head>
```

It is important to understand that search engines are not all the same, and that they index, spider, and display different search results for the same Web site. For example, Google ignores the description tag and generates its own description based on the content of the Web page. Although some major engines may disregard your description tags, it is highly recommended that you include the tag on each Web page since some search engines rely on the tag to index your site.

The Keywords Tag

A keyword is a word that may be used by Internet users when searching for information on the Internet. It is also a critical component to developing your pay-per-click campaign, which we will discuss in great detail in later chapters of this book. Using the best keywords to describe your Web site helps get those searchers to find your site in search engines. The keywords tag allows you to provide relevant text words or word combinations for crawler-based search engines to index. Although we maintain that the keyword tag is vitally important and should be included on every page, many crawler-based engines may use your page content for indexing instead of the contents of the keywords tag. In truth the keywords tag is only supported by a few Web crawlers. Because most Web crawlers are content-based, in other words, they index your site based on the actual page contents, not your meta tags, you need to incorporate as many keywords as possible into the actual content of your Web pages. For the engines that support the description tag, it is beneficial to repeat keywords within the description tag with keywords which appear on your actual Web pages. This increases the value of each keyword in relevance to your Web site page content. You need to use some caution with the keywords tag for the few search engines that support it, as repeating a particular keyword too many times within a keyword tag may actually hurt your Web site rankings.

If you look at the example earlier, you will notice that the keywords tag is the one that says <meta name="keywords" content=." The keywords you want to use should go between the quotation marks after the "content=" portion of the tag. It is generally suggested that you include up to 25 words or phrases, with each word or phrase separated by a comma.

To help you determine which keywords are the best to use on your site, visit **www.wordtracker.com**, which is a paid service that will walk you through this process. Wordtracker's suggestions are based on more than 300 million keywords and phrases that people have used over the previous 130 days. A free alternative to determining which keywords are best is Google Rankings at **http://googlerankings.com/dbkindex.php**.

The Robots Tag

The robots tag lets you specify that a particular page within your site should or should not be indexed by a search engine. To keep search engine spiders out, add the following text between your tags: <META NAME="ROBOTS" CONTENT="NOINDEX">. You do not need to use variations of the robots tag to get your pages indexed, as your pages will be spidered and indexed by default. However, some Web designers include the following robots tag on all Web pages: <meta name="robots" content="ALL">

Other Meta Tags

Many other meta tags exist; however, most provide amplifying information about a Web site and its owner and do not have any impact on search engine rankings. Some of these tags may be utilized by internal corporate divisions. In our example earlier you can see some examples of other meta tags which can be incorporated, note that this is not a complete list of all possible meta tags:

```
<meta name="language" content="en-us">

<meta name="rating" content="SAFE FOR KIDS">

<meta name="distribution" content="GLOBAL">

<meta name="contentright" content="(c) 2008 APC Group, Inc">

<meta name="author" content="Gizmo Graphics Web Design">

<meta name="revisit-after" content="30 Days">

<meta http-equiv="reply-to" content="info@crystalriverhouse.com">

<meta name="createdate" content="4/8/2008">
```

You may also use the "comment" tag, which is primarily used by Web designers as a place to list comments relative to the overall Web site design; this primarily is to assist other Web developers who may work on the site in the future. A comment tag looks like this:

```
<!-begin body section for Crystal River Vacation House>
```

ALT Tags

The ALT tag is an HTML tag that provides alternative text when non-textual elements, typically images, cannot be displayed. The ALT tag is not part of the head of a Web page, but proper use of the ALT tag is critically important in SEO. ALT tags are often left off Web pages; however, they can be extremely useful for a variety of reasons.

- They provide detail or text description for an image or destination of a hyperlinked image.

- They enable and improve access for people with disabilities.

- They provide information for individuals who have graphics turned off when they surf the Internet.

- They improve navigation when a graphics-laden site is being viewed over a slow connection, enabling visitors to make navigation choices before graphics are fully rendered in the browser.

Text-based Web content is not the only thing that increases your ranking in the search engines. Images are just as important because these images can include keywords and key phrases that relate to your business. If any visitors to your Web site should happen to have the image option off when hitting your site, they will still be able to see the text that is associated with your images. ALT tags should be placed anywhere there is an image on your Web site. It is important to remember not to use descriptions that are too lengthy when describing your images, but do include accurate keywords within the ALT tag. The keywords and key phrases you use in the ALT tag should be the same keywords and phrases you used in meta description tags, meta keyword tags, title tags, and the content of your Web pages. A brief description of the image, along with one or two accurate keywords and key phrases, is all you need to optimize the images on your Web pages for search engines.

Most major Web design applications include tools to simplify the process of creating ALT tags. For example, in Microsoft Frontpage 2003, right click on the image, choose properties and the general tab, and you can enter ALT tag text information. To enter ALT tag information directly into a Web page, go to the HTML view and enter it after the IMG tags in the following format:

```
<img border="0" src="images/cftec.jpg" width="300" height="103" alt="Whether you're a chef, restaurant owner, caterer, multi-unit manager or other foodservice professional, ChefTec Software helps you stay on top of your business"></b></font></p>
```

A great feature of Microsoft Expression Web is that it prompts you for ALT tags when you add images to your Web site.

How to Use the Correct Keywords

When it comes to keywords, you need to choose the words or word combinations your potential customers are using when they look for products or services using a search engine on the Internet. If you start to optimize keywords that are incorrect, you may be wasting your time because your potential customers search use keywords that do not put you up there in the top rankings of search engines. You will need to do some market research to find out what keywords are being used by people in search engines to find similar products or services to what you are selling. There are software tools on the market that you can use to find out just what these keywords are so you can implement them into your Web content and meta tags. The importance of the keyword meta tag has faded over the years, but using keywords within the content of your individual Web pages is critical and is the key to high Web site rankings. The use of keywords in your pay-per-click advertising campaign is critical, however. I will explain pay-per-click keywords in depth later in this book.

SEO means that every page of your Web site will be optimized to the greatest extent possible for search engines. Keywords will vary based on the individual Web page content. By using the wrong keywords, you risk sending your potential customers in an entirely different direction than to your Web site. Always keep in mind that if you are not listed in the top rankings of search engines, your customers may have difficulty finding you and your competition will have the advantage. Unfortunately, there is no magic formula to develop SEO and effective search phrases.

As mentioned previously, you will have to have a different list of keywords and key phrases for each Web page you are optimizing for the Internet based on the content of that individual page. Keywords that work for some of your Web pages may not work for others. This is why you need to constantly assess how your SEO campaign is progressing and be prepared to make changes along the way.

A good way to keep on top of keywords is to keep an eye on your competition. Use a search engine yourself and use some of the keywords and key phrases that you know target your type of product or service. Take a look at the top-ranking Web sites and view the source HTML code as well as the keywords they have used in their meta tags. The HTML code will show you the keywords that the site's creator used. You not only will be able to come up with more keyword ideas, but you will be able to keep up with your competition so that you rank at the top of search engines as well.

Optimization of Web Page Content

Relevant Web page content is by far the single most important factor that will affect and determine your eventual Web site ranking in search engines. Visitors to your Web site are going to read your content when they find your site and start to browse your Web pages, whether they browse to a page directly or via a search engine. You need to optimize your Web site with all the right keywords within the content of each Web page so that you can maximize your rankings within search engines.

Not only are the visitors to your Web site reading the content on these pages, but search engine spiders and Web crawlers are reading this same content and using it to index your Web site among your competitors. It is important that you have the right content so that search engines are able to find you and rank you near the top of the listings for similar products that people want to buy. Search engines are looking for keywords and key phrases to categorize and rank your site; therefore, it is important that you focus on just as many key phrases as you do keywords.

The placement of text content within a Web page can make a significant difference in your eventual search engine rankings. Some search engines will only analyze a limited number of text characters on each page and will not read the rest of the page regardless of length; therefore, the keywords and phrases you may have loaded into your page may not be read at all by the search engines. Some search engines do index the entire content of Web pages; however, they typically give more value or weight to the content that appears closer to the top of the Web page.

Optimize Your Web Site

If you want to get the best results from search engines, here are some tips that you should follow to optimize your Web site.

- Make sure that you have at least 200 words of content on each page. Although you may have some Web pages where it may be difficult to put even close to 200 words, you should try to come as close as you can since search engines will give better results to pages with more content.

- The text content of your Web pages should contain the important keywords and key phrases that you have researched, know will get you competitive rankings, and are the most common phrases potential customers might use to search for your products or services.

- No matter how much content you have after incorporating keywords and key phrases, make sure that your content is still understandable and readable in plain language. A common mistake is to stack a Web site full of so many keywords and key phrases that the page is no longer understandable or readable to the Web site visitor — a sure bet to lose potential customers quickly.

- The keywords and key phrases you use in the content of your Web site should be included in the tags of your Web site, such as meta tags, ALT tags, head tags, and title tags.

- Add extra pages to your Web site, even if they may not seem directly relevant. The more Web pages you have the more pages search engines will have to search, link, and find you. Extra pages can include tips, tutorials, product information, resource information, and any other information or data that is pertinent to the product or service that you are selling.

Optimizing your Web content and Web pages is one of the most important tips you can use to ensure the success of your Web site. If you are unable to optimize your Web site yourself, you should hire an expert so that you get the most out of the Web content that you have on your Web site.

Web Site Optimization Tips, Hints, and Secrets

It is critically important that you explore and implement the wide range of tips, suggestions, and best practices we have provided in this book to give your Web site the most competitive edge and obtain the highest possible rankings with search engines, especially in conjunction with your pay-per-click advertising campaigns. The following pages contain various best practices, tips, and secrets.

- It is important to use your keywords heavily on your Web pages. Use key phrases numerous times, placing them close to the top of the page. Place key phrases between head tags in the first two paragraphs of your page. Place key phrases in bold type at least once on each page. Repeat keyword and key phrases often to increase density on your pages.

- Design pages so they are easily navigated by search engine spiders and Web crawlers. Search engines prefer text over graphics and also prefer HTML over other page formats. You must make your page easy to navigate by the search engines.

- Do not use frames. Search engines have difficulty following them, and so will your site visitors. The best advice I can give on frames is to NEVER use them.

- Limit the use of Macromedia Flash and other high-end design applications. Most search engines have trouble reading and following them, and it will hurt you in search engine listings.

- Consider creating a site map of all pages within your Web site. While not necessarily the most useful tool to site visitors, it does greatly improve the search engine's capacity to property index all of your Web site pages.

- Many Web sites use a left-hand navigational bar. This is standard on many sites. However, the algorithm that many spiders and Web crawlers use will read this before the main content of your Web site. Make sure you use keywords within the navigation, and if using images for your navigational buttons, ensure that you use the ALT tags loaded with appropriate keywords.

- Ensure that all Web pages have links back to the home page.

- Use copyright and about us pages.

- Do not try to trick the search engines with hidden or invisible text or other techniques. If you do the search engine will likely penalize you.

- Do not list keywords in order within the content of your Web page. It is perfectly fine to incorporate keywords into the content of your Web pages, but do not simply cut and paste your keywords from your meta tag into the content of your Web pages. This will be viewed as spam by the search engine, and you will be penalized.

- Do not use text on your Web page as the page's background color; for example, white text on a white background. This technique is known as keyword stuffing and all search engines will detect it and penalize you.

- Do not replicate meta tags. In other words, you should only have one meta tag for each type of tag. Using multiple tags, such as more than one title tag, will cause search engines to penalize you.

- Do not submit identical pages with identical content with a different Web page file name.

- Make sure every Web page is reachable from at least one static text link.

- Make sure that your title and ALT tags are descriptive and accurate.

- Check for broken links and correct HTML.

- Try using a text browser such as Lynx to examine your site. Features such as JavaScript, cookies, session IDs, frames, DHTML, or Flash keep search engine spiders from properly crawling your entire Web site.

- Implement the use of the robots.txt file on your Web server. This file tells crawlers which directories can or cannot be crawled. You can find out more information on the robots.txt file by visiting **www. robotstxt.org/wc/faq.html.**

- Have other relevant sites link to yours. We will cover the use of cross-linking your Web site with others later in this chapter, as this is an often-overlooked, but extremely important way of increasing your search engine rankings. This is known as back-linking, and is critically important to gain search engine visibility.

- Design Web pages for site visitors — not search engines.

- Avoid tricks intended to improve search engine rankings. A good rule of thumb is whether you would feel comfortable explaining what you have done to a Web site that competes with you. Another useful test is to ask, "Does this help my users? Would I do this if search engines didn't exist?"

- Do not participate in link schemes designed to increase your site's ranking. Do not link to Web spammers. If you do, your own ranking will be negatively affected by those links.

- Do not create multiple pages, sub-domains, or domains with substantially duplicated content.

- Do not use doorway pages created for search engines.

- Consider implementing cascading style sheets into your Web site to control site layout and design. Search engines prefer CSS-based sites and typically score them higher in the search rankings.

Web Design & Optimization Suggestions

Shelley Lowery, author of the acclaimed Web design course, Web Design Mastery, **www.webdesignmastery.com** and eBook Starter.com, Give your eBooks the look and feel of a REAL book... **www.ebookstarter.com**, offer valuable tips and suggestions for Web design and Web site optimization. You can visit **www.web-source.net** to sign up for a complimentary subscription to eTips and receive a copy of the acclaimed *eBook Killer Internet Marketing Strategies*, **www.web-source.net.**

ESTABLISH LINKS WITH REPUTABLE WEB SITES

You should try to find quality sites that are compatible with and relevant to your Web site's topic and approach the Webmaster of that site for a link exchange: Do not link to your competitors. This will give you highly targeted traffic and improve your score with the search engines. Your goal is to identify relevant pages that will link to your site, effectively yielding you quality inbound links. You need to be wary of developing or creating a link farm or spam link Web site, which offers massive quantities of link exchanges, but with little or no relevant content for your site visitors or the search engines.

HOW TO ESTABLISH A RECIPROCAL LINK PROGRAM (BACKLINKS)

Begin your link exchange program by developing a title or theme that you will use as part of your link request invitations. Your title or theme should be directly relevant to your site's content. Because most sites use your provided title or theme in the link to your Web site, be sure you include relevant keywords, which will improve your Web site optimization and search engine rankings. Keep track of your inbound and outbound link requests. Begin your search for link exchange partners by searching a popular engine such as Google and entering key phrases such as link with us, add site, suggest a site, add your link, and so on. If these sites are relevant they are ideal to be your reciprocal link program as they too are actively seeking link partners. Make sure that the Webmaster of other sites actually links back to your site, as reciprocal links commonly are not completed. If they do not link back to you in a reasonable time, remove your link to them because you are only helping them with their search engine rankings.

You may want to use **www.linkpopularity.com** as a free Web source for evaluating the total number of Web sites that link to your site.

Reciprocal links play an important part with affiliate networks. This may be a factor in determining what software you will use if you are going to install an affiliate program on your Web site. Some allow you to link directly to your Web site, that is your URL, so in theory by allowing this and multiplying the links times the number of affiliates you have, you may see exponential improvement in search engine ranking due to reciprocal links to your site. If the software does not allow this feature, your links go to the affiliate hosting servers first, and then your site, and you do not benefit from the links in terms of search engine visibility or rankings.

ESTABLISH A WEB SITE PRIVACY POLICY

Internet users are becoming more and more concerned with their privacy. You should establish a privacy Web page and let your visitors know exactly how you will be using the information you collect from them. This page should include the following information.

- How do you plan on using their information?

- Will their information be sold to or shared with a third party?

- Why do you collect their e-mail address?

- Do you track their IP address?

- You should notify site visitors that you are not responsible for the privacy issues of any Web sites you may be linked to.

- Notify them that you have security measures in place to protect the misuse of their private or personal information.

- Provide site visitors with contact information in the event they have any questions about your privacy statement.

ESTABLISH AN, ABOUT US, PAGE

An about us page is an essential part of a professional Web site for a variety of reasons. One reason is that your potential customers may want to know exactly who you are, and second, it is a great opportunity to create a text-laden page for search engine visibility. An about us page should include the following:

- A personal or professional biography

- A description of you or your company

- Company objectives or mission statement

- Contact information, including your e-mail address

- A photograph of yourself or your business

ESTABLISH A TESTIMONIALS PAGE

Another way to develop credibility and confidence among your potential customers is to include previous customer testimonials. You do need to make sure your testimonials are supportable so include your customer's name and e-mail address for validation purposes.

ESTABLISH A MONEY-BACK GUARANTEE

Depending on the type of Web site you are operating, you may wish to consider implementing a money-back guarantee to completely eliminate any potential risk to customers in purchasing your products. By providing them with a solid, no-risk guarantee, you build confidence in your company and your products with potential clients.

ESTABLISH A FEEDBACK PAGE

There are many reasons to incorporate a feedback page into your Web site. There are times when potential customers will have questions about your products and services or may encounter problems with your Web site, and the feedback page is an easy way for them to contact you. Additionally, it allows you to collect data from the site visitor such as their name, e-mail address, or phone number. A timely response to feedback is critical to assuring customers that there is a living person on the other end of the Web site; this personal service helps increase the likelihood that they will continue to do business with you.

ESTABLISH A COPYRIGHT PAGE

You should always display your copyright information at the bottom of each page. You should include both the word Copyright and the © symbol. Your copyright should look similar to this: **Copyright © 2008 Gizmo Graphics Web Design**

How Do Search Engines Work?

There are several different types of search engines, including crawler-based, human-powered, and mixed. We will discuss how each one works so you can optimize your Web site in preparation for your pay-per-click advertising campaign.

CRAWLER-BASED SEARCH ENGINES

Crawler-based search engines, such as Google, create their listings automatically. They crawl or spider the Web and index the data which is then searchable through Google.com. Crawler-based search engines will eventually revisit your Web site. As your content is changes, as does that of your competitors, your search engine ranking may change. A Web site is added to the search engine database when the search engine spider or crawler visits a Web page, reads it, and then follows links to other pages within the site. The spider returns to the site on a regular basis, typically once a month, to search for changes. Often, it may take several months for a page that has been spidered to be indexed. Until a Web site is indexed the results of the spider are not available through the search engines. The search engine then sorts through the millions of indexed pages to find matches to a particular search and rank them based on a formula of how it believes the results to be the most relevant.

HUMAN-POWERED SEARCH DIRECTORIES

Human-powered directories like the Open Directory, depend on humans for their listings. You must submit a short description to the directory for your entire site. The search directory then looks at your site for matches from your page content to the descriptions you submitted.

HYBRID OR MIXED SEARCH ENGINES

A few years ago, search engines were either crawler-based or human-powered. Today, a mix of both types of results is common in search engines results.

Using a Search Engine Optimization Company

If you are not up to the challenge of tackling your Web site's SEO needs, it may be to your benefit to hire an SEO company so that the optimization techniques you use are properly implemented and monitored. There are many SEO companies on the Internet that can ensure your rankings will increase when you hire them. Be wary of anyone who guarantees you top 10 ranking in all major search engines; these claims are baseless. If you have the budget to hire an SEO company, it may be extremely beneficial for you since (a) you will know that the experts at SEO are taking care of you, and (b) you can focus your energies on other important marketing aspects of your business. To find an SEO company, follow these basic rules.

- Look at the business reputation of the SEO companies you are thinking about hiring. Ask the company for customer references you can check out on your own. Also contact the Better Business Bureau in their local city or state to confirm their reputation, **www. bbb.org.**

- Do a search engine check on each company to see where they fall in the rankings of major search engines such as AOL, MSN, and Google. If the company you are thinking about hiring to manage your own SEO does not rank high in these search engines, how can you expect them to launch you and your business to the top of the ranks?

- You want to choose an SEO company that actually has people working for them and not just computers. While computers are great for generating the algorithms needed to use search engine programs, they cannot replace people when it comes to doing the market research to ensure that the company uses the right keywords and key phrases for your business.

- You need to make sure that the SEO company uses ethical ranking procedures. Some ranking procedures are considered to be unethical. Some search engines will penalize you or ban your business Web site from their engines if they find out that you or the SEO company you have hired are using these methods; unethical ranking procedures include doorway pages, cloaking, or hidden text.

- The SEO company you decide to hire should be available to you at all times by phone or e-mail. You need to be able to contact someone when you have a question or a problem.

Once you have decided to hire an SEO company, it is important that you work with the company instead of just handing over all the responsibility to them. How much control of your Web site you should allow your SEO company is an area of debate. Because you will be controlling your pay-per-click advertising campaign, however, you must maintain control over your SEO efforts. Use these tips to work effectively with your SEO provider.

- Listen carefully to the advice of the SEO account manager. They should have the expertise for which you hired them and typically can provide factual and supportable recommendations. SEO companies are expected to know what to do to increase your ranking in the search engines; if they fail to deliver you need to choose another company.

- If you are going to make changes to your Web site design, let your SEO account manager know. Any change you make can have an effect on the already optimized Web pages. Your rankings in search engines may start to plummet unless you work with your SEO account manager to optimize any changes you feel are necessary.

- SEO companies can only work with the data and information you have on your Web pages. If your Web site has little information it will be difficult for any SEO company to improve your business' search engine rankings. SEO relies on keywords and key phrases contained on Web pages that are filled with as much Web content as possible. This may mean adding two or three pages of Web content that contain tips, resources, or other useful information that is relevant to your product or service.

- Once they have been optimized never change any of your meta tags without the knowledge or advice of your SEO account manager. Your SEO company is the professional when it comes to making sure that your meta tags are optimized with the right keywords and key phrases needed to increase your search engine ranking. You do not want to change meta tags that have already proven successful.

- Be patient when it comes to seeing the results of SEO. It can take anywhere from 30 to 60 days before you start to see yourself moving into the upper ranks of search engines.

- Keep a close eye on your ranking even after you have reached the top ranks. Information on the Internet changes at a moment's notice, and this includes your position in your target market in search engines.

Search Engine Registration

It is possible to submit your Web site for free to search engines as I showed you for the Google Search Engine, but when you use paid search engine programs, you will find that the process of listing will be faster and will bring more Web traffic to your Web site more quickly. Other than pay-per-click and other advertising programs, such as Google Adwords, it is not necessary to pay for search engine rankings if you follow the optimization and design tips contained in this book and have patience while the search engine Web-crawling and indexing process takes place. At the end of this chapter, we have provided a wealth of tools and methods to submit your Web site to search engines for free. If you decide to hire a third-party company to register you with search engines, here is some basic guidance to ensure you get the most value for your investment.

SUBMITTING TO HUMAN-POWERED SEARCH DIRECTORIES

If you have a limited advertising budget you need to make sure you have at least enough to cover the price of submitting to the directory at Yahoo!. It is called a directory search engine because it uses a compiled directory assembled by human hands, not a computer. For a one-time yearly fee of approximately $300, you can ensure that crawlers, a search engine that goes out onto the Internet looking for new Web sites by following links and meta tags, will be able to find your Web site in the Yahoo! directory. It may seem like a waste of money to be in a directory-based search engine, but the opposite is true. Crawlers consistently use directory search engines to add to their search listings. If you have a large budget put aside for search engine submissions, you might want to list with both directory search engines and crawler search engines, such as Google. When you first launch your Web site, you may want it to show up immediately in search engines and do not want to wait the allotted time for your listing to appear. If this is the case, you may consider using what is called a paid placement program. Remember that your pay-per-click advertising campaigns will show up with the top search engine rankings based on your keyword bidding.

SUBMITTING TO CRAWLER SEARCH ENGINES

Submitting to crawlers means you likely will have several Web pages listed within the search engine. The more optimized your Web site, discussed previously in this chapter, the higher your ranking will be within the search engine listings.

USING SEARCH ENGINE SUBMISSION SOFTWARE

There are dozens of software applications that can submit your Web site automatically to major search engines and others. We have reviewed most of these products extensively and recommend Dynamic Submission, **www.dynamicsubmission.com**; although, you will find that many search engines including Google recommend you do not use any automated submission software. Dynamic Submission, currently in version 7.0, is a search engine submission software product which claims to be, "a multi-award-winning Web promotions software package, the best on the market today." Dynamic Submission software was developed to offer Web site owners the ability to promote their Web sites to the ever-increasing number of search engines on the Internet without any hassles or complications. Dynamic Submission helps you submit your Web site to hundreds of major search engines with just a few button clicks; driving traffic to your Web site. To use Dynamic Submission enter your Web site details into the application as you follow a wizard-based system culminating in the automatic submission to hundreds of search engines.

Since nearly 85 percent of Internet traffic is generated by search engines, submitting your Web site to all the major search engines and getting them to be seen on the search engine list is extremely important, especially in concert with your pay-per-click advertising campaign. It is essential to regularly submit your Web site details to these Web directories and engines. Some search engines de-list you over time, while others automatically re-spider your site. Dynamic Submission is available in four editions, including a trial edition which I highly encourage you to try, to fit every need and budget. Here are the major features of Dynamic Submission 7.0:

- Automatic search engine submission

- Supports pay-per-click (PPC) and pay-per-inclusion (PPI) engines

- Support for manual submission

- Keyword library and keyword builder

- Link popularity check

- Meta tag generator

- Web site optimizer

- Incorporated site statistics service

PAYING FOR SEARCH ENGINE SUBMISSIONS

You may choose to use a fee-based service to have your Web site listed in popular ranking directories. Also, be sure to manually submit your site to the Open Directory, **www.dmoz.org**, which is free.

Search Engine Optimization Checklist

There are many aspects to SEO you need to consider to make sure it works. I have covered each of these in depth earlier in this chapter, but the following checklist can serve as a helpful reminder to ensure that you have not forgotten any important details along the way.

- **Title tag.** Make sure your title tag includes keywords and key phrases that are relevant to your product or service.

- **Meta tags.** Make sure your tags are optimized to ensure a high ranking in search engine lists. This includes meta description tags and meta keyword tags. Your meta description tag should have an accurate description so that people browsing the Internet are interested enough to visit your Web site. Do not forget to use misspelled and plural words in your meta tags.

- **ALT tags.** Add ALT tags to all the images you use on your Web pages.

- **Web content.** Use accurate and rich keywords and key phrases throughout the content of all your Web pages.

- **Density of keywords.** Use a high ratio of keywords and key phrases throughout your Web pages.

- **Links and affiliates.** Make sure that you have used links, and affiliates, if you are using them, effectively for your Web site.

- **Web design**. Your Web site should be fast to load and easy to navigate for visitors. You want to encourage people to stay and read your Web site by making sure it is clean and looks good.

- **Avoid spamming.** Double-check to make sure you are not committing any spamming offenses on your Web site. Some spamming offenses include cloaking, hidden text, doorway pages, obvious repeated keywords and key phrases, link farms, or mirror pages.

Always be prepared to update and change the look, feel, and design of your Web pages to use SEO techniques wherever and whenever possible.

Free Web Site Search Engine Submission Sites

http://dmoz.org Open Directory Project

http://tools.addme.com/servlet/s0new

www.submitexpress.com/submit.html

www.ineedhits.com/free-tools/submit-free.aspx

www.submitcorner.com/Tools/Submit

www.college-scholarships.com/free_search_engine_submission.htm

www.quickregister.net

www.global.gr/mtools/linkstation/se/engnew.htm

www.scrubtheweb.com

www.submitaWebsite.com/free_submission_top_engines.htm

www.nexcomp.com/weblaunch/urlsubmission.html

www.submitshop.com/freesubmit/freesubmit.html

www.buildtraffic.com/submit_url.shtml

www.mikes-marketing-tools.com/ranking-reports

http://selfpromotion.com/?CF=google.aws.add.piyw

www.addpro.com/submit30.htm

www.website-submission.com/select.htm

FREE WEB SITE OPTIMIZATION TOOLS

www.websiteoptimization.com/services/analyze contains a free Web site speed test to improve your Web site performance. This site will calculate page size, composition, and download time. The script calculates the size of individual elements, and sums up each type of Web page component. On the basis of these page characteristics, the site then offers advice on how to improve page load time. Slow load time is the number one reason potential customers do not access Web sites.

www.sitesolutions.com/analysis.asp?F=Form This is a free Web site which analyzes your page content to determine if you are effectively using meta tags.

www.mikes-marketing-tools.com/ranking-reports This Web site reveals search engine rankings, offering instant online reports of Web site rankings in seven top search engines, including Google, Yahoo! Search, MSN, AOL, Teoma (Ask Jeeves), AltaVista, AllTheWeb, and the top three Web directories, Yahoo! Directory, Open Directory (Dmoz), and LookSmart, all for free.

www.keyworddensity.com Free, fast, and accurate keyword density analyzer.

www.hisoftware.com/accmonitorsitetest A Web site to test your Web site against accessibility and usability: Section 508, Complete WCAG, CLF, XAG standards.

www.wordtracker.com The Leading Keyword Research Tool. It is not free, although there is a limited free trial.

https://adwords.google.co.uk/select/KeywordSandbox Gives ideas for new keywords associated with your target phrase but does not indicate relevance or give details of number or frequency of searches.

http://inventory.overture.com/d/searchinventory/suggestion Returns details of how many searches have been carried out in the Overture engine in a month and allows a drill down into associated keywords containing your keyword phrase as well.

www.nichebot.com Wordtracker- and Overture-based tools as well as a nice keyword analysis tool, which focuses on Google's results.

www.digitalpoint.com/tools/suggestion Gives search numbers on keywords from Wordtracker and Overture sources.

OTHER TIPS FOR INCREASING WEB SITE/BLOG TRAFFIC

- Prominently feature RSS/ATOM feeds on your Web site and blogs. They need to be easily found and easy to subscribe to. This is one of most powerful marketing and communication tools you have to increase Web site traffic.

- Write articles on anything related to your Web site or blog. Distribute them freely, but make sure anyone who publishes gives you credit and links to your blog and Web site. You will be amazed at the blog and Web site traffic this can bring in.

Things NOT to Do on a Web Site or Blog

- Do not ever use frames.

- Do not use pop-ups.

- Do not use bold colored backgrounds with white font.

- Do not forget about your site and let it grow stagnant and dated. The same applies to your blog — even more so.

- Do not have any dead or broken links. Check for them and eliminate them.

- Do not use an image as a page background. It looks bad, loads poorly, distracts your site visitors, and does not work well as resolution grows higher. I advise a white background.

- Do not use animated icons. They are annoying, unnecessary, and distracting.

- Do not use those annoying flash pop-ups that scroll across your screen in front of the page content.

8 Affiliate Program Software

If you have decided to establish and operate your own affiliate program on your Web site and blog, you are making an exciting decision which can reward you with increased sales volume and revenues and the knowledge that you are in full control over a network of affiliates around the world, all working on your behalf. You could join an affiliate network, which would provide you with the functionality and ease to sell your products through an established program. Having your own program however is exceptionally rewarding, and rather simple to maintain.

There are dozens of outstanding affiliate software packages available. Some are shareware which are free, but come with no support, to full-featured products which will meet and probably exceed your needs. In this chapter, I will highlight several options for you and provide you with contact information so you can make the most informed choice.

You will find there is a significant difference in many of the software programs available. Typically there is an installation or setup fee, but this is not always the case, and often there is a recurring monthly maintenance fee. Because most of the actual software resides on the affiliate software company servers, they are really doing most of the work for you. On your Web site, typically all you have installed are the tracking mechanisms which notify the affiliate company when a click or conversion is completed. The small monthly fee provides you with this service. This is not the only way it can be done; several companies charge no fee other than the initial setup, and the software resides entirely on your Web site. Another model is site replication, in which you replicate your site for others so they can stand up an identical copy of your store, with their affiliate URLs embedded, on their domain name; truly a turn-key solution.

The fact is that online advertising continues to boom. With the explosion of blogs, online advertising has grown at an explosive pace. Most merchants are either part of an affiliate network or have their own affiliate program. The key to success with your own affiliate program is choosing the right software, and putting in the time to manage your program and your affiliates. To be honest, that is the easy part; the difficult part is choosing which software package is best for you.

A key part of running a successful affiliate program is being able to manage your affiliates efficiently and cost-effectively. Thankfully, there are software products to help you do this. The trouble is, with dozens of different affiliate software suppliers offering a wide range of features, functionality, and pricing, how do you choose the right one?

Types of Affiliate Marketing Software

There are several choices in types of affiliate marketing software available to you. Some may not be appropriate based on your Web site configuration, but let's review each.

- **Affiliate Network:** We have discussed affiliate networks in the past, but they need to be considered — from both the merchant and affiliate perspective — because they are a great choice depending on your goals. In this case, the software is provided and hosted by the affiliate network. You simply join the existing network and offer your products for sale to other members of the affiliate network.

This is probably the easiest solution as no technical changes to your Web site are required, and you do not do anything other than join. They handle the program administration, reporting, commission payments, and more. The downside of an affiliate network is that you are limited by the number of affiliates of the network and there are dozens of affiliate networks all competing with each other. Another downside is that an affiliate network is typically the costliest in terms of transaction and monthly fees. An example of an affiliate network is Commission Junction, **www. cj.com.**

- **Hosted Affiliate Network Software:** I prefer this option. The software is not provided to you or installed on your Web server; instead, software providers host it on their servers and you pay a fee, usually monthly, for support and maintenance. This option is quick and simple to get running. Because all you have on your Web site is a small piece of tracking code, your work is minimal. Because they own and host the software, you instantly benefit from software upgrades, patches, and enhancements. They also are responsible for all the servers, backups, and reliability. Additionally, you get technical support included with the package. Your initial costs are very low because you are not buying the software package, and the recurring fees are typically low. There are two models of recurring fees: flat rate or volume-based. I like the flat rate because I know my costs up front and volume-based can get expensive if you have a thriving affiliate network that is generating lots of conversions.

- **Affiliate Network Software — Stand-Alone:** You buy the software package and own the license to use as you see fit. This is a one-time fee and can be expensive. You install it on your Web server; although, often, this is included for free or for a small fee and you integrate it with your shopping cart or inventory management system. This software is typically very robust and packed with features, as is the previous option. Often, there are no recurring fees unless you want to sign up for upgrades and patches or other support which is typically limited or not included. The downside is that you own it, and when it breaks, you have to fix it or pay someone to fix it. If you do not own your Web server, you must ensure that the host provider is compatible and allows you to install the software and that you have appropriate access to enable the changes to make it functional. Unless you own and operate your own Web server, this option is less desirable.

There are some other options, such as all-in-one inclusive providers who will sell Web hosting, Web site development, e-commerce or shopping cart capabilities, and affiliate management packages as a complete package. This model is expensive, and you have no control or choice in product or features. I do not recommend this option.

Another option is to purchase shopping cart software with built-in affiliate tracking functionality. Most shopping carts have some limited affiliate capabilities, but in general, they require additional software, plug-ins, or external software to maximize their functionality. From my experience, you are much better off avoiding the use of affiliate tracking capability within shopping carts. However, you do need to confirm that if you choose a software package, your affiliate software is 100 percent compatible with your shopping cart software. I tend to exclude this option because in most cases, while they have the capability to track sales by an affiliate, they do not have a robust system to manage the affiliates, commissions, sales, and so on. One advantage is that this capability, if built into your software, is available to you at no charge or for a one-time add on fee.

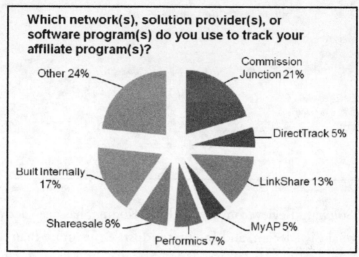

Which network(s), solution provider(s), or software program(s) do you use to track your affiliate program(s)?

- Other 24%
- Commission Junction 21%
- DirectTrack 5%
- LinkShare 13%
- MyAP 5%
- Performics 7%
- Shareasale 8%
- Built Internally 17%

Reprinted with Permission Copyright 2008 Shawn Collins
http://blog.affiliatetip.com

Another feature to consider is fraud protection. Many companies offer fraud protection, which has been a major problem with the affiliate community for many years. Let's take a look at some of the affiliate software packages available:

A great resource for comparing and reviewing affiliate software products is Affiliate-Software-Review.com, **www.affiliate-software-review.com**. Did you know there are more than 70 affiliate management solutions? With their comprehensive affiliate platform database and advanced comparison system, combined with carefully researched data regarding affiliate management solutions, you can easily compare, contrast, and search the various options available so you can choose the best affiliate tracking system for your needs. You can use their Web site as a comparison shopping engine before making an affiliate software purchase decision. Reviewing the listings is currently free of charge to merchants researching affiliate tracking solutions. If you are serious about quickly finding the right system for you and want to compare them side-by-side or search, you can upgrade to a Gold membership for a low one-time fee, which is located here: **www.affiliate-software-review.com/membershipupgrade.**

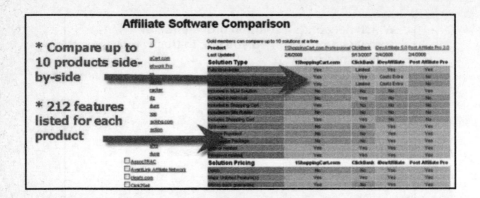

Affiliate-Software-Review.com owner, Peter Koning, has been active in the international IT, telecom, and Internet industries for more than 20 years. Peter has worked in key functional areas such as software development, project management, new product introduction, marketing and sales, and affiliate tracking software. With a major in Computer Science and an International MBA, Peter uses advanced techniques to research the important features and various sources of affiliate tracking software and management solutions for his merchant clients. As a founding member of Affiliate Software Review, Peter is responsible for vendor and merchant relationships, business development, operations management, and arranging the extensive reviews of affiliate tracking systems.

AFFILIATE MARKETING SOFTWARE AND NETWORKS SUMMARY

This section provides you with a brief introduction to some of the affiliate software packages and affiliate networks available to you. It is certainly not an inclusive list. I was surprised by the variety of software on the market and sophistication of affiliate networks, as well as the high degree of functionality and features in many of them. There is clearly a difference among the options as some are very refined and polished, while some are clearly home-grown solutions or the efforts of a single developer without the bells and whistles of others. The bottom line is that you need a product that will be compatible with your Web site, your hosting package, and your shopping cart. Ensure that any software meets these requirements before you even start comparing which software package to purchase. If you are uncomfortable with installing software or managing your own affiliate program, you may wish to consider joining an affiliate network instead of managing your own affiliate program on your Web site. Let's take a brief look at some of the software options available to you.

www.trackingsoft.com — ROIAdvantage is TrackingSoft's state-of-the-art tracking solution for affiliate program and advertising campaign management. ROIA represents the culmination of more than seven years experience in the affiliate tracking and Web advertising market by incorporating technological advances, client feedback, and innovation. The result is a comprehensive solution which provides not only tracking of traffic and conversions, but also an advanced interface, multi-level drill-down reporting, publisher management, support for multiple ad campaigns, advanced Web site analytics, and much more.

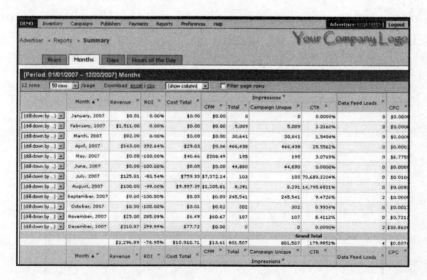

Month ▲	Revenue	ROI	Cost Total	CPM	Total	Campaign Unique	CTR	Data Feed Loads	CPC
(drill-down by ...)	January, 2007	$0.01	0.00%	$0.00	$0.00	0	0	0.0000%	0	$0.000
(drill-down by ...)	February, 2007	$1,511.00	0.00%	$0.00	$0.00	5,009	5,009	2.2160%	0	$0.000
(drill-down by ...)	March, 2007	$92.00	0.00%	$0.00	$0.00	30,641	30,641	1.5404%	0	$0.000
(drill-down by ...)	April, 2007	$143.00	392.64%	$29.03	$0.06	466,439	466,439	25.5562%	0	$0.000
(drill-down by ...)	May, 2007	$0.00	-100.00%	$40.66	$208.49	195	195	3.0769%	0	$6.775
(drill-down by ...)	June, 2007	$0.00	-100.00%	$0.05	$0.00	44,880	44,880	0.0000%	0	$0.000
(drill-down by ...)	July, 2007	$125.01	-93.54%	$759.33	$7,372.14	103	103	70,689.3204%	0	$0.010
(drill-down by ...)	August, 2007	$100.00	-99.00%	$9,997.39	$1,205.81	9,291	9,291	14,795.6921%	0	$0.008
(drill-down by ...)	September, 2007	$0.00	-100.00%	$0.03	$0.00	245,541	245,541	9.4726%	2	$0.000
(drill-down by ...)	October, 2007	$0.00	-100.00%	$0.01	$0.02	802	302	0.9934%	0	$0.001
(drill-down by ...)	November, 2007	$25.00	295.09%	$6.49	$60.67	107	107	8.4112%	0	$0.721
(drill-down by ...)	December, 2007	$310.97	299.99%	$77.72	$0.00	0	0	0.0000%	2	$39.860
	Grand Total									
		$2,296.89	-76.95%	$10,910.71	$13.61	801,507	801,507	179.9852%	4	$0.007

Key features include:

- Clean linking

- Track performance of individual links, banners, and creatives

- Completely customizable commissions

- Multiple currency support

- Excellent fraud prevention

- Multiple campaign and program support

- Cookieless tracking

- Customizable templates for automatic mailings

- Network publishers

A detailed listing of features can be found here: **http://trackingsoft.com/tracking_solution_features_list.shtml.**

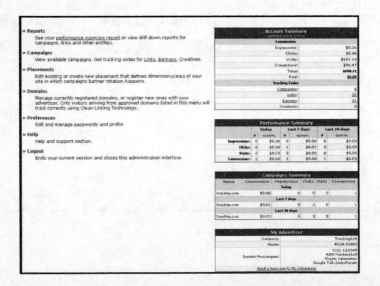

www.myaffiliateprogram.com — MYAP v9 is affiliate tracking and management software delivered through an ASP model. This means that the software sits on their servers, and you and your affiliates log in to view reports, manage links, and control your accounts. A complete list of features can be found at **www.myaffiliateprogram.com/features.asp.**

www.darkblue.com — DarkBlue is an innovative, new affiliate network set to raise the standard of current online marketing solutions. Since its beginning, DarkBlue has grown to become a leading force in affiliate marketing with more than 60 staff and support members. The network currently boasts more than 12,000 affiliates producing more than one billion impressions per month. Advertising on DarkBlue is strictly Cost-Per-Action/Acquisition (CPA), so there is zero risk for advertisers. The DarkBlue Affiliate Network is a trusted third party between advertisers and affiliates, providing services such as free ad serving, tracking, statistical reporting, real-time service and support, and a quick turnaround for advertisers.

www.marketingtips.com/assoctrac — Founded in 1996 by Internet marketing expert, Corey Rudl, The Internet Marketing Center, Inc. focuses on researching, developing, and testing cost-effective e-business marketing strategies and automation solutions that small and home-based business owners can immediately apply to their businesses and profit from. After more than five years in development, AssocTRAC 4.0 incorporates all the features any online businessperson needs to make sure their affiliate program is streamlined and successful.

AssocTRAC 4.0 is a powerful Web-based service that allows you to quickly and easily start generating substantial affiliate income, even if you have no experience with affiliate programs. With AssocTRAC 4.0, it is easy to start signing up new affiliates to promote your products and services on their Web sites, no matter how many affiliates you recruit or how many different products you sell.

AssocTRAC gives you total control of your affiliate program. You choose:

- The affiliate commission amount for each product you sell

- The resources you will include in the welcome package for your new affiliates

- The links and banners your affiliates will use to advertise your products

- How and where new affiliates will sign up

- How and when you will pay your commissions.

I am not truly convinced that this software is still available as I see no way to order the product through their Web site. A complete list of features is available at **www.marketingtips.com/assoctrac/faq.html#G2.**

www.affiliatewiz.com — Affiliate Wiz™ is ASP.NET affiliate tracking and marketing software for managing an affiliate marketing program. Affiliate Wiz™ was developed exclusively for use on Windows servers running the .NET 2.0 framework, and is written in ASP.NET/VB.NET. Affiliate Wiz is compatible with most shopping carts, signup forms, and online ordering systems. Affiliate Wiz is a completely Web-based affiliate tracking software solution. Once installed all affiliate administration is performed through your browser. Their software is purchased for a one-time license fee, and installed on your Web server. Main features of Affiliate Wiz are available at **www.affiliatewiz.com/features.asp.**

www.directtrack.com — DirectTrack is an affiliate software used to build, operate, and manage your entire affiliate program. In addition you can configure DirectTrack to handle all ad serving needs and track the effectiveness of your online media buys. The Professional Version includes several advanced modules and can be used for up to five different Web sites.

As with the Merchant Standard, the Pro Version can be privately branded to match the look and feel of your company. You can also configure DirectTrack to handle all ad serving needs and to track the effectiveness of your online media buys. There are three versions of DirectTrack depending upon your needs and business model. Each version has a one-time startup fee and monthly minimum hosting fee. Features for each version may be found at **www.directtrack.com/pricing.html.**

www.cj.com — Commission Junction is the largest affiliate network and certainly the most well known. Ashley Devan, Director of Marketing, provided me with a fantastic interview in Chapter Fifteen. Commission Junction, a ValueClick company, is a global leader in the online advertising channels of affiliate marketing and managed search. Commission Junction operates the only truly global network in affiliate marketing while setting the industry standard for network quality, and providing the most sophisticated reporting tools available.

www.adserversolutions.com — Ad Server Solutions provides automated self-serve ad management software applications and remotely hosted ad serving services for online advertising. Buy and sell advertising space, manage, track and report all advertising. Using Ad Server Solutions and ad server software for all of your ad management needs will help lower costs, increase efficiency, and maximize revenue.

Ad Server Solutions provides marketing and technology solutions for online marketers and publishers which are used for managing rich media ad delivery, ad inventory, geographical ad targeting, revenue generation, live statistics and real-time reporting. Their products and services are designed to meet the needs of every Web site owner. They provide award-winning online advertising, automated self-serving ad management software (ad server software), ad network software, affiliate software, and banner exchange software. A complete list of features is available at **www. adserversolutions.com/features.html**. A screenshot is available on the following page.

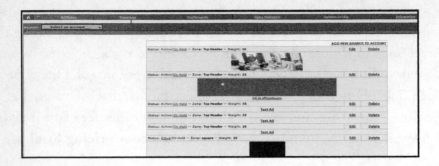

www.dhsoftwares.com — DH-MLM is their primary product, and they have developed a variety of add-ons to increase the functionality of DH-MLM. Price is $197 without support, or $377 with unlimited support. Software features are as follows:

- Manages affiliates up to nine levels deep

- Sets payment amounts at each of these levels in either a flat rate amount or as a percentage of the item price

- Makes recurring payments to affiliates as long as they remain a subscriber to your service

- Retrieves refunds from affiliates who have already received a payment for referring a customer

- Automatically generated yet fully customizable affiliate FAQ pages; can be further customized to add more FAQs

- Fully customizable header and footer; place your own logo and links on each of the affiliate control panel pages

- Customize automated e-mails sent to affiliates and customers, which automatically will let the affiliates and/or customers know what steps need to be taken next, no manual intervention necessary

- Ability to set cookie expiration dates so affiliates will still get credit for the sale even if the customer decides to sign up at a later date; perfect for potential customers who need to sleep on it before making a purchase; a point worth noting when recruiting affiliates

- Sort list of affiliates by activity, sales, name, or ID; see which of your affiliates are generating traffic and sales

- Customize the title of your affiliate pages and the affiliate control panels to improve your rankings in search engines

- Manual entry feature to enter sign-ups and credit the upline as though they signed up for themselves

- Administrative control panel to manage all affiliates and set preferences for DH-MLM

- Affiliate control panel to track statistics and modify contact information; extremely easy to use for anyone at all.

- Increased security for control panels

- Use of sessions for control panel log-ins

- Increased affiliate search functionality.

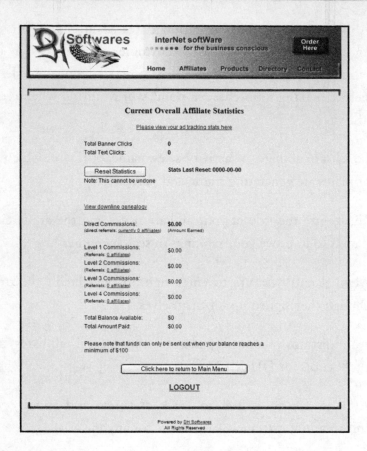

www.fusionquest.com — FusionQuest is a full-featured yet affordable affiliate tracking system known for innovation and exceptional support that has been in continuous operation since the summer of 2000.

Their primary innovation is UltraLinks. This is a unique linking technology that allows the affiliate links to be direct links to the sales site. Normally, affiliate links are very long and cumbersome URLs that do not even contain the merchant's domain name. These links are called redirect links because they actually link to a program on the affiliate tracking provider's server that initiates the tracking and then forwards the visitor to the destination sales site.

UltraLinks uses a sophisticated technology that allows the links from an affiliate to be direct links to the merchant's site. No redirection, no query string, nothing to get in the way. They are simple, regular links to the site.

This technology offers advantages for both the affiliates and the merchants.

- Links from affiliate pages count toward search engine link popularity.

- Click-through rates have proven to be higher when the links are not obviously affiliate links. With UltraLinks the link is a direct, regular link. There is no way to tell if it is an affiliate link.

- Affiliates are protected from both commission highjacking and having their affiliate ID removed when linking from a Web page.

- The links brand the merchant's Web site domain rather than the affiliate tracking solution provider's domain.

- Links provided for e-mail and plain text applications are short and easy to type, opening up the program to offline promotions, something not possible with redirection links.

In addition to UltraLinks, the following are a few other highlights.

- FusionQuest pays your affiliates for you anywhere in the world using direct deposit or a Master Card-based cash card.

- FusionQuest takes care of all 1099 tax reporting on affiliates when utilizing the network option.

- The network currently consists of more than 50,000 affiliates.

- Customizable affiliate areas to brand and match your Web site. It can be made to look like affiliates never leave your site.

- Advanced communication with affiliates. Send personalized e-mail to all affiliates anytime. Use the power of an automated set of welcome e-mails that can be used to motivate and train affiliates all automatically.

- No limits to the number of affiliates or clicks.

- Support recurring commissions and multi-tier commission structures; no limit to number of tiers.

- Custom integration for special situations.

- Basic shopping cart included.

- Time-tested, proven tracking system.

You have your affiliate program running and now you need to promote it. If no one knows it is there, no one will join it. This is definitely where the power of an affiliate network comes in. Because your products are offered to all the network affiliates, you have instant promotion limited to the members of the network, of course. In Chapter Seven, we discussed organic search engine optimization and other methods to maximize the visibility and page rankings in the major search engines. This advice is critical and ties directly to this chapter. You must optimize your site for search engine visibility as well as promote your new affiliate program.

Affiliate Directories

First, start plugging your affiliate program into affiliate or associate directories. One of the best is at Associateprograms.com. You can find the submission URL at **www.associateprograms.com/pages/How-to-submit-an-affiliate-program**. Another great one is Affiliate Scout, which is located at **www.affiliatescout.com/add**. Another good one is AffiliateRanker. com which is available for submission of your affiliate program at **www. affiliateranker.com/submit.jsp**. I recommend you simply do a search for affiliate directory and carve out an afternoon submitting your affiliate program to the many directories out there. Some will require you to put a reciprocal link on your Web site to their Web site. Because these typically link directly to your listing, I have no problem with this.

Promoting Your Affiliate Program

In addition to promoting your Web site through organic search engine optimization, essentially making sure your site is indexed by search engines, and optimizing your site design, there are many more things you can do to promote your affiliate program. Many of these promotional ideas will be discussed in Chapter Twelve; however, this chapter will provide you with general guidelines to follow.

The golden rule before announcing your brand-new affiliate program is to ensure that you have fully tested it; it is completely functional, easy to find and easy to navigate; and the support mechanisms are in place to support it. A promotional opportunity is a great way to recruit new affiliates, such as a cash bonus for signing up. In the case of Atlantic Publishing, they offered a free $50 gift voucher for their products. Make sure your promotional advertisement has an expiration date. Likewise they can use this promotional period to promote your affiliate program for you and recruit other affiliates.

You can initiate campaigns within your affiliate program to promote sales volume, total sales amount, or other incentives to inspire affiliates to promote your program and encourage sales. This is a great thing to consider around holiday periods when shoppers are looking for good bargains.

If you are offering discounts or other promotional materials, which your affiliates can promote for you, also consider adding them to the many big coupon Web sites that promote coupons, discounts, and special sales. My favorite is **www.dealnews.com.**

Embrace e-mail marketing as a method to promote your affiliate program. Atlantic Publishing Company produces a monthly newsletter that announces new book releases to their customers. Include details about your affiliate program in your e-mail marketing campaigns. I provide detailed information about e-mail marketing in my book, *The Complete Guide to E-mail Marketing: How to Create Successful, Spam-Free Campaigns to Reach Your Target Audience and Increase Sales.* One word of caution, use your trusted e-mail list. Spam does not work, and you will not get quality affiliates by sending out bulk spam e-mails. Keep in contact with your affiliates and customers through regular e-mails which contain useful information as well as promotional offers.

Consider integrating pay-per-click advertising into your overall marketing strategy and promote you affiliate program. I recommend you read my book, *The Ultimate Guide to Search Engine Marketing: Pay Per Click Advertising Secrets Revealed,* which gives you detailed introduction and advice on Pay-per-click, as well as how to select keywords which will in turn drive potential customers (and new affiliates) to your Web site.

Consider purchasing ad space on Web sites or in e-mail marketing campaigns that have content relevant to your products. Although these will cost money, they do have a good return on investment and can promote your company, products, and affiliate program opportunities.

Establish a blog for your company. Use it to promote communications and viral marketing, and disseminate information through this medium. A blog is very powerful and incredibly popular. For more information on blogs, check out my book, *The Secret Power of Blogging: How to Promote and Market Your Business, Organization, or Cause with Free Blogs.* Promote your products and affiliate program through co-workers, friends, other blogs, and other Web sites and the viral effect, particularly with blogs, will have a measurable positive effect on your overall and affiliate sales.

Make your affiliate program, Web site, and blog appealing to visitors and potential customers. It really does not matter how cool your Web site or affiliate program is if no one clicks on the links or buys from you. You need to give them a reason to want to join your affiliate program or buy your products. Create this interest and you will be successful. Do not stuff your Web pages and blog with useless advertisements and links. Nothing is worse than a page crammed with flashing banners and graphics all over it. If you have products to sell, put good descriptions by each one:

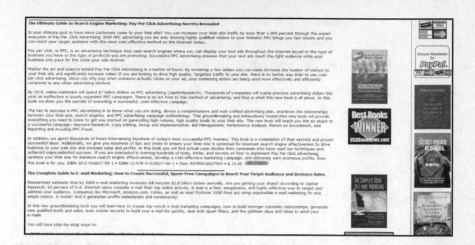

Organize your Web site so that the navigation is logical and simple, the information is clearly presented, and visitors find the information they would expect on the Web page.

Consider writing articles related to your products. Atlantic Publishing Company produces press releases for each product. Additionally, the authors write articles which are distributed through the Internet promoting the book, the author, and Atlantic Publishing. This type of marketing draws in customers as well as other potential affiliates to your Web site or blog.

You can offer an incentive for signing up with your affiliate program. I, personally, am turned off by many of the affiliate Web sites that offer a free download of — the secrets to making millions online— and so on. Offer a free product sample or something tangible, not another useless download people will toss in the deleted bin.

Subscribe and participate in online forums and blogs related to your product or marketplace. You can shamelessly plug your products and your affiliate program. Create a link to your Web site and affiliate program in your signature on the forums. Blog and offer advice, articles, or respond to others with information which will pique interest in your company, Web site, products, and blog.

These are just some ideas to get you started. As with any online promotions or long-term plan to promote your Web site, blog, or affiliate marketing campaign, it does take patience and determination. If something is not working, change direction, remain persistent and you will eventually realize the benefit of your hard work.

MARKETING: RECRUITING AND MANAGING AFFILIATES

By Michael Bloch

www.tamingthebeast.net

In affiliate marketing, there is an abundance of myths on both sides of the fence. Many affiliates believe that it is simple to make a killing from promoting other people's services; likewise, many merchants think they'll generate massive sales through an affiliate program.

Like any aspect of marketing, this can be the case, but not without some blood, sweat, and tears. Even if you have a network of thousands of affiliates, chances are that just a small percent of those marketing your products will be responsible for more than 90 percent of affiliate-generated sales.

Before we move onto recruiting and managing affiliates, you will need to have given plenty of thought to the components of a good affiliate program, and have your affiliate software in place. Manual recording of referrals just doesn't cut it these days, and most good affiliates will not be interested in your program if you do not have an automated system with good reporting mechanisms.

MARKETING: RECRUITING AND MANAGING AFFILIATES

Once your software is set up, you need to start recruitment. This should not just be left to having a — Join our affiliate program — link on your site; you'll need to put in a bit more effort than that.

Affiliate Content Pages

On-site content is very important, not only to explain your program to potential affiliates, but also to give search engines some fodder to chew on. Many affiliates will use a search engine to search for new programs; so ideally, you will optimize your affiliate pages for terms such as "(product) affiliate program," "best (product) affiliate program," and "similar."

Ensure that you have plenty of content spread over a few pages; I suggest the following pages at the very least:

- Program overview

- Terms

- Rates

- Signup

The rates page should not just have "Earn x%," but also examples of earnings based on referral levels. Stay realistic with projected earnings.

By the way, on your terms page, make it ultra-clear that you have zero tolerance for spamming and the use of malware for promoting your program, and make sure you enforce those policies.

As with any sales process, it is important to have calls to action scattered throughout your content; after all, you are trying to sell your program to other marketers. Have plenty of signup links throughout and make sure that the signup process is simple.

Marketing Your Program

Once you have taken care of your marketing materials, go beyond your site and start spreading the good word. Treat this exercise much the same as you would convincing a client to purchase your products. Slapped-together spiels with little thought put into them will not attract the kinds of affiliates you want.

Affiliate Program Directories and Forums

There are many affiliate directories and forums around and these are an excellent place to begin advertising your program. Simply run a search on the terms affiliate directory and affiliate forum and you will be on your way. Some forums and directories will allow you to list your program in exchange for a link back to them, but some may charge you for a listing or want a cut of any earnings generated by the affiliates they refer. It is important to have selected appropriate affiliate software and second-tier payment functions are very handy in these situations. A second tier is where an affiliate is paid not only on the sales they generate, but also a slice of the sales of any referrals made by affiliates they refer. It is a bit like MLM (Multi-Level Marketing), but only a second level rather than multiple levels as many MLM programs often have.

When submitting to an affiliate directory, be sure to read the instructions very carefully. Incomplete or incorrect submissions are usually discarded.

You will be competing with many other program listings so pay special attention to crafting attention-grabbing descriptions.

Submitting to affiliate directories is a rather time-intensive task; it can take days to complete. If you can spare the cash, I strongly recommend using an affiliate submission service such as AffiliateFirst, which will submit your program to about 50 directories for $59. This is one of the cheapest services around, but by no means does the price reflect the quality. I have submitted a few programs via AffiliateFirst and have been very happy with their service.

Once your program is listed in affiliate directories, visit them all and see if there is a way to get a premium listing at a reasonable rate. With so many thousands of programs listed in most good directories, if you can raise the profile of your listing somehow, you will do better with recruitment.

Affiliate Networks

These are the powerhouses of affiliate marketing, as they usually have thousands of registered affiliates, some with hundreds of thousands. Prices can range from a few hundred dollars as a one-time payment to thousands of dollars a month. Most affiliate networks will also handle fraud screening and payments. The way it usually works is that for each sale referred by a network, the network gets a certain dollar amount or percentage, so it is something you need to factor in when calculating how much commission you wish to pay if you choose to use a network.

Selecting and dealing with affiliate networks is a huge topic, one better left to an article of its own, but some of the most reputable networks include **cj.com** and **ShareASale.com**. CJ has a huge reach and prices to match, and while ShareASale is smaller, they are much cheaper; they are great folks to deal with too. If you choose to go with a network, you will not need to have your own affiliate software, but it can be of benefit to run an in-house program as well as through a third party.

Personal Approaches

If you are looking for power or super affiliates, it is important to remember that they do not have to spend a lot of time looking for affiliate programs — merchants come to them. Seek out the authority sites in your genre and approach them with a personalized note. One of the easiest ways to do this is to run searches on industry-related keywords via your favorite search engine. You are looking for authority sites, not competitors, so add terms like "articles," "reviews," "resources," "community," "blog," and "forum" to your searches.

Having found a target, remember that the more popular a site is, the more likely that they would already be aware of affiliate partnerships, so you do not need to define affiliate programs. Power affiliates are concerned with a number of issues:

- Revenue share levels

- Good lines of communication

- Tracking accuracy

- Extensive promotion resources

- Payment reliability

- Discount offers for people they refer

- Quality of product/service

- Merchant reputation

- Money-back guarantees for people they refer

Address each of these points briefly in your recruitment note. It is fine to be excited about your program, but do not overdo it or exaggerate potential earnings. All the information you provide should be realistic. An experienced affiliate can see through any spin you put on it.

Buying Lists

Trawling through search engine listings is incredibly time-consuming, so buying lists of contacts in your industry is an option worth considering. The key here is to buy lists from a reputable list broker. Before buying leads, look at the history of the company. How fresh is the data? How often is it updated? Most important, how is the data gathered? Many list brokers are just fronts for spamming operations. What you pay for is what you get; expect to pay a minimum of twenty-five cents a lead record, when buying thousands of leads, and also ensure that the records contain site URLs.

Screening Affiliates

Once affiliates start signing up, even if you automatically approve them, it is wise to audit your network on a regular basis. The FTC is now making marketers responsible for the actions of their affiliates. If your affiliates run amok, it could cost you thousands of dollars in fines.

You will have all sorts of affiliates signing up for your program, from hobbyists to spammers to legitimate career Webmasters and marketers. It is important that you review every affiliate on a regular basis to ensure that the way they are promoting you is acceptable to your company, and more importantly, legal.

The following is a brief list of screening tips.

- Affiliates must have an active site. If they do not they may be a spammer. This is not necessarily the situation in all cases, as some affiliates use PPC (Pay-per-click). So if you find an affiliate signing up without having specified a Web site, contact the person and find out what his plans are.

- Affiliate site content should be relevant to your product.

- The site should have appreciable levels of content. Web sites that primarily contain ads should be avoided, unless they are a popular destination.

- Watch for gambling and adult-related advertising on the affiliate's site. If you are not geared toward a market oriented to adult goods and services, then you probably do not want to be associated with an affiliate who is.

- Be very clear with your affiliates about what content they can use from your site. I have seen cases where affiliates have basically copied all the content from a merchant's site. This not only causes confusion for potential clients, but also can have an impact on your search engine rankings. By supplying quality content and promotional materials to your affiliates, the incidence of this will be minimized.

- Misrepresentation of your products and services. If an affiliate has over hyped your products and made outlandish claims, there is a possibility that the people they refer will not even bother to read the content on your own site — they will just go ahead and purchase. You may find yourself in an unpleasant position when the client discovers that the product or service didn't perform "as advertised."

Combating Affiliate Fraud

Affiliate fraud unfortunately has increased over the past couple of years, which is another good reason to regularly screen your affiliate base.

The main types of fraud:

- **Malware and stealware:** Some affiliates have developed software that is installed on a user's machine, usually as part of a freebie download. When a person clicks on an affiliate link, the true affiliate's ID is replaced with the fraud's. If the malware application is widely used, this can result in genuine affiliates losing interest in your program. Be sure to mention in your terms that malware and stealware are not tolerated, as this also will help to reassure genuine affiliates. If you see a particular affiliate generating a large number of sales from various sites that are not listed in their profile, this may be the result of malware. Learn more about stealware — it is a major problem.

- **Fake purchases:** If you have a high-value product that returns large commissions to affiliates, you may find some unscrupulous parties signing up for your program, then using stolen credit card information to purchase products via their affiliate links.

To combat this, ensure that payment of commissions occurs well after the sale, but not so long that other affiliates are discouraged from signing up. Thirty days (a.k.a. NET 30) after the end of the month in which a sale is made is sufficient and pretty much industry standard. If you offer a refund period on your goods and services, then the commission pending period should at least equal that.

Communicating With Your Affiliates

Good affiliates are usually busy people; they can easily forget about your products and services. Over time, your offers can wind up accidentally deleted or in less-visited areas of sites.

It is important to stay in contact with your affiliates, especially the high performers. Do not wait for them to contact you because if you do, it usually means they are reporting a problem. By taking the time to regularly make contact with your affiliate marketing sales force, you are demonstrating that you recognize their efforts, and you are interested in the partnership.

You do not have to have a new product as an excuse to contact your power affiliates. Even just a brief note to say hello and ask if they need anything can go a long way. Also use the opportunity for feedback on your program. A regular newsletter will also help keep your brand at the forefront of your affiliate sales force's mind. Most good quality affiliate management software has newsletter features.

Going the Extra Mile

Most affiliate managers know that in order to keep good affiliates happy, you need to offer them a little more than what is offered for the majority of the affiliate sales force. Be prepared to go the extra mile — for example, priority response times, custom creatives better suited to their site, special commission rates based on volume, or maybe even sending them gifts occasionally.

Everyone likes to feel important, so the better you treat your super-affiliates, the more likely they are to stick with your program and be productive. Super-affiliates tend to flock together, so if you impress one, they likely will tell their peers about your program.

Visit **www.tamingthebeast.net** for free Internet marketing and Web development articles, tutorials and tools. Subscribe for free to our popular e-commerce/Web design e-zine.

USING YOUR HOMEPAGE TO TELL A STORY

By Michelle Howe

A Web site is more than a brochure; it is an opportunity to start building a relationship with your perspective client or customer. The best way to do this is tell a story.

Everyone loves a story. As small children, before we could read, our teachers and parents used to read us stories. But even after we acquired the ability to read, a story captures our attention and imagination. The most successful professional speakers are known for telling engaging stories to their audiences.

A good Web site tells a story and engages the reader. The homepage of a Web site is probably the most important place to tell a good story. What you want to do is grab the attention of your visitor, and keep them reading through the content of your homepage.

When you tell a story on a Web site, you are presenting the information with a beginning, a middle, and an end, as if you were telling a story to group of people seated in front of you.

USING YOUR HOMEPAGE TO TELL A STORY

Here is a simple plan that will help you write better content for the home page of your Web site.

(1) Decide What the Purpose is for Your Homepage.

This is probably the biggest mistake people make when putting together a Web site. Instead of targeting the homepage for a specific purpose, it becomes convoluted, and the visitor becomes confused by multiple ideas presented in a disorganized fashion.

The information on the homepage may be excellent, but if it is put in the wrong order without the right emphasis, the message is not clear.

Right now I am working with a client who has excellent information throughout the whole Web site. However, that is the problem. In order for visitors to find all the information they need to make a decision, they need to click through page after page to gather information. The homepage only answers some of the questions a visitor might have. It forces the reader to click from page to page to get answers. This is a big problem because people don't want to take the time to click from page to page.

The first thing I did was ask the client what she wanted to accomplish as a result of having a Web site. The answer she gave me told me what was most important to emphasize on the homepage.

(2) Grab the Reader's Attention.

When someone lands on your Web site's homepage, they need to immediately know that they have arrived at the right place. So make sure you have a headline that immediately captures the attention of your Web site visitor.

Create a headline that lets visitors know you understand their pain or problem. You want a headline that in essence says to them, "Stop right here; you've arrived at the right place to get the answers to all

USING YOUR HOMEPAGE TO TELL A STORY

your questions. We know what your problems are, and we have the solutions."

One way to do this is to ask a question. "Are You Looking for Innovative Sales Training?" is the type of headline that engages readers and causes them to think.

Another type of headline technique is to use startling statistics such as "Did You Know That One Out of Three Women Will Have Heart Disease in Her Lifetime?" Headlines like this will pique readers' interest and make them want to learn more.

(3) Decide on a Logical Order to Present Information.

A homepage contains many ideas. It is an opportunity for a company to give an overview of who they are, what they do, and why you should do business with them.

Because you are going to be presenting multiple ideas, it becomes very important that you have a logical order to your information. Here is where you use the template or outline for creating a story to put together the content for your homepage.

The content of the homepage needs to have a beginning, a middle, and an end. Each of these three pieces needs to be tied together so that there is a smooth flow and logical progression. One idea needs to flow naturally into the next idea without awkward breaks or disturbances.

Imagine you are telling someone a story about how you discovered a new grocery store with all sorts of interesting food. Just as you are getting to a really funny part, your cell phone rings. You stop telling your story and answer the call. The person who had been listening to your story with great interest is now bored and walks away.

The same thing happens on a Web site. If you stick information in the wrong place on the homepage, it becomes like a cell phone ringing;

USING YOUR HOMEPAGE TO TELL A STORY

the visitor becomes bored and leaves the site.

In conclusion, use the storytelling technique for your homepage as a way to shorten the sales cycle. Give your audience the information they need to make a decision by keeping them engaged and entertained. Gently guide them to the right sales path without interruptions.

About the Author:

Michelle Howe, MBA, president of Internet Word Magic, specializes in writing for Web sites and creating irresistible copy to sell a company's product or service. A former university professor, she is the author of the award-winning book, *Turn Browsers Into Buyers: Secrets for Turning an Internet Profit*. Visit her Web site at **www.InternetWordMagic.com** for a free report, "The Five-Step Plan to Article Success."

Affiliate marketing is great when done correctly. It will generate revenue and sales. However, as I have said in every book, any technique you utilize should be part of an overall marketing and advertising strategy. I have touched on Google AdSense and Pay-Per-Click advertising in previous chapters of the book, and in this section I will cover them in depth so you can consider adopting and implementing these into your Web site and blog.

Google AdSense

Google AdSense lets you place Google advertisements on your Web pages or blog, earning money for each click by site visitors. Instead of paying per click, you actually earn revenue per click just for hosting the advertisements on your Web site. Google.com states, "Google AdSense is the program that can give you advertising revenue from each page on your Web site — with a minimal investment in time and no additional resources. AdSense delivers relevant text and image ads that are precisely targeted to your site and your site content. And, when you add a Google search box to your site, AdSense delivers relevant text ads that are targeted to the Google search results pages generated by your visitors' search request."

The concept of Google AdSense is very simple: You earn revenue potential by displaying Google ads on your Web site or blog. Essentially, you become the host site for someone else's pay-per-click advertising. Since Google puts relevant CPC, cost-per-click, and CPM, cost-per-thousand impressions, ads through the same auction and lets them compete against one another, the auction for the advertisement takes place instantaneously, and Google AdSense subsequently displays a text or image ad that will generate the maximum revenue for you.

Becoming an AdSense publisher is very simple. You must fill out a brief application form online at **www.google.com/AdSense**, which requires your Web site to be reviewed before your application is approved. Once approved, Google will e-mail you HTML code to place on your Web pages. Once the HTML code is saved onto your Web page or blog and is activated, targeted ads will be displayed on your Web site.

You must choose an advertisement category to ensure that only relevant, targeted advertisements are portrayed on your Web site. Google has ads for all categories of businesses and for practically all types of content no matter how broad or specialized. The AdSense program represents advertisers ranging from large global brands to small local companies. Ads are targeted by geography also, so global businesses can display local advertising with no additional effort. Google AdSense also supports multiple languages. In addition, you can earn revenue for your business by placing a Google search box on your Web site, paying you for search results. This service may help keep traffic on your site longer since site visitors can search directly from your site. It is available to you at no cost and is very simple to implement.

HOW TO SET UP YOUR GOOGLE ADSENSE CAMPAIGN

The first step is to complete the simple application form which is on the Web at: **www.google.com/AdSense/g-app-single-1**. It is critical that you carefully review the terms of service. In particular, you must comply with and agree that you will not:

- Click on the Google ads you are serving through AdSense.

- Place ads on sites that include incentives to click on them.

In other words, you cannot click on your ads or place text on your Web site asking anyone to click on your advertisements. The reason for this is simple: You cannot click or ask anyone else to click on your own advertisements to generate revenue.

Screenshots (C) Google Inc. and are reproduced with permission

Google AdSense Program Policies

Since a successful Google AdSense campaign must be in compliance with all the program policies, you should review the Google policy at **www. google.com/adsense/support/bin/answer.py?hl=en&answer=48182**.

Setting Up Google AdSense on Your Web Site

When you first sign up for your account, you will see the Today's Earning text along with any action notices such as on the one in the screenshot to release payment. Also, you can navigate to your AdSense setup and My Account. To set up your initial AdSense account, click on the My Account tab. Because Google will be paying you, you must complete several steps before your account is activated; providing W-9 tax data and choosing your form of payment, either electronic transfer or check. You may review or edit all of your account settings, including payment options, and review payment history data from the My Account tab.

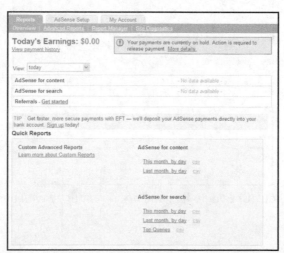

Screenshots (C) Google Inc. and are reproduced with permission.

Click on Account Setup to begin setting up your advertisements. The following screen will be displayed:

Screenshots (C) Google Inc. and are reproduced with permission.

Choose the product you would like to add to your Web site. You may choose either AdSense for content or AdSense for search or referrals. We will set up a Google AdSense for content advertisement on our Web site. Now choose your ad type. Choose either ad unit, the drop-down menu to choose text and image ads, text only, or image only ads, or link unit which displays a list of topics relevant to your Web page. Ad unit with text and images is the default and recommended setting. Click on ad unit to continue.

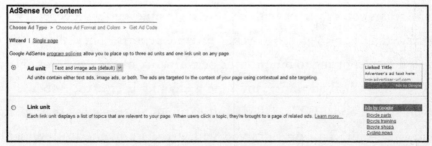

Screenshots (C) Google Inc. and are reproduced with permission.

You will be presented with several options to choose from including unit format, colors, and other options. Choose your desired options using the drop-down menus; note that this is not the actual advertisement which will be displayed on your Web site, but merely a sample of how it may appear.

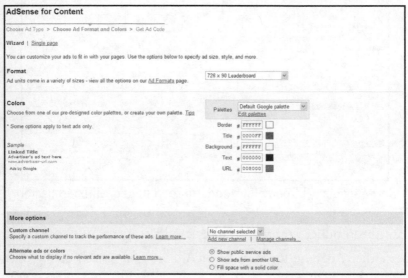

Screenshots (C) Google Inc. and are reproduced with permission

You may utilize More Options to enable Custom Channels or elect to alternate ads or colors, including the option to show public service ads if there is no advertisement ready to be displayed on your Web site. Google states that, "it is common for publishers to report significant increases in revenue from changing factors like ad formats, color palettes, and placement — increases you can track with channels. Channels offer a deeper level of analysis than is provided by overall revenue reports. They allow you to break down reporting to monitor the performance of sites, sections of sites, or even individual ad units. Any time a channel is created, AdSense will record impressions, CTR, CPM, and earnings statistics for that specific page or ad unit. This provides you with a precise method of evaluating which sites and locations will enable you to realize your maximum earning potential."

After choosing your selections you will be provided with HTML code which needs to be placed in the HTML code on your Web site. You are free to place the code on one or more pages within your Web site.

AdSense for Content

Choose Ad Type > Choose Ad Format and Colors > Get Ad Code

Wizard | Single page

Click anywhere in this box to select all code.

You may paste this code into any web page or website that complies with our program policies.

For more help with implementing the AdSense code, please see our Code Implementation Guide. For tips on placing ads to maximize earnings, see our Optimization Tips.

Your AdSense code:

```
<script type="text/javascript"><!--
google_ad_client = "pub-2693250782343896";
google_ad_width = 120;
google_ad_height = 240;
google_ad_format = "120x240_as";
google_ad_type = "text_image";
google_ad_channel ="";
//--></script>
<script type="text/javascript"
   src="http://pagead2.googlesyndication.com/pagead/show_ads.js">
</script>
```

Screenshots (C) Google Inc. and are reproduced with permission.

When you insert the HTML code into your Web site, your campaign is activated, and advertisements are immediately served to your site. Remember: Do NOT click on your advertisement at any time, even to test them. Google provides a preview mode for testing. The ad below was created and set up on our Web site in less than five minutes.

Screenshots (C) Google Inc. and are reproduced with permission.

How to Set Up Your Google Referrals

Google AdSense program policies allow you to place one referral per product, for a total of up to four referrals, on any page. You simply click on the referral link to choose your referrals.

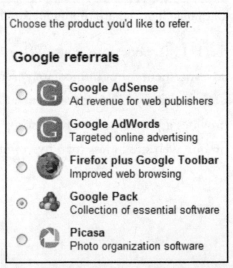

Screenshots (C) Google Inc. and are reproduced with permission

Google AdSense will generate the HTML code for your Web site. Once the code is placed on your Web pages, your referral will be activated and displayed on your Web site as shown below. You have a variety of options in size, color, and wording to choose from, and you are free to change your referral advertisements at any time:

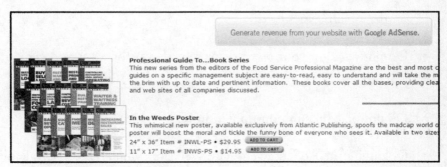

Screenshots (C) Google Inc. and are reproduced with permission.

Google AdSense is simple to implement, non-intrusive to your Web site, and allows you to open channels to earning potential revenue for your business.

Hints and Tips for Maximizing Google AdSense on Your Web Site

Google AdSense is an outstanding way to generate Web site traffic, attract advertisers, and create a revenue stream for your business. Use these hints and tips to maximize your earning potential:

- Always follow the Google AdSense Guidelines.

- Do not modify or change the Google AdSense HTML code you place on your Web site.

- Do not use colored backgrounds on the Google AdSense ads. If you have a Web site with a colored background, modify the advertisement to match your background.

- Place your ads for maximum visibility. If someone needs to scroll down to see your ads, you will likely not get any clicks on them.

- Do not include incentives for anyone to click on your ads (i.e. "Click here," "Click on my ads," etc.). This is a violation of the Google AdSense guidelines. Do not have friends, family, or co-workers click on the advertisements.

- Do not click on your own ads or reload your browser and click on your ads.

- Do not place ads in pop-up windows.

- Do not buy an AdSense Template Web site, which is readily available on eBay and other online marketplaces. These get-rich click campaigns are against Google's policies and do not make money.

- Text ads typically do better than image ads. If you insist on image ads, keep them a reasonable size: I recommend only using the 300x250 medium rectangle.

- You can modify the URL link color in the advertisement through the Google AdSense account panel. This makes it stand out among your ads and attracts the eye of the site visitor.

- If you have a blog, have others place advertisements in it. You will need to get Google approval for your blog, and when you do, this is a successful areas to insert advertisements.

- If your Web site has articles that you wish to embed advertisements in, use these guidelines: short articles — place the ad above the article, long articles — embed it within the content of the article.

- Wider format advertisements are more successful. The paying advertisement format is the large rectangle.

- Distribute ads on each Web page. Combine ads with referrals and search boxes so your Web site does not look like a giant billboard.

- Put the Google Search box near the top right-hand corner of your Web page.

- If your advertisements are based on content, the first lines of the Web page determine your site content for ad-serving purposes.

- Set the Google AdSense search box results window so that it opens in a new window. This will keep your browser open, and visitors will not navigate away from your Web site.

For more details on how to implement Google AdSense, you may wish to purchase my book, *The Complete Guide to Google Advertising — Including Tips, Tricks, & Strategies to Create a Winning Advertising Plan*, which covers extensively the secrets to a successful Google AdSense campaign.

Introduction to Pay-Per-Click Advertising

The key to pay-per-click advertising is that, unlike other paid advertising campaigns where you pay for the campaign itself in hopes of generating customers and revenues, you are not paying for any guarantees or promises of sales, Web site traffic, or increased revenues. You are not paying for traditional advertising campaigns hoping for a one or two percent return on your investment, and you are not paying for placing a banner advertisement on a Web site hoping that someone actually sees it, is interested, and clicks on it. Google makes Pay-Per-Click advertising easy with Google AdWords.

In the early days of the web, Banner advertising was the largest type of advertising, and it still holds a small market share. However, the main disadvantage of banner advertising is that the ads are embedded within pages, and you have to rely on Web designers to put your banner ad on a page that has similar or complementary content. A banner advertisement for dog food will not do well if it is placed on a Web site that talks about computer repairs. Enter the beauty of pay-per-click advertising: You do not pay to have your advertisement loaded on a Web page or listed at the top of search engines, and you only pay for results. In other words, pay-per-click advertising is entirely no cost to you, minus potential setup costs, even if your advertisement is viewed by millions of Web site visitors.

You will only pay when someone actually clicks on your Google AdWords advertisement. When that happens Google charges your account based on a formula price, and the visitor will be navigated to the page on your Web site which you preset when you created your pay-per-click advertisement. The click in no way guarantees you any sales; it merely means that someone has clicked on your advertisement. Do not underestimate the importance of having a user-friendly, information-rich Web site to capture the attention of the site visitor to help close the deal. Not all pay-per-click campaigns must result in a purchase. Many advertisers use pay-per-click advertising to sell products; however, many more use them to sell services, promotional material, news releases, and other media all intended to build business or disseminate information.

As an advertiser, Web site owner, or corporate manager, you will admire the simplicity and functionality of pay-per-click advertising, which allows you to have significant control over your campaign and is a perfect companion to your affiliate program. One of the success factors in creating and managing a Google AdWords pay-per-click campaign is the effective selection and use of keyword and advanced statistical reporting tools from

Google, as well as your Web hosting company. To ensure the potential for success of a Google AdWords pay-per-click campaign, you must choose the most effective keywords, design an effective and captivating advertisement, and have a well-designed, information-rich Web site with easy navigation.

Pay-Per-Click Advertising Walkthrough

As the advertiser you pay a rate which you specify for every visitor who clicks through from the search engine site to your Web site. Every keyword has a bid price, depending on the popularity of the keyword in search engines. You set your own budget and financial limitations, and you are done. Here is a step-by-step walkthrough:

- As the advertiser, you join Google AdWords and with a credit card put money on your account to get started.

- You create your ad as you want it to appear with your own selected keywords that you wish to target.

- Based on the keyword value, you set how much you are willing to spend on each keyword. Obviously, the more popular keywords are more costly per click than others.

- Upon completion, your ad is now ready to appear in the Google Search Engine.

- When someone searches through Google by using one of your keywords, the advertisement is matched to the keyword query, and the ad is displayed in the Google Search Engine results.

- If the person clicks on your advertisement, they are navigated to your Web site, and you are charged for the click.

The search engine will return a rank-ordered list of the most popular Web sites matching your search criteria. They may display your advertisement if it also matches the search criteria and keyword. One of the benefits of Google AdWords pay-per-click advertising is that your advertisement will be placed right up there with the top-ranked Web sites in your search category.

In general, the rules for most pay-per-click search engine applications operate on the same principle: The advertiser with the highest bidder gets top billing in the search engine return. A combination of experience, knowledge of the market, and some trial and error lets you balance keywords and phrases to deliver optimal results, and the tools provided by Google AdWords help you achieve that goal.

Google AdWords Pay-Per-Click Benefits

- Instantaneous and easy to implement.

- Results are clearly measurable.

- Cost-effective in comparison to other types of traditional and online advertising programs.

- For both large and small businesses.

- Ideal for testing market response to new products or services.

- Gives you full control of your budget — you can set systematic budgetary limits to minimize your overall financial risk and investment.

- More effective than banner advertising.

- Delivers a higher click-through rate than banner advertising.

- Ideally placed with top search engine results on the world's most popular search engine.

- Only delivered to your potential customers when they are actually searching for keywords related to your products or services contained in your pay-per-click ad.

- Delivered immediately based on keyword searches; dramatically increases chance of turning potential customers into actual customers.

- Allows you to design your ad, which is strategically placed in a prominent location on the Web site, instead of flashy, annoying banner advertisements which turn off potential customers.

- Can be delivered in search engine results — which is the most common — or within the content of a Web page.

Cost of Google AdWords Pay-Per-Click Advertising

Google AdWords pay-per-click advertising is, of course, limited by the size of your advertising budget. You will know in advance how much you will pay per click. Most start out with a minimum price per click, such as ten cents, and can quickly escalate to significantly more money depending on the keyword; even as much as $100 per click.

Let us say you want to sell a particular product by utilizing a pay-per-click advertising campaign. For the sake of this example we will sell Atlantic Publishing Company's award-winning book, *The Restaurant Manager's Handbook*, and have decided to use the keyword phrase, Restaurant Management, in our Google AdWords pay-per-click advertisement. Restaurant management is a fairly common topic. There are many others who want to use restaurant management as the keyword phrase, and all of us want to be the top-ranked listing. Essentially, we bid against our competitors with the amount we are willing to pay for each click on our advertisement. It may be cost-prohibitive to be the top bidder because our advertising budget will be consumed much quicker than if we were the #2 or #3 bidder. There are times, however, when it is more critical to be the #1 bidder regardless of the cost. Your bid is the maximum amount you are willing to pay for the Web site visitor to click on your advertisement. Be careful what amount you are willing to bid per click, as you may have to pay it. We will discuss bidding in detail later in this book.

Tips, Tricks, and Secrets for Google AdWords Pay-Per-Click Advertising

- Design Google AdWords ads so they target potential customers who are ready to buy. Rarely will banner ads or pay-per-click ads draw in the curious Web site browser and result in a sale.

- Make sure that your Google AdWords ad is very specific.

- Target one product for each Google AdWords ad if possible, instead of a generic ad which targets a large market segment.

- Make your ad links directly to the product page with a link to buy the product on that page, instead of a generic page or the Web site home page.

- If your Google AdWords ad targets a very specific product, you may see a reduction in actual clicks because your advertising segment is very narrow. However, those clicks are probably extremely profitable since you are only getting clicks from individuals seeking information on your specific product. This means your advertising cost may actually be reduced, while your sales go up.

- Be willing to bid for a good position. If you do not want to spend much money and are willing to settle for the bottom of the bids, no one is going to see your ad.

- Bid enough to gain the exposure you need, but balance exposure to stretch your advertising budget. It is not often worth the cost to have the #1 bid, and it is significantly less costly if you are in positions 2-10.

- Being the #1 listing on search engines may not be all it is cracked up to be. The top listing is the one that is clicked the most often, but it also has the worst percentage of converting clicks into actual sales. Many click-happy people click on the top listing without ever converting a sale. Those clicks will quickly eat up your advertising budget. You may have better luck by being below the #1 listing since serious potential customers screen all the advertisements, instead of just clicking on the first one.

- Use the provided tracking tools to monitor performance and adjust keywords and bidding as necessary.

- Chose very specific keyword phrases and you will lower your overall costs while increasing the potential conversion rate by choosing multiple highly targeted words or phrases instead of generic terms in an attempt to get tons of traffic. For example, use Crystal River Florida Vacation Rental Home instead of Florida Rental.

- Use capital letters for each word in the title and description fields of your pay-per-click ad.

- Use demographic targeting with your Google AdWords ad. If your intended audience is in the United States, there is no reason to allow your pay-per-click advertisement to be viewed elsewhere and eat up your advertising budget with worthless clicks.

- Use Google AdWords ad targeting if you are trying to specify a geographic area, such as the Washington D.C. area only.

- Use the Google Keyword Suggestion Tool to help you determine which keywords are most effective for your campaign.

- Keep an eye out for fraud. Although Google has fraud detection and prevention, if you suspect your competition is clicking on your ads, you may want to invest in additional protection such as, **www. whosclickingwho.com.**

- Check the spelling in your Google AdWords ad to ensure it is correct.

- Embed keywords within your actual Google AdWords pay-per-click advertisement. This may help them stand out among competitor ads when scanned by potential customers.

This is a brief introduction to the basic concepts of pay-per-click marketing. You can read about this topic in more detail in my book, *The Ultimate Guide to Search Engine Marketing: Pay Per Click Advertising Secrets Revealed.* You also are not limited to Google AdSense or Google AdWords because both Microsoft and Yahoo! have similar programs. The main point you should carry away from this chapter is that there are a variety of tools you can implement on your Web site and blog to enhance your affiliate marketing campaign, draw in new Web site traffic and potential customers, and generate even more revenue.

MAKING AFFILIATE MARKETING SUCCESSFUL FOR YOU

By Michael Bloch

Taming the Beast: **www.tamingthebeast.net**

WHAT IS AN AFFILIATE PROGRAM?

With the proliferation of goods and services now available on the Internet, advertisers look to individuals and companies to help sell their products by utilizing Webmasters and others to spread the word.

This can be in the form of banner advertising on affiliate sites, text links, reviews written by affiliates, direct e-mail, and so on. The advertisers compensate Webmasters by paying them for displaying the ads, for click-throughs sent to them, or, as is most common these days, a commission on sales resulting as a referral from their Web site or e-mail message. For a more detailed look at getting involved with affiliate programs, view the learning resources and tutorial links at the end of this article.

HOW CAN I MAKE MONEY FROM BEING AN AFFILIATE?

There are many thousands of affiliate programs out there all claiming to be the best. Some of them will give you the impression that all you have to do is implement their banners and links, and wait for the commission checks to start rolling in. This can be the case, but this scenario usually applies only to very large sites with massive Web traffic that is relevant to the offered product or service. For most of us, being a successful affiliate requires a little more work.

MAKING AFFILIATE MARKETING SUCCESSFUL FOR YOU

The range of goods and online services offered via the Internet has grown at an incredible rate over the past few years, and so has the competition. Web site visitors need to have a very good reason for clicking on a link or banner.

CHOOSING THE RIGHT BANNERS

In most affiliate programs, you are offered a wide variety of banners to place on your site, and very few of them will be effective. If you can attain a click-through rate of two percent you are doing very well. It has been my experience that graphics-rich banners do not perform as successfully as their simpler counterparts. The main reason for this is download time. If a banner is the last thing to load on your page, and the banner ad is excessively byte-heavy, by the time it has loaded, your visitor may already have scrolled down the page missing it entirely. Heavy banner ads can slow down the loading or critical elements of your page, and you can lose your visitors altogether. A graphically rich banner can confuse the actual message if the artwork and marketing blurb are imbalanced. For these reasons the banners you implement should be no more that 15kb whenever possible.

Banners with extreme animation, such as rapid flashing, are also something to consider very carefully. While these do achieve high click-through rates, they are also extremely annoying. If you decide to implement this form of banner advertising, use it very sparingly.

When selecting any form of graphic advertising, keep the theme of your site in mind. While graphic ads are meant to stand out and catch a visitor's eye, it should not be to the point that everything else on the page is totally ignored. Wherever possible, ensure that all banner ads, and any other advertising for that matter, use a link that opens in a new window. That way if visitors choose to visit one of your advertisers, it is easy for them to return to your page and review what they actually came to your site for.

MAKING AFFILIATE MARKETING SUCCESSFUL FOR YOU

POP-UPS AND POP-UNDERS

Many companies, mostly agencies representing a number of advertisers, now give their affiliates the options of using pop-up and pop-under ads. My opinion is that pop-ups are evil. They annoy visitors and are usually closed before they even have a chance to load. Go for pop-unders instead, preferably those that only display once per visit. See below for further articles on this subject.

USING TEXT LINK ADS

One of the most successful forms of advertising are text link ads. They are band-width friendly, do not take up a lot of space, and can be easily implemented into most page layouts. Good text link ads do not just scream, Buy me!; they offer some information why your Web site visitor should investigate the offer. A company should supply you with very short text links which only state the product or company name. You simply implement the links directly into the content of related articles and reviews.

ARTICLES AND PRODUCT OR SERVICE REVIEWS

This is where a bit of hard work comes in. Your regular site visitors will view you as an authority on particular subjects, so why not write a review on a product or service you are advertising? This also supplies excellent content for search engine spiders to latch onto. We have attracted many visitors to our site using what I call ad-articles.

However, there is a catch: If you are going to use the ad-article concept to promote products, you need to believe in what you write. Research the product and company well. Contact the company and let them know what you are doing, and ask for further resources and assistance. Once you have created the review, send them the link. You may be surprised at the response you get.

MAKING AFFILIATE MARKETING SUCCESSFUL FOR YOU

One of our advertisers was so impressed with the effort we put into promoting his company's product that he gave us an extra 15 percent commission on each sale. This form of Web site advertising is a bit time-consuming so choose your products carefully. The information that you supply to your Web site visitors will help them formulate a decision, so be honest in your sales copy. If you are successful in this promotion strategy, over time your reviews will not be seen as hype and bluster, but as a reliable source of information. Everybody wins.

E-MAIL ADVERTISING AS AN AFFILIATE MARKETING TOOL

Direct promotion via e-mail has boomed over recent years but has brought with it mountains of spam. If you intend on using e-mail as a method of advertising products and services, stand behind the products you are promoting and make yourself available to answer any questions.

An effective promotion technique I have found is to combine e-mail with the ad-article strategy. In our e-zine we occasionally put a summary of a product or service, just enough information to stir the curiosity of our readers. The summary then contains a link to the ad-article on our site. The benefit of this is not only that you have a good opportunity to promote the product or service, but while visitors are on your site they may also look at other sections. The advertiser benefits through having highly targeted potential clients visit their site.

ORIGINAL MARKETING STRATEGIES

Using the two above strategies combined, you can tailor your own campaign. Visitors sometimes become blind to the advertising resources supplied by companies, and your efforts in coming up with something original may spark their, and the company's, interest.

MAKING AFFILIATE MARKETING SUCCESSFUL FOR YOU

As an example, our hosting company has provided great service to us over the past 18 months, which made us very confident in promoting their hosting solutions. So, we approached them and negotiated a great deal for all parties involved. They have increased visibility on our site, and we receive fantastic benefits in return while promoting a service we really believe in. Using this example, you can make many of your alliances and business partnerships more beneficial to all concerned.

SUCCESSFUL AFFILIATE MARKETING REQUIRES PATIENCE

If you are certain that your Web site can generate fantastic sales for a particular company, contact them to negotiate a tailored arrangement. If they are not too enthusiastic to begin with, be patient; companies are approached every day by affiliates wanting to cut a better deal.

The reality is that many affiliates cannot deliver what they promise, and the companies are aware of this. Implement their links and banners, go the extra mile with ad-articles and other unique strategies, generate some sales, and then approach them again. You probably will find that they have a change of heart. Good affiliates are scarce, and if you are performing well, they will be very keen to keep you.

Most forms of advertising take some time to kick into gear. Putting up a link for a couple of days and then pulling it down because it is not generating any interest may not be a reflection on the product, just in the way it is being presented to your Web site visitors.

If you have run successful campaigns before, try to remember the elements that made it a success. What works for one product may not necessarily work for another, but it is worth a try. Again, if you are having problems with promotion, contact the company. They will more than likely have thousands of affiliates and will know what strategies are working. A good advertiser may even go to the trouble

MAKING AFFILIATE MARKETING SUCCESSFUL FOR YOU

of reviewing your site and provide you with some tips and hints based on their observations.

NETWORK ADVERTISING AGENCIES VS. INDIVIDUAL ADVERTISERS

One of the easiest ways to get involved with affiliate programs is through one of the major advertising agencies. They will offer you hundreds or thousands of advertisers to choose from, and payment will be consolidated.

It can be quite difficult to keep track of a number of individual advertisers, but this should not turn you away from considering individual companies to represent on your Web site. If the company is well known, has a good product, offers excellent affiliate support, and commits to regular payments with a low payout threshold, they can actually perform better than some of your agency associations.

This is particularly the case if the company offers residual income where you receive monthly commissions from referred clients to services such as Web hosting, magazine subscriptions, etc., for as long as the client is with the company. Affiliation with these individual advertisers, over time, can build a steady stream of income for you.

By the way, be extremely wary of affiliate programs that you have to pay to join; they are really multi-level-marketing (MLM) associations. There are some successful and respectable MLM offers, but many are scams. Research the company offering the program.

SUCCESSFUL AFFILIATE MARKETING, UNPLUGGED

Be careful of who you advertise for. Many companies set a minimum payout level they know not many will achieve. They greatly benefit from the fact that thousands of affiliates will not make any real money from the association. Over time these affiliates will drop off when they

MAKING AFFILIATE MARKETING SUCCESSFUL FOR YOU

cannot hit the target, but the company has benefited from the traffic, with minimum outlay. One sale here, two sales there: it all adds up for them.

Consider this: A company launches an affiliate program with a minimum payout level of $25 which is industry standard. They then recruit more than 20,000 affiliates. Only the top 1,000 affiliates actually generate enough sales to receive payouts on a regular basis. The remaining 19,000 only average one sale each, lose interest, and drop away. These 19,000 affiliates made nothing, but the company still raked in what could turn into millions of dollars in sales.

Successful affiliate marketing boils down to survival of the fittest, the fastest, and the wisest, but mainly those who put the most effort into it. Do not be discouraged if after a couple of months you have not made enough money to retire — it does take time.

Looking back over our figures, it was approximately six months after we got involved with affiliate programs that our efforts really started to pay off. The longer you are involved with affiliate marketing, the more savvy you will become about what will and will not work. Your effort versus return eventually will reap greater income in shorter periods of time.

Affiliate marketing can be exciting and frustrating, with many highs and lows, but one thing is for sure — it is never boring.

Affiliate Mistakes

I have compiled a long list of mistakes, lessons learned, and best practices through my research, as well as through personal mistakes, errors, and affiliate application shortcomings. I specifically kept this chapter in bullet format to give you chunks of information you could quickly absorb and incorporate into your affiliate marketing strategy.

- **Building an unattractive or non-functional Web site:** Your Web site is your image; make it professional, sharp, and content-rich, and get your point across efficiently. It should be easy to navigate, intuitive, and user-friendly.

- **Graphic or ad-intensive Web pages:** Graphics need to load quickly, and affiliate ads need to be seen, but not in excess. Do not create pages full of advertisements; they do not equate to conversions.

- **Difficult site navigation:** Navigation should be easy enough for a 5-year–old child. If a 5-year-old can navigate to the pages you want your visitors to see, you are probably in good shape. If site visitors cannot get to where they want to go, they will surely go elsewhere to spend their money.

- **Joining way too many affiliates:** The theory of the more the better does not necessarily apply. It is great to have multiple income streams as an affiliate of others, but start out slowly and build from there.

- **Failing to convince others to buy the products:** Do not just cut and paste the affiliate content from the merchant site to yours. You are not convincing anyone to buy the product if you do this. Add a personal testimonial, telling them why you think it is a great product.

- **Spam:** Do not use bulk or spam e-mail to promote products or your affiliate program unless you know the list is spam-free and double opt-in.

- **Overuse of cross-selling or up-selling:** This is when you try to sell one product and also push your potential customers to buy several others at the same time. Sometimes this is actually nice — I really like the way Amazon does it with their recommendations — but do not force it on a customer in an overly intrusive manner or make them click their way out of an up-sell. If they want it, they can buy it; if not, do not make them work to get out of the sale.

- **Changing the commission rate:** If you advertise a commission rate of 20 percent, you need to pay a commission rate of 20 percent. Do not realize you cannot afford it and switch mid-stream; you will lose your affiliate base.

- **Choosing the wrong affiliate network:** Do your research. There are many affiliate networks: some great, some not so great. There are plenty of reviews available online, so do your research and choose one that is reputable, trustworthy, and provides good customer service and technical support.

- **Choosing the wrong affiliate software:** This one needs some serious research and consideration. The product you choose must work on your Web site, work with your shopping cart, provide the features you need, and be simple enough for you and your affiliates to use. I have showcased several here for you to consider, but always do the research.

- **Ridiculous commission rates:** No one will join your affiliate program to earn two percent; make it worthwhile to them.

- **Make sure your affiliate software has provisions for commission theft and fraud protection:** As with PPC marketing, this is a tough area, but there are some basic methods that affiliate marketing software can implement to protect and cloak affiliate links from being manipulated or fraudulently altered, robbing you of precious commission payments.

- **Promoting only one product:** I know I told you not to promote too many products, but do provide a good pool of products for someone to choose from. Comparison shopping is popular, even online. People want to spend their money wisely, so give them alternatives and suggestions.

- **Excessive use of banner ads:** This is just my personal opinion, but I hate them. I will not click on them, and they are typically useless. They do not tell me anything. I want to know about the product — why I should buy it, details, reviews, etc. — not a flashing banner ad that says to click here.

- **Unreliable reports and late commission payments:** Pay on time, every time. Make sure your reports are accurate and dependable, and that they match your payment amounts.

- **Not capturing e-mail addresses:** Offer opt-in newsletters or other means to legally capture e-mail addresses. This builds your customer database so you can use your e-mail marketing strategy to bring in customer sales. Make sure you only engage in spam-free e-mail marketing, which I discuss later in this chapter.

- **Relying on one marketing strategy:** Affiliate marketing is great, but use your Web site and blog effectively, develop good SEO practices, and embrace PPC marketing and Google AdSense to increase visibility, ranking, and revenue.

- **Submitting affiliate site URLs to FFA directories:** FFA (Free For All) Web sites are nothing more than Web directories with random links, typically sorted by category. There are many free programs that submit your URL to FFA Web directories and Web sites, along with your e-mail address, resulting in no real increase in Web site traffic but a define increase in spam e-mails. There is no advantage or reason to subscribe to FFA Web sites.

- **No support:** It may seem simple to you, but others may struggle. Make sure the help they need is there when they need it. A visitor may become your most profitable affiliate.

- **The Build-it–and-they–will-come mentality:** This applies across the spectrum for online marketing, but particularly for Web sites and affiliate marketing. You can build a great site and even achieve great search engine rankings, but if no one has an interest in or enough knowledge about your products, they will not buy from you. You have to inform and educate as well as convince others they should buy from you or visit your Web site or blog.

- **Data feeds with outdated products, prices, or information:** Data feeds make the affiliate's life easy, but not if it is outdated information. It is your responsibility to maintain this.

- **Choosing the wrong product:** Do your research on products, perform market research, review the products yourself. Would you buy them? Is there a market for these products? Are you trying to convince your site visitors to buy the products? Are they relevant to your type of business, blog, or Web site?

- **Bad e-mails and bad e-mail accounts:** Make sure your e-mail accounts are working, and that your outgoing affiliate e-mail has the correct e-mail addresses built into them. Make sure the links in the e-mail are correct. This seems like common sense, but often an account approval e-mail is not functional, full of spelling errors, or broken links. Also, use e-mail associated with your domain name.

- **No communication:** Many affiliate programs have e-mail capability. Communicate with your affiliates once a month or more; offer them support, assistance, and encouragement.

- **Promoting unrelated or non-relevant products:** Do not promote automobile parts on your Web site about Boston terriers; promote dog-related products, not car parts.

- **The hard sell:** Do not be like those crazy infomercials with hyperactive, obnoxious spokespersons making ridiculous claims about their life-changing products. Convince people why they should consider buying your product; do not tell them to buy it.

- **Ridiculous prices:** 50 percent commission is great. However, 50 percent commission of a product that is 200 percent overpriced will generate a net revenue of zero. Price your products to be competitive if you want them to sell. If you have a ten percent commission, you cannot increase prices by ten percent to compensate and expect great sales results.

- **Failure to collect names and e-mail addresses:** Do not just sell your products; build a database of customers and potential customers. Ask, "Would you like to join our mailing list for future offers and promotions?"

- **Questionable credit adjustments:** Be up front and forthcoming when making commission adjustments. You may think the affiliate understands why you are doing it, but they will think you are stealing their money.

- **Extended delays in approving affiliates:** Do not make them wait any longer than 24 hours, one business day — it is not a tough decision.

- **Sudden death:** This is when your affiliate program dies and you cannot resurrect it, recreate the files, and track what commissions were yet to be paid. It is not likely, but have a reliable backup plan just in case.

- **Log-in or password problems:** Ninety-nine percent are due to user error, but still provide the support or automated means for correction.

- **Bad links:** These are not broken links. These are links that go to the merchant Web site but are not properly coded to give you the credit for the conversion. Make sure your links are properly coded.

Spam and Phishing

Wikipedia.com states, "E-mail spam is the most common form of Internet spamming. It involves sending unsolicited commercial messages to many recipients. Unlike legitimate commercial e-mail, spam is generally sent without the explicit permission of the recipients, and frequently contains various tricks to bypass e-mail filtering." One of the biggest mistakes new affiliates make is engaging in bulk or spam e-mail, hoping it will draw in new customers, and result in huge conversions and sales.

Most spammers buy bulk e-mail addresses from disreputable resellers, or through a variety of means such as harvesting them from Usenet postings, domain name DNS listings, or Web pages. They may use commonly used e-mail addresses with your domain, such as sales@, admin@, support@, service@, etc., or use specialized Web spider software to steal e-mail addresses from Web sites and other lists.

Another major concern with spamming is the spoofing of e-mail addresses. Spoofing is a method for concealing the identity of the sender, making you believe the e-mail is in fact from a reputable business. With spoofing the spammer modifies the e-mail message so it appears to come from another e-mail account. Spoofing can occur with any e-mail account or domain name. For example, you may get an e-mail from Bruce Brown at bruce@e-mail.com. This may seem to be a legitimate e-mail account. It avoids spam filters and gives you peace of mind because you believe the e-mail is legitimate from a reputable or known source.

Spoofing can cause you a multitude of headaches. You can become bombarded by spoofed e-mails which appear to be legitimate. Dealing with spoofed e-mails is frustrating and time-consuming. As the Web site or domain name owner it is much worse. Bounced e-mails usually are sent back to the spoofed domain e-mail account — yours. You may find you are receiving replies, bounced e-mails, and nasty responses to an e-mail you never sent. The main goal behind spoofed e-mails is to release privacy information or passwords to third parties who use them against your business.

Most spammers are after privacy and/or financial data, or offer illicit activities such as pornography, get-rich-quick schemes, pirated software, or overseas business scams. The best defenses against spam are anti-spam filters, junk mail filters, and specialized software at the e-mail server and the mail client to protect your e-mail accounts. The best advice for affiliates is to not engage in spam. It only creates problems, and does not result in sales.

PHISHING

Another major threat to your affiliate program is phishing. Phishing is actually a variation on the word fishing, which means that phishers throw out baited Web sites hoping someone will bite. Webopedia.com defines Phishing as: "The act of sending an e-mail to a user falsely claiming to be an established legitimate enterprise in an attempt to scam the user into surrendering private information that will be used for identity theft. The e-mail directs the user to visit a Web site where they are asked to update personal information, such as passwords and credit card numbers, Social Security and bank account numbers, that the legitimate organization already has. The Web site, however, is bogus and is set up only to steal the user's information. For example, 2003 saw the proliferation of a phishing scam in which users received e-mails supposedly from eBay claiming that the user's account was about to be suspended unless he clicked on the provided link and updated the credit card information that the genuine eBay already had. Because it is relatively simple to make a Web site look like a legitimate organization's site by mimicking the HTML code, the scam counted on people being tricked into thinking they were actually being contacted by eBay and were subsequently going to eBay's site to update their account information. By spamming large groups of people, the phisher counted on the e-mail being read by a percentage of people who actually had listed credit card numbers with eBay legitimately."

Phishing hurts affiliates for several reasons. First, many potential customers are very wary of any site with which they are not personally familiar, and many will not click on links if they are unsure where they are headed. Instead, many will simply type in the URL of the product's Web site, eliminating the possibility for you to earn a conversion and commission for any resulting sale.

CAN-SPAM ACT

The CAN-SPAM Act of 2003, Controlling the Assault of Non-Solicited Pornography And Marketing Act, establishes requirements for those who send commercial e-mail, spells out penalties for spammers and companies whose products are advertised in spam if they violate the law, and gives consumers the right to ask e-mailers to stop spamming them. The law, which became effective on January 1, 2004, covers e-mail with the primary purpose of advertising or promoting a commercial product or service, including content on a Web site. A transactional or relationship message, e-mail that facilitates an agreed-upon transaction or updates a customer in an existing business relationship, may not contain false or misleading routing information, but otherwise is exempt from most provisions of the CAN-SPAM Act, according to the Federal Trade Commission.

The Federal Trade Commission (FTC), the nation's consumer protection agency, is authorized to enforce the CAN-SPAM Act. CAN-SPAM also gives the Department of Justice (DOJ) the authority to enforce its criminal sanctions. Other federal and state agencies can enforce the law against organizations under their jurisdiction, and companies that provide Internet access may sue violators as well.

Several years ago a former client chose to launch an ill-advised e-mail campaign. They bought numerous e-mail lists from mostly disreputable list clearing houses, and imported more than 100,000 e-mail addresses into their e-mail management program. Then they sent multiple e-mails, with surprising and disturbing results. They had an almost 40 percent bounce rate, not uncommon for harvested lists, and another 30 percent that had requested to be removed or had removed themselves. Many of these unsubscribe requests were extremely nasty and threatening. Within a week they found that the e-mail marketing provider had shut down their account for suspected spam activity, and a few days later their Web site hosting company had terminated their Web site under threat of legal action from the backbone provider. This meant that their entire online business was shut down within days just for being accused of spam. Luckily, they had backups of their entire Web site and were able to move their domain name to another Web hosting company, and re-establish their Web site. However, this process left them essentially out of business for nearly 72 hours, and permanently out of the e-mail marketing business.

You may find this tip invaluable to your Web-based business. When you establish a new Web site, you often buy the domain through your Web hosting company. They purchase it and put it in their name, meaning they are the administrative and technical contact on it and only they can access it to change important information such as DNS entries. If you find yourself in a disagreement with a Web hosting company, and need to move fast, you will find yourself dead in the water if they control your domain names. Always buy your own domain names. Register them for yourself or your business, and list yourself as the administrative, technical, and billing point of contact with a good e-mail address. The only domain name registrar I recommend is GoDaddy, **www.godaddy.com**. They have the best prices, best service, and most advanced control panel, giving you complete control over all your domain names within a single, easy-to-navigate interface.

In fact, if you want to consolidate all your existing domain names from multiple registrars, you can combine them into one GoDaddy.com account, and you will even add a year onto each registration just for moving them to GoDaddy.com. Although this is not really related to the subject of Spam, this tip will ultimately save you headaches down the road.

Let us take a close look at what comprises the Can-Spam Act.

CAN-SPAM ACT REQUIREMENTS

- **Bans false or misleading header information.** The From, To, and routing information of your e-mail, including the originating domain name and e-mail address, must be accurate and identify the person who initiated the e-mail.

- **Prohibits deceptive subject lines.** The subject line cannot mislead the recipient about the contents or subject matter of the message.

- **Requires that your e-mail give recipients an opt-out method.** You must provide a return e-mail address or another Internet-based response mechanism that allows a recipient to ask you not to send future e-mail messages to that e-mail address, and you must honor the requests. You may create a menu of choices to allow a recipient to opt-out of certain types of messages, but you must include the option to end any commercial messages from the sender. Any opt-out mechanism you offer must be able to process opt-out requests for at least 30 days after you send your commercial e-mail. When you receive an opt-out request, the law gives you ten business days to stop sending e-mail to the requester's e-mail address. You cannot help another entity send e-mail to that address or have another entity send e-mail on your behalf to that address. Finally, it is illegal for you to sell or transfer the e-mail addresses of people who choose not to receive your e-mail, even in the form of a mailing list, unless you transfer the addresses so another entity can comply with the law.

- **Requires that commercial e-mail be identified as an advertisement and include the sender's valid physical postal address.** Your message must contain clear and conspicuous notice that the message is an advertisement or solicitation and that the recipient can opt out of receiving more commercial e-mail from you. It also must include your valid physical postal address.

Penalties for each violation of the CAN-Spam Act are subject to fines of up to $11,000. Deceptive commercial e-mail also is subject to laws banning false or misleading advertising. Additional fines are provided for commercial e-mailers who not only violate the rules described above but also:

- Harvest e-mail addresses from Web sites or Web services that have published a notice prohibiting the transfer of e-mail addresses for the purpose of sending e-mail

- Generate e-mail addresses using a dictionary attack — combining names, letters, or numbers into multiple permutations

- Use scripts or other automated ways to register for multiple e-mail or user accounts to send commercial e-mail

- Relay e-mail through a computer or network without permission: for example, by taking advantage of open relays or open proxies without authorization.

The law allows the Department of Justice to seek criminal penalties, including imprisonment, for commercial e-mailers who do or conspire to the following:

- Use another computer without authorization and send commercial e-mail from or through it

- Use a computer to relay or retransmit multiple commercial e-mail messages to deceive or mislead recipients or an Internet access service about the origin of the message

- Falsify header information in multiple e-mail messages and initiate the transmission of such messages

- Register for multiple e-mail accounts or domain names using information that falsifies the identity of the actual registrant

- Falsely represent themselves as owners of multiple Internet Protocol addresses that are used to send commercial e-mail messages.

The FTC has issued additional rules under the CAN-SPAM Act involving the required labeling of sexually explicit commercial e-mail and the criteria for determining the primary purpose of a commercial e-mail. See the FTC Web site at **www.ftc.gov/spam** for updates on implementation of the CAN-SPAM Act.

SOURCE: FEDERAL TRADE COMMISSION

Most recipients of bulk e-mail, spam, or unsolicited advertisements view them as unwelcome, unpleasant, or offensive. They key to utilizing e-mail as a tool for marketing or advertising your Web site or affiliate marketing program is to build your customer lists using opt-in methods (or double opt-in) to ensure that your e-mail lists comply with the requirements of the CAN-Spam Act.

12 Ideas to Grow and Stimulate Your Affiliate Program

This chapter contains information about media exposure, off-line or traditional marketing, and other ideas to promote and stimulate the success of your affiliate program. Please consider adopting these ideas wherever appropriate as you develop your marketing and advertising goals in conjunction with your affiliate marketing program.

Media exposure is one way you can boost your Web presence visibly, and increase the amount of Web site traffic. You need to strive to get as much media coverage as possible without spending too much of your advertising budget. This is a great way to promote your business, Web site, and affiliate program. Your potential and existing customers are only going to buy products and services from a business they feel is trustworthy. To earn that trust and reliance, you have to make the most of media exposure so that you can build your credibility and find a secure position for your business as an expert in your target market.

You need to develop a combination of effective online and offline publicity and public relations that is geared toward affirming your corporate trustworthiness, reliability, and credibility. You need to learn how to develop your own public relations and media campaigns so that you can build up the value, credibility, and trust that create satisfied and repeat customers. When you gain credibility and trust, you get more sales and increased confidence from your customers, and you gain the public profile you want and need for your business. This is particularly true when promoting Web sites, blogs, and affiliate programs.

Many businesses pay thousands of dollars for media exposure, publicity, and advertising. You can get free publicity and PR for your business Web site by using proven, inexpensive, and often free methods. You want to merge the proven success of positive media coverage and a successful online presence to give yourself the winning edge over your competitors and promote a highly effective and desirable affiliate program. The combination of successful online and offline publicity and promotion will guarantee your credibility, trustworthiness, and dependability, all of which to greater sales and/or interest in your products. Your success will lead to more sales, increased client confidence, increased exposure at speaking appearances, and the positive public profile you want for your online business. People who look on the Internet for merchants will only buy from someone they feel they know and trust; if you earn that trust, it extends exponentially as your affiliate program grows.

Promoting Your Business in the Media

There are several things you can do to promote your offline media exposure.

- Approach your local chamber of commerce and request that they write a short article about you and your business. Publish that article on your Web site and blog as another promotional tool or use it in an e-mail marketing campaign.

- Offer to speak at a seminar or lead a workshop in your area of expertise. This will get media exposure that is incredibly positive and community-oriented and establish credibility and trust among potential clients. Circulate your Web site and blog URL at the seminar, and hand out information about your affiliate program. Put your Web site URL on everything you distribute (flyers, promotional items, business cards, letterhead).

- Follow up any correspondence or phone calls with a letter or phone call. Make sure to leave your Web site URL on their voicemail. This strategy builds a reputation as a conscientious and courteous entrepreneur.

- Share your knowledge by writing articles and professional opinions for online publications, and upload them to automated syndication sites. These syndication sites are perfect for having immediate hotlinks back to your Web site and blog, and you can promote your affiliate program in them. Remember to include your e-mail and contact information in the byline as well as brief biographical information on yourself and your business. The more exposure you generate, the more success.

- Offer coupons such as buy-two-get-one-free offers to stimulate sales, or offer 20 percent off one-day-only sales promotions.

- Offer a commission increase for reaching sales goals.

Develop tactics to make media exposure and coverage work for you. Keep in mind that most columnists will give their e-mail address in their byline at the conclusion of their article. Send them a note with your comments and views while offering your expertise as a source for future quotes. Optimize your media exposure whenever possible; the returns for your business will be substantial.

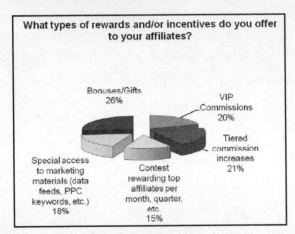

Reprinted with Permission Copyright 2008 Shawn Collins
http://blog.affiliatetip.com

Gaining the Trust of Customers and Clients

Gaining the trust of your customers and clients is extremely critical in developing a continuing relationship that rewards your online business with repeat customer sales. The one-time sale may boost your immediate sales numbers, but return customers take your business from mediocre to fantastic profits. Your affiliates also are striving to have repeat customers as well improve their commission. There are several rules you should remember when it comes to building a relationship with your customers and gaining their trust: be honest, be up-front, and always do what you say you are going to do. By following these three simple guiding principles, you will have satisfied customers.

Increasing Your Public Profile

Your public profile is your trademark for success and profits. Your online profile and business rating is critically important to how customers perceive you. Your local and state Better Business Bureaus are great organizations to join, and obtain positive ratings. Other online business profile ratings services worth considering are **www.resellerratings.com**, **www.epinions.com** and **www.consumerreports.org**.

Your goal when it comes to sharing your expertise is to publish for free, thereby allowing many other organizations, news services, and publications or magazines to distribute your article throughout their network in return for links back to your Web site and blog. There are ways that you can publish a full-page ad promoting yourself and your business without spending a dime. Contact editors of publications and offer them your press release to add content to their next publication. Many editors are looking for useful and relevant content so that they can meet deadlines. You need to take advantage of this opportunity and create the perfect article for publication. You should target newspapers, magazines, newsletters, Web sites, and Web magazines as ideal opportunities for displaying your article. Magazines that have both an offline and an online presence are excellent for increasing exposure and driving customers to your Web site.

Ideas to Improve Your Web Site and Affiliate Program

- **Site design:** Make sure your Web site is professional and has a great design. You want your Web site to have a clean, tight look so that customers are compelled to return. Professional site design means having a Web site that is (1) easy to navigate, (2) has appropriate logos, (3) has up-to-date information, (4) answers customer questions, and (5) does not look like an amateur site.

- **Honesty:** Do not hide anything from your customers or affiliates. To maintain credibility and trust, follow through on what you say you offer with your affiliate program. You do not want to be identified and exposed as running a fraudulent affiliate program.

- **Testimonials and product reviews:** Using customer testimonials and product reviews is a great way to promote the quality and reliability of your products. This is an amazingly effective tactic which **Amazon. com** has perfected with their product reviews. The strongest and most effective referral comes from direct customer testimonials. You can add **Amazon.com**-style product reviews to your Web site by visiting **www.review-script.com.**

- **Tiered commissions:** If you have very successful affiliates, you may wish to reward them with higher commission rates. You also may wish to have other affiliates in special categories with higher commission percentages. For example, Atlantic Publishing Company offers a 30 percent commission to authors, while other affiliates still earn an impressive 20 percent for each sale.

- **Contests:** Stimulate competition and reward programs within your affiliate base. Offer a monthly bonus to the affiliate with the highest conversions, a bonus reward to your most-improved affiliate, or a gift to your top performing affiliate. Communicate with them, shower them with encouragement and praise, and inspire them to achieve higher levels of success. If you do not, they will simply put your products on their site and forget about them, or do nothing and forget about being your affiliate.

- **Tier bonuses:** For example, the first affiliate in the month to reach $1,000 in conversions or the first affiliate to have 25 or more conversions in a month gets a bonus.

- **Double or triple commission days:** You likely will lose some money in this, but you will inspire your affiliates to push your products and convince their customers to buy your products so they can earn the short-lived commission bonus. This goes a long way with earning the trust and respect of your affiliates.

- **Bonus for up-selling:** If an affiliate promotes one product on their site but sells it and more through your Web site, reward them with a bonus or other incentive.

- **Promote your URL:** Include your Web site URL on all correspondence such as e-mail signatures, stationery, business cards, and blog posts.

13 Summary

When I first started out writing books, I had envisioned creating a set of books which would cover the gambit of online advertising and marketing, all specifically geared to the individual or small business with limited advertising and marketing budgets. This latest chapter of the series covers the final major areas of marketing which I had only briefly touched on in my previous books. I am convinced that affiliate marketing can be both profitable and successful. As an affiliate who is selling products for other merchants, or the merchant who is establishing an affiliate program or joining an affiliate network — both offer unbound potential for significant increase in sales volume, boost in profits, and immense personal gratification and satisfaction.

As an experienced affiliate who has installed and managed an affiliate program, and been an affiliate of others, both through individual Web sites and affiliate networks, I know that affiliate marketing is not the golden ticket to untold riches. Trust me, there are many Web sites offering you the secrets, for a price of course, but the real secrets are held within this book when combined with determination, persistence, great communication skills, and lots and lots of hard work. Believe me, the results are worth the work, and affiliate marketing has the potential to provide you with a substantial increase in sales volume or a supplemental income stream. As with all my previous books, I wanted a practical book which you could refer to often for advice and guidance, eliminate the fluff, and provide accurate, factual, and useful information specifically geared toward the small business or individual with limited budgetary resources and technical support staff. You do not need to be an expert affiliate marketer to establish and run your own successful affiliate marketing campaign, and this book will walk you through the process to ensure you are prepared and ready to achieve your maximum success potential.

No matter what, have fun with affiliate marketing. It is incredibly gratifying to receive your commission checks or watch your affiliate program network grow and prosper under your management. I hope you can use this book to reach and exceed all of your affiliate marketing goals.

Affiliate Marketing Case Studies

This chapter will feature real-life case studies of how affiliate marketing transforms organizations, increases customer base, grows revenue, and is one of the most powerful marketing tools available today.

CASE STUDY: PANDA SECURITY

www.pandasecurity.com

Panda Security is a global leading provider of IT security solutions, with millions of clients in more than 200 countries and products available in 23 languages. Panda's mission is to develop and supply global security solutions to keep clients' IT resources safe from the damage inflicted by viruses, intruders and other Internet threats at the lowest possible total cost of ownership. Panda Security proposes a new security model specially designed to firmly combat new types of cyber-crime. This results in technologies and products with much greater detection and efficiency rates than the market average, providing a higher level of security to users.

Panda Security has various product lines for companies and home users: security software, security appliances, and managed security services. All Panda's solutions are backed by tech support, made up of an expert team of professionals available at all times. Panda's corporate slogan, "One step ahead," sums up the competitive advantage that has characterized the company from the start: a commitment to continuous innovation and change, a capacity to keep one step ahead in the fight against computer threats.

CASE STUDY: PANDA SECURITY

2007 saw the development of a new security model based on the combination of HIPS + In-depth Audits, which complements the traditional signature-based model and provides a much more effective response to new types of cyber-crime.

Situation:

When Panda Security USA first contacted AMWSO in 2005, the affiliate program had already been running for more than a year on Commission Junction. The affiliate program was getting very little traction through the network and had lost large amounts of money due to affiliate fraud.

Panda Security determined that its affiliate program would be better managed by a professional affiliate management company. An exhaustive research and selection process was executed to find an organization with the capacity, professionalism, and track record to manage their program. There was only one company that continually showed all of these abilities to Panda: AMWSO. In June 2005, AMWSO was awarded with the contract to manage the Panda Security USA affiliate program.

Proposal

AMWSO conducted an exhaustive needs assessment review of the Panda Security affiliate program. After AMWSO came to a thorough understanding of Panda's overall goals for its affiliate program, it was decided that a full-time AMWSO affiliate manager would manage the program.

The following issues needed to be addressed immediately.

Affiliate recruitment/activation: Panda wanted AMWSO to recruit super-affiliates and boost sales through the affiliate channel. Additionally, Panda wanted to see results through the 2,000+ affiliates who had signed up for the affiliate program through Commission Junction but were not driving impressions, clicks, or sales.

* Cleanup: It was recommended that Panda Security formulate a progressive anti-parasite stance and remove any affiliates who may have been participating in parasitic activity. Additionally, AMWSO would work with Panda to eliminate affiliate fraud.

CASE STUDY: PANDA SECURITY

- Develop creative inventory: The affiliate program had few tools available for affiliates to promote Panda's software. Panda also wanted assistance with developing tools to offer affiliates, and therefore, boost conversion rates through the affiliate channel.

- Trademark protection: Panda wanted AMWSO to protect the Panda trademark through the affiliate channel.

- Coupon campaigns: It was recommended that Panda create and distribute coupons.

Results

A contract was designed that tied the affiliate manager dedicated to the Panda Security contract directly to the revenue earned by the affiliate program. Resources were brought to bear on developing the creative needs of the contract as well as key support tools for affiliates, including Commission Junction trackable 30-day trials of Panda's software, Commission Junction trackable video files that promoted Panda and the software, an affiliate support site, a dedicated forum through **ABestWeb. com**, and more.

To date, the Panda Security affiliate program has grown by more than a thousand percent in total affiliate-generated sales a month. In March 2008, the total increase peaked to more than 1800 percent in affiliate-generated sales. The number of earning affiliates and the number of active affiliates has grown exponentially from when AMWSO took over the management of the affiliate program. There have been very few months since July 2005, when either the number of earning affiliates or the number of active affiliates has dropped off in numbers.

Future

Panda Security and AMWSO look forward to a promising future together with a number of new projects on the horizon, and the prospect of growing the program into new and emerging affiliate segments. The Panda Security affiliate program continues to be fully managed by AMWSO.

AMWSO.com was founded in 1996 as a Web design and development company with a focus on the gem and jewelry industry. Throughout the late

CASE STUDY: PANDA SECURITY

1990s its focus was on developing brochure-style sites for jewelry firms worldwide. In 1999 the firm launched Gemkey.com, a Business to Business site for the jewelry and diamond industry; in 2000, it launched **Mondera.com**. Until 2002 the company's focus was on supporting these two sites.

In 2002 the company's focus changed from internal projects to managing external developments, which included the development of sites for such firms as ACCOR, Michelin Asia, Exxon Mobil, and other large firms. At the same time the company launched its first affiliate management project, taking on the Mondera affiliate program.

Mondera was an immediate success and won multiple awards from LinkShare and the affiliate community as a whole. From that success, AMWSO expanded the affiliate team to take on more affiliate management projects. From 2002 to 2006, the AMWSO team took on a wide number of affiliate management clients and has managed the majority of our core clients for three or more years. In 2006 AMWSO transformed into a dedicated affiliate management firm and has focused purely on developing its skills and processes as it continues to grow.

www.amwso.com

http://feeds.feedburner.com/AMWSO - RSS News Feed

Tel: UK 0161 408-6624 / Tel: USA 904-350-0510

Tel: INTL 66 81 807 2093 / FAX : USA 604-608-5580

CASE STUDY: MACECRAFT SOFTWARE

www.macecraft.com

Macecraft.com once had an affiliate program promoted through Commission Junction that did not perform very well. The Webmaster had already hired a graphic designer who made a new banner, which did not improve performance.

CASE STUDY: MACECRAFT SOFTWARE

After reading the affiliate offer, the "Get Easy Money" speech seemed out of place and disconnected. So I began researching the company. I discovered that Macecraft is a Finnish developer that has been producing registry cleaning software for more than a decade. This seemed like a much bigger selling proposition, so I used it instead. The new message was focused on the product's credibility with a large, already established public. But this still didn't seem strong enough, so I dug further. It turns out that Macecraft's flagship program has a rather unique feature: It is compatible with every version of Windows ever conceived. This was the unique selling point I was looking for. I targeted the software's compatibility with Windows Vista, and its ability to make Vista run smoother and faster. Basically, I made the program look trustworthy and sellable.

Once I finished writing the copy, I needed to deal with the usability issue. When you are promoting a product on a Web site like CJ, you are competing for the attention of potential affiliates with many other developers. So I used a bullet list and spaced out the text as much as I could, making it more prominent.

The last piece of the puzzle was the banner. The tag line they used was out of sync with the copy, so I decided on a more subtle approach. The idea was to convey the potential winnings but also to stand out and make the potential affiliates read the offer more closely. I ended up with an image of a hand holding a wad of dollars and a tag line that said "GO GET THEM." Immediately after the new ad was put online, the number of affiliates attracted daily jumped by 70 percent.

George Cozma works as a consultant for online entrepreneurs who wish to boost the conversion ratio of their Web sites, and attract more sales and more affiliates with the same amount of traffic. Most of his experience lies in copywriting, but he also conducts usability studies. His favorite quote is, "If it wasn't tested, it didn't happen." He can be contacted and from time to time even hired by sending an e-mail to geegelc@yahoo.com.

CASE STUDY: MYTEMPLATESTORAGE.COM

www.mytemplatestorage.com

The MyTemplateStorage affiliate program presently combines two projects from TemplateMonster network: **www.templatemonster.com** and **www. templatetuning.com**. Founded in 2003, this affiliate program has become one of the most advanced affiliate programs available online, and the best template affiliate program going. Thousands of affiliates have joined this program since 2003, and this afflux never stops.

TemplateMonster project

TemplateMonster is the most advanced project, and the core of the MyTemplateStorage affiliate program. **TemplateMonster.com** is the world's leading Web site templates supplier with a constantly growing database of more than 20,000 products. TemplateMonster is a framework for Web pages and Web sites, providing a number of files (graphics, code, flash, fonts, etc.) that allow you to easily build your Web site without ordering a high-cost design from custom design studios. Most important, you will definitely find a template to your liking, as new templates are added to TemplateMonster's collection every other day. TemplateMonster is all about making your Web life as easy and pleasant as possible. The only thing you have to do after purchasing the template is replace the texts with your own and change the images; after that, your Web site is ready to go online.

TemplateMonster was founded in 2002. With templates getting more and more popular, in 2003 the TemplateMonster affiliate program was created, which included only one TemplateMonster project at that time. The affiliate program was named MyTemplateStorage, symbolizing that you can have a templates store on your Web site. This system works on a custom-developed engine not connected with any other affiliate programs or networks.

Several different tools are available for affiliates working with the TemplateMonster project. The first and most effective tool is a templates shop, which allows selling TemplateMonster templates on an affiliate's

CASE STUDY: MYTEMPLATESTORAGE.COM

Web site under their own branding and receiving a 20 percent commission for every sale made. The templates are displayed on the Web site by simple Java script code generated in the administrative area of the affiliate program.

For those affiliates who have no experience working with code, MyTemplateStorage offers the ready-made affiliate shops. These are the entire affiliate Web sites ready to go online, but the affiliate still has to register the domain name and buy the hosting package to upload the ready-made affiliate shop files. The sales are tracked based on the randomly generated ID that every template's shop script or ready-made affiliate shop has as the part of code. This ID is unique for every affiliate. The template shops are available in English, German, French, Spanish, Dutch, Turkish, Portuguese, Czech, Italian, Polish, and Danish.

The second tool for affiliates is the affiliate link redirecting customers directly to TemplateMonster's Web site while the affiliate cookie is saved to the customer computer. The affiliate link is unique for every affiliate. It can be used as a special offer in the newsletter or sent to your customers directly, placed in the links section of your Web site, or linked to your custom banner. The affiliates also receive 20 percent commission for all the sales made via their affiliate link. Once the cookie is set, it never expires.

The third tool is presented by TemplateMonster affiliate banners. Both static and animated banners are offered, and you can choose among different sizes and types of products. You still will earn 20 percent commission. There is also an option available for advanced programmers to look into: **www.templatemonster.com/webapi.**

For the convenience of MyTemplateStorage affiliates, they can get the templates for themselves without making the actual purchase. There is a Get Template Tool with which affiliates can request the template with the 20 percent discount, while the template cost will be deducted from their commission.

TemplateTuning.com

TemplateTuning.com is the second project of MyTemplateStorage affiliate program. TemplateTuning.com is a template customization studio staffed

CASE STUDY: MYTEMPLATESTORAGE.COM

by professionals capable of tweaking and custom-fitting Web sites based on templates from any of the world's leading templates providers. Their staff is responsive and communicative, and most tuning processes take less than 24 hours. You are assigned your own project manager who keeps you updated on all the details until project completion and makes sure you get what you need.

In the affiliate program, this project is presented with affiliate link and banners. When a Web surfer clicks through your affiliate link or banner, a cookie containing your affiliate number is set in his Web browser, and your affiliate number is recorded in the database, while your customer is sent to **TemplateTuning.com**. When a customer places an order on TemplateTuning.com, affiliate script looks for the cookie to identify the affiliate who will be awarded the commission.

Visitors redirected to TemplateTuning.com through your affiliate link may place an order in the future and your commission will still be awarded if the cookie is presented in their browser. You will earn 25 percent of all orders at TemplateTuning.com.

General Information and Registration

Registration with MyTemplateStorage is free, and no fees are required for setting up the affiliate account. The registration process is easy; it takes no longer than two to three minutes to fill out the registration form and follow the registration confirmation link. Once registered, affiliates get access to the affiliate program administration area with the available in-depth Help Center.

You can register with the program even if you do not have a Web site and create it at a later date. You can register at **https://secure. mytemplatestorage.com/join.php.**

Help and Support

Affiliate Help Center is available from the affiliate administrative area. Affiliate support is provided by phone, an online help ticket system, support e-mail, and an affiliate program manager.

Customer support for affiliate customers is available 24-7 by phone, online

CASE STUDY: MYTEMPLATESTORAGE.COM

billing, customers chat, and help ticket systems (support, billing, and customer care). There is also a Help Center available at **www. template-help.com.**

How commissions are paid

Commissions are paid upon your request by wire transfer, money bookers, and automated clearing house after you have earned at least $100. A statistics section is available in the administrative area allowing you to track your sales.

More opportunities

MyTemplateStorage.com program is two-tier, meaning you can assign more people to your affiliate program and receive five percent of their sales. There is a special supervisor link that TemplateMonster will provide.

Template purchase process

When the affiliates set up their template shops, they do not have to worry about fraud, payment processing, or sending the template. MyTemplateStorage's billing department will take care of the payments, and our customer support department will send your customer the template and provide any support if needed.

New projects

MyTemplateStorage's management team is always looking for new projects to add to the affiliate program that would benefit the affiliates. In the near future they plan to add a custom design studio, a tutorials project, and a hosting project. They are also working on the new version of **www.site2you.com/ sitebuilder**, which is an advanced Web site builder that enables anyone to create and handle a successful Web site quickly, professionally, and affordably.

Kara Hoffman is currently the head of the MyTemplateStorage affiliate program. She joined TemplateMonster in the spring of 2006 as the sales manager of **www.templatetuning.com**. She can be contacted at **www. mytemplatestorage.com**, e-mail: kara@templatemonster.com, phone: 518-312-4162.

CASE STUDY: MYTEMPLATESTORAGE.COM

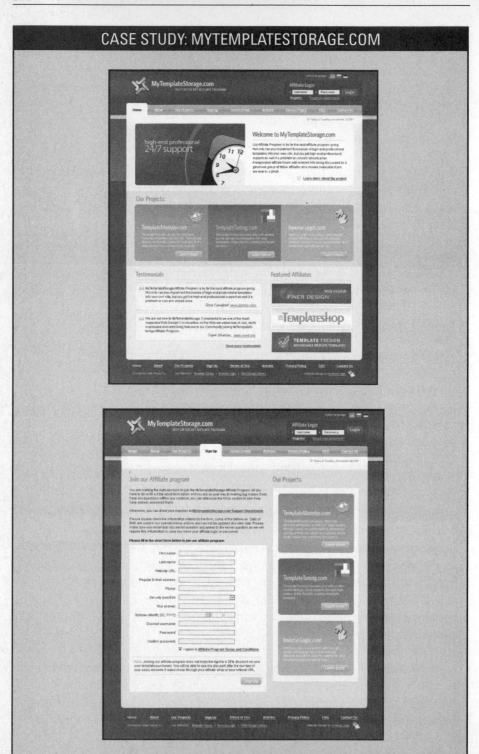

CASE STUDY: IMPLIX AFFILIATE PROGRAM

www.implix.com

by Ola Kudzin, Implix Affiliate Manager

The Multi-Product Advantage

I was recently interviewed by one of our affiliates who was writing a post on his blog about our affiliate program. He asked me what was unique about Implix's affiliate program. Not how it worked, not when it was set up, not how much it paid – only what was unique about it.

The first thing that came to my mind is that Implix Affiliate Program is six programs rolled into one. That is because we have six distinctive products that help small businesses solve six different problems. And you can promote (and profit from) all six of them.

	GETRESPONSE - a turn-key "do it yourself" e-mail marketing solution that lets you build your e-mail list, send newsletters, and install follow-up e-mail autoresponders.
	WEB SITE WIZARD – an easy-to-use online Web site builder which lets you create your own great-looking Web site without any technical, programming, or design skills.
	TALKSTREAM – a simple but powerful online tool that lets you add audio and video to your Web site and to your e-mails. All you need is a microphone for audio and a Webcam for video.

CASE STUDY: IMPLIX AFFILIATE PROGRAM

CLICKCONFERENCE (coming soon)- revolutionary web conferencing software which will let you host conference phone calls, online meetings, training, and presentations.

EBOOKGOLD – eBook creation software which lets you create and sell your own eBook. Sharing your knowledge has never been easier.

HYPERTRACKER - online tracking service that shows you which of your ads and marketing campaigns generate results and which are expendable.

Most affiliate programs have only one product. So why does offering six products give you an advantage? Let me put it this way.

These are six complimentary products that each of your prospective customers can use to solve their different marketing and business challenges. This gives you up to six sales per customer. Your cost for acquiring the new sale stays the same as with other affiliate programs, but the profit may be six times more. Implix affiliate commissions are residual and tracked for as long as the customer remains active.

We have run our multi-product affiliate program for more than six years now, since 2002; currently we have 70,000+ active affiliates. Most affiliates who joined us several years ago are still actively promoting our products today. Six years is an eternity on the Internet, and we are confident that our experience lets us provide you with the best possible tools and services you need to make your affiliate presence a lasting success. Can you think of any other multi-product affiliate program that has been out there for more than six years and has paid millions of affiliate commissions?

CASE STUDY: IMPLIX AFFILIATE PROGRAM

Up to 6 times more profit opportunities

6

6+ years of experience in helping of **70,000+ affiliates and paying out millions of dollars** of residual commissions

6 complimentary products that help small businesses solve **6 different business challenges,** and make you money at the same time.

Combining six income opportunities has one powerful advantage: simplicity. You do not have to worry about maintaining six different log-ins and panels to check your statistics; you get all the information you need in one place. You do not have to worry about getting six commission checks; you get one check every month combining all your affiliate commissions for that month.

There you have it: one affiliate account, one set of log-in credentials, no multiple passwords to remember, one affiliate check, and one set of statistics that lets you view your results.

1 affiliate account
One set of rules that you need to follow, one password to remember and one easy-to-use web interface.

1

1 set of statistics
You can see in the statistics which product is your bestseller. You can track your marketing campaigns to find out which of your initiatives are bringing you most profit

1 check with all your affiliate payouts
Commissions from all 6 products are combined and paid out to you on one check.

CASE STUDY: IMPLIX AFFILIATE PROGRAM

Cross-promotion

Each of our six products complements each other, which creates a great profit opportunity for you. For example, someone who is interested in sending newsletters via GetResponse may need a Web site provided by WebsiteWizard, or if they already have one they may want to enhance it with audio/video content, TalkStream.

Similarly, a customer who purchases eBookGold to create his first eBook may then need a Web site to sell that eBook, WebsiteWizard; a newsletter to promote the Web site, GetResponse; a way to track his various campaigns, HyperTracker; and perhaps even an audio/video service, TalkStream, to enhance his presence.

The list of examples goes on and on. Can you imagine how these cross-selling and cross-marketing opportunities can be profitable for you?

Best of all, you do not have to lift a finger except for picking one product you like the most and promoting it like crazy. We will cross-sell others for you using our proven marketing techniques that we have developed over 6+ years. The result is up to six times more profit opportunity for you, and a solid compensation plan that generates $5,000, $12,000, and even in excess of $20,000 a month for some of our affiliates. Do you have what it takes to be our next super-affiliate?

Do not delay; start benefiting from the multi-product advantage. Sign up at **www.implix.com/affiliates** and start promoting today. You will be glad you did.

Ola Kudzin, Implix Affiliate Manager

www.implix.com

Interviews with Affiliate Marketing Experts

In this Chapter I interviewed numerous affiliate marketing experts. I found their guidance and insight invaluable additions to this book, and I am sure you will as well as you delve into affiliate marketing.

INTERVIEW WITH ALLAN GARDYNE

What is your experience with Affiliate Marketing?

I began affiliate marketing in 1997 and went full-time in 1998. I hired my first assistant that year, and we now have a team of people in three countries and an office in Burleigh Heads, Queensland, Australia.

For a decade I was purely an affiliate promoting other people's products. In 2007 we launched our own product, SpeedPPC, and we now have a team of affiliates promoting it. We have SpeedPPC customers in more than 60 countries.

AssociatePrograms.com, which I launched in 1998, offers a wide variety of information on affiliate marketing, including a comprehensive, searchable affiliate directory, a helpful affiliate forum, affiliate advice articles, newsletter archives, and an affiliate Knowledge Base — a sort of extended FAQ.

Other sites we own include PayPerClickSearchEngines and **KeywordWorkshop.com**, which both review their namesakes. We also own other affiliate-driven sites promoting various products.

INTERVIEW WITH ALLAN GARDYNE

When just starting out as an affiliate, what advice can you give someone?

I strongly advise you to start with something simple. Start with a small site in a fairly non-competitive niche. Do not worry if you do not earn a fortune from it. See the experience as serving your apprenticeship in the affiliate marketing industry.

Just by owning one small site, you will learn a wide variety of useful skills, such as how to attract links to your site, how to write to sell, how to publish a newsletter, how to increase conversion rates, and so on.

I think it is a mistake to aim too high in the beginning. I know they say, "Aim for the stars and you'll reach the moon." However, I have often seen new affiliates begin with a grand, imaginative plan for a huge Web site; two or three months later, when they are still struggling to build it and no money is coming in, they get frustrated and give up.

If, instead, they start with a much more modest goal, quickly get a Web site up, get a few links on it, and get a few dollars coming in, then they are more likely to feel good about what they are doing and continue.

Earning your first dollar quickly is very important. It is a way of proving to yourself that affiliate marketing actually works and is something worth investing time and effort in.

For a small business that wants to start their own affiliate program, what words of wisdom can you give them?

The most important thing is to produce a high-quality product that affiliates will be keen to promote. The second most important thing is to create a Web site with a high conversion rate, and you need to do that before you launch your affiliate program. Experienced affiliates hate being used as guinea pigs. I have seen far too many new affiliate merchants rush to the market with a scrappy, badly designed site and then wonder why experienced affiliates don't want to promote their products.

What advice would you give someone who is considering joining affiliate programs?

It is a wonderful industry to be in. My wife, Joanna, and I love being able to work from wherever we are in the world.

INTERVIEW WITH ALLAN GARDYNE

One of the most valuable tips I can give is that you need to remember you are dealing with real people, not just sales statistics. Newcomers to affiliate marketing often make the mistake of grabbing an affiliate program, dashing off a few words, plunking an affiliate link or some banners on a page, and hoping they will make sales.

They need to remember that real, live, thinking, feeling people will visit their Web site. One of the most effective things an affiliate can do is try to imagine what those visitors are thinking. Try to imagine what problems they have and solve them, or tell them about a product that will solve them.

Your job as an affiliate is to help people decide what to buy. To do that, you need to know as much as possible about the products you are promoting and as much as possible about the people who are likely to buy them.

Can you suggest three things merchants could do to help drive more sales from their affiliates?

Pay high commissions, as high as you can possibly afford. This helps make affiliates enthusiastic. Pay promptly. Pay bonuses for good performances.

But there is a lot more to it than that. What you really need are loyal affiliates who keep promoting your products year after year.

Here is a link to an article I wrote with more tips on this:

28 Ways to Inspire Affiliate Loyalty

www.AssociatePrograms.com/articles/144/1/28-ways-to-inspire-affili-ate-loyalty

As a potential affiliate, what qualities should I look for in merchants, and how do I find them?

The number one thing I look for is an excellent product. I feel more comfortable if I already know the vendor and trust him or her.

If I do not know the vendor, I look for product endorsements from people I think I can trust. I like to see testimonials on the site with people's photos and Web sites.

INTERVIEW WITH ALLAN GARDYNE

The product should be priced competitively, commissions should be fair, and it helps if the affiliate merchant offers affiliates strong support and useful marketing materials. I also like to promote products which pay residual commissions; for example, a Web host or private membership site which pays each time the customer pays. LifetimeCommissions.com reviews affiliate programs that pay residual and lifetime commissions.

You can search in the affiliate directory at AssociatePrograms.com, and you can also search on our forum to see if anything bad has been said about the product or affiliate program.

If you are thinking of promoting a certain merchant, it is a good idea to do a Google search for productname scam and see what turns up. However, watch out. These days, some cunning affiliates will write productname scam in a headline to catch your eye, and then turn the article around and say the product is NOT a scam and advise you to buy it through their link.

If the product has huge sales, it is quite likely that there will be a very small percentage of disgruntled customers or odd characters saying nasty things about it — perhaps even anonymous competitors. So do not jump to conclusions just because you see one complaint about a product.

You can also ask on affiliate forums like ours if anyone has had any bad experiences with a company.

What is the relationship between Pay-Per-Click (PPC) and Affiliate Marketing? Should an affiliate use PPC in tandem with affiliate marketing?

PPC marketing can be used either to buy traffic and send it directly to the merchant via an affiliate link, or it can be used to send traffic to a carefully crafted landing page on a site owned by the affiliate. This page presells (warms up the visitor ready for a purchase) before the visitor arrives at the merchant's site.

PPC marketing may also be used to collect e-mail addresses for a list or newsletter so the affiliate can do follow-ups, and therefore have multiple chances to make a sale.

INTERVIEW WITH ALLAN GARDYNE

The affiliate can use that e-mail list to generate subsequent sales of other products.

So, yes, it is definitely beneficial for affiliates to use PPC marketing. However, PPC marketing can be a quick way to lose money because you spend more than the income you generate. PPC is not a good place for beginners to start. It is a very good thing to learn and experiment with once you have conquered the basics.

Our SpeedPPC system, available from SpeedPPC.com, is designed to help marketers, including affiliates, do PPC marketing much faster, with higher conversion rates and lower costs. It is aimed at people who are already doing PPC marketing, not at newcomers.

Is it realistic for someone to make a living entirely on affiliate programs?

Most affiliates do not achieve that level of income, but it definitely can be done if you are determined enough.

For a small business which has products to sell online, what advice can you give them before they deploy an affiliate program?

Test and tweak. Get everything working smoothly and make sure your site has achieved the highest conversion rate you can manage before you launch your affiliate program. One way to do this quickly is to buy PPC traffic and see if your site makes sales. If it does not, you have a serious problem you need to fix before you launch your affiliate program.

Read Jimmy D. Brown's eBook, *Sales Army Secrets.* It has a lot of excellent advice and is written by an experienced affiliate vendor.

What is the best thing a small business or individual can do to increase online income?

After you have tested and tweaked and made sure you have a decent conversion rate, you need to get traffic to your site. An affiliate program is ideal for this because you pay only on results, only when the affiliate makes a sale.

INTERVIEW WITH ALLAN GARDYNE

How do you see affiliate marketing changing in the next five years?

I think it is fairly obvious that the industry will become even more frantically crowded and competitive. People who are talented at getting attention should do well. Guerrilla marketing tactics will become more important.

The safest place to be may be out on the edges, in overlooked non-competitive niches, if you are fortunate enough to find them.

What kind of Web sites does affiliate marketing work best for?

Just about every product you care to name could be sold via an affiliate program.

Are there any types of products that are particularly well-suited for affiliate marketing?

Digital products such as eBooks and software work particularly well because the vendors can afford to pay very high commissions; 50 percent or maybe even 75 percent. Occasionally I have seen 100 percent commissions, when the digital product is being used as a lead to sell another product.

We are paying $248.50 commissions on sales of SpeedPPC. That is a very powerful incentive for affiliates to put some solid work into promoting our product.

What is the most important thing to remember when beginning or promoting an affiliate program?

That real people are involved, with real hopes and dreams. They are not just statistics. I know I have already said that, but so many people don't get this that I think it needs to be repeated.

Also, as a wiser man told me once, people like buying from people they know, like, and trust. So it is a really good idea to help your customers get to know you. One way to do this is by publishing a newsletter in which you gradually reveal your personality and information about you. Publishing videos and podcasts would also help.

What is the relationship (if any) between blogging and affiliate marketing?

INTERVIEW WITH ALLAN GARDYNE

Some high-profile bloggers earn thousands of dollars a month from affiliate programs and advertising. For example, I read in the Wall Street Journal that **Celebrity-Babies.com** earned $500,000 in 2007 from advertising. I assume that includes the site's affiliate commissions.

However, there are millions upon millions of blogs out there, and most of them do not get much traffic or generate much revenue.

What affiliate marketing or industry sites do you read regularly?

Rather than visiting Web sites, I tend to scan marketing newsletters, and I use an RSS reader to keep an eye on a few dozen blogs. I scan the blog headlines and occasionally click on one or two that look interesting.

I learned long ago that it is very easy to click on a link, and then another link... and pretty soon your whole day has vanished and you have not achieved anything useful. So these days I am usually very disciplined.

One of my favorite private membership sites is Planet Ocean. For years, I have been a paid subscriber to the Planet Ocean newsletter and private Web site, which is a good way to keep up to date with what the search engines are doing.

What is your favorite affiliate development tool or application?

Well, of course, I would have to say SpeedPPC. My business partner, Jay Stockwell, was doing some experiments in PPC marketing for us, and found it frustratingly time-consuming. He developed a script to help us do things faster, more efficiently, and more profitably. That was the first version of SpeedPPC. We went public with Version 2. We are now on Version 3.

However, I would like to emphasize that affiliate marketing can be done with very simple tools. For example, for more than 10 years I have published the Associate Programs Newsletter simply by writing it in TextPad, a very simple plain text editor. Most of the time, I am not using anything more complicated than e-mail.

For anyone just getting started in affiliate marketing, I recommend they read my free Affiliate Program Tutorial at **www.AssociatePrograms.com/articles/188/1/Affiliate-Program-Tutorial.**

INTERVIEW WITH ALLAN GARDYNE

I wrote it for our bookkeeper when he began asking us questions about how we generate our affiliate revenue.

Allan Gardyne is the founder of AssociatePrograms.com, a comprehensive directory of affiliate programs, forums, marketing tips, and newsletters. Since 1998 his Web site and newsletter have been helping affiliates succeed in affiliate marketing. His company also owns other Web sites, including SpeedPPC.com, **KeywordWorkshop.com**, and **PayPerClick-SearchEngines.com**, as well as a growing number of affiliate-driven niche sites. Allan's business partner, Jay Stockwell, who invented SpeedPPC, runs the company's office in Burleigh Heads, Queensland, Australia. You can contact Allan at **www.AssociatePrograms.com/pages/Contact-Us**.

INTERVIEW WITH FRANCK SYLVESTRE

What is your experience with Affiliate Marketing?

I started affiliate marketing on a shoestring budget of zero in early 2006. I had just lost my job and needed to make money to take care of my wife and two children. I bought an affiliate marketing eBook, and a few weeks later I got into an affiliate program with coaching from a top marketer. The fee was $197, but I managed to get in at no cost.

I made my first commission, $250, a few weeks later. Since I was on a budget, I had no other choice than to become a SEO expert. My main affiliate marketing Web site is now on the first page of Google for the very tough key phrase affiliate marketing. In fact, now I can easily get top ten rankings for any of my Web sites.

I also specialize in article marketing. Many people do not know this, but writing and submitting articles to directories is still one of the best ways to drive traffic to your Web sites and make affiliate commissions.

When just starting out as an affiliate, what advice can you give someone?

The first advice I would give to a new affiliate is to understand that this is a business. Do not think that you are going to make easy money or become rich overnight. That will not happen.

INTERVIEW WITH FRANCK SYLVESTRE

Affiliate marketing is just a matter of choosing the right market and promoting the right products. Testing and tracking are also main factors of success.

For a small business that wants to start their own affiliate program, what words of wisdom can you give them?

Starting their own affiliate program is one of the best things they can do. As for wisdom, I would say: Let people who are more experienced than you help you grow your business faster. By this I mean that it is better to hire a good affiliate manager than doing it yourself because he will already have many contacts and insider secrets you cannot discover on your own. Do not try to do everything yourself.

What advice would you give someone who is considering joining affiliate programs?

I would advise him to stick to one niche and one Web site until he becomes profitable. People are struggling to find a profitable niche, while it is one of the easiest thing to do on the Internet. Here is a hint for a million-dollar niche: the golf market.

I also would advise him to always promote his own Web site, and try to build a list of subscribers.

Can you suggest three things merchants could do to help drive more sales from their affiliates?

1. Help your affiliates by providing them all the tools they need to promote your Web site. As an example, Joebucks.com's affiliate program even gives a free Web site to their affiliates so they can start right away.

2. Increase the commission. The more the merchant pays, the more his affiliates will be willing to promote because they know they will earn more. One of my mentors, who earns $20 million a year, gives a 200 percent commission to his affiliates. They promote an e-book that costs $20, and they earn $40 in commission. Do you see how powerful this is? Believe me, this works very well. You will blow your competition out of the water, as this is something that only a few insiders do.

INTERVIEW WITH FRANCK SYLVESTRE

3. Another thing that works very well is to run special promotions and reward your top affiliates. Host a contest with prizes. As an example, I just received a three-day autoresponder series for a special promotion in the weight loss market. I will earn more money, and the merchant will, too. Without this promotion, I would have promoted like usual. Also, affiliates like to be the sales leader.

As a potential affiliate, what qualities should I look for in merchants, and how do I find them?

You should look for the following:

1. High commission

2. Support

3. High conversion rate

You can find them within affiliate networks like clickbank.com, Commission Junction, or Linkshare. You can also find merchants in good affiliate directories or by doing a Google search for Your Niche + Affiliate Programs.

What is the relationship between Pay-Per-Click (PPC) and Affiliate Marketing? Should an affiliate use PPC in tandem with affiliate marketing?

PPC is not specific to affiliate marketing. I earn four figures a month from affiliate programs using my own search engine optimization methods and article marketing. I do not use PPC, although it is in my plan to earn even more.

Is it realistic for someone to make a living entirely on affiliate programs?

Yes, this is realistic. Hundreds are doing it. It was my goal at first, but I found that it is more lucrative to create your product and have hundreds of affiliates promoting it for you. Plus, promoting your own products makes it even easier to earn money from affiliate marketing because you build a list of buyers on autopilot. All you need is to send them good related affiliate products.

INTERVIEW WITH FRANCK SYLVESTRE

For a small business that has products to sell online, what advice can you give them before they deploy an affiliate program?

They first need to understand how affiliates think. In fact, those who already have an experience in affiliate marketing will do better because they know affiliate marketers' hot buttons.

What is the best thing a small business or individual can do to increase online income?

Get a mentor. That is how I increased mine.

How do you see affiliate marketing changing in the next five years?

Well, I do not predict the future. Only God can do this. I think that only serious affiliates who treat their online venture as a business will really make a killing, while others will still be struggling.

What kind of Web sites does affiliate marketing work best for?

Review and pre-sell Web sites are known to be highly effective.

Are there any types of products that are particularly well suited for affiliate marketing?

Every product works. There is no limitation here. Anything that can be sold online can have an affiliate program.

What is the most important thing to remember when beginning or promoting an affiliate program?

The most important thing to remember is that you need to understand how your niche market thinks. Create a buyer persona for your promotion, and always talk to this person. The good thing is that the merchant already did this for you in most cases.

What is the relationship, if any, between blogging and affiliate marketing?

INTERVIEW WITH FRANCK SYLVESTRE

Blogging is a powerful affiliate marketing weapon because search engines love blogs. You will receive thousands of visitors to your Web site and affiliate links if you do this properly. Anyone doing affiliate marketing or any kind of business online should have a blog.

What affiliate marketing or industry sites do you read regularly?

I do not read about affiliate marketing because I'm very busy promoting, developing my own products, and putting my business on autopilot.

What is your favorite affiliate development tool or application?

My favorite tool is autoresponders. Building a list is an essential aspect of affiliate marketing, and autoresponders will help to do this. I use the Ultimate Marketing Center, which has many other features as well as autoresponders.

Franck Silvestre makes thousands of dollars a year by writing articles and promoting various affiliate programs related to languages, Forex, weight loss, and many other lucrative niches.

Franck also wrote a search engine optimization eBook that can be found at **www.seoseductionsecrets.com**. Visit **www.mynetmarketingland.com** to register for his affiliate marketing newsletter and learn how easy it is.

INTERVIEW WITH JAMES NARDELL

What is your experience with Affiliate Marketing?

Two years as an affiliate and three years as an affiliate manager.

When just starting out as an affiliate, what advice can you give someone?

There is not an easy way to make money online, grab affiliates and entice them to sell your products, or start a new site, whether you use a data feed or not, and make money tomorrow.

INTERVIEW WITH JAMES NARDELL

There is a way, though, to do all of the above: hard work, patience, participating in forums, and plenty of research, followed with trial and error until you get hold of the "holy grail" — cheap, extremely targeted, high converting traffic.

For a small business who wants to start their own affiliate program, what words of wisdom can you give them?

If you plan to start your business with zero investment, the odds are that you will fail like any other bricks and mortar company. Also, while you can get free traffic through organic search, in many cases it makes sense to also pay for traffic.

What advice would you give someone who is considering joining affiliate programs?

1) Research the affiliate programs and/or the product(s) being sold.

2) Before signing up with an affiliate program, read all of the associated rules, restrictions, or guidelines.

3) Go through an affiliate network. The companies that use an affiliate network to manage their program have to jump through some hoops in order to qualify to have their product(s)/company advertised in the network, and they also have to be well funded. The caveat here is that an affiliate program that is run through a network will almost always pay less than an independent program because they have to give the network a piece of the action, plus an array of fees depending on what features are being utilized by the program. Basically, you trade a few commission percentage points for security.

4) Ask around on the message forums about the affiliate program you are considering joining.

5) Contact the affiliate manager. They can help you with copy, affiliate tools, and much more besides.

Can you suggest three things merchants could do to help drive more sales from their affiliates?

INTERVIEW WITH JAMES NARDELL

1) Make sure that the content you offer affiliates is up to date and compelling.

2) If you have a large product inventory, offer a data feed. However, if you offer a data feed, make sure it is not peppered with errors.

3) Offer discount coupons if this strategy fits your business model.

As a potential affiliate, what qualities should I look for in merchants, and how do I find them?

Ask the following questions:

- Does the merchant/affiliate manager answer his e-mails?

- Does the merchant have suitable materials/content to market their products, i.e., banners, data feeds, coupons, etc.?

- Has the merchant been in business for a long time? If so, what feedback is already published on the Internet?

- Is the pricing for the product(s)/service(s) compelling?

- Are other affiliates already marketing the merchant's product/ service? If so, how? Also, does the merchant have a high/low EPC (where available)?

- Is the merchant listed in the major networks: CJ, Linkshare, Shareasale, Performics, etc.?

- Does the affiliate program tracking work? (Run a test transaction to be sure.)

What is the relationship between Pay-Per-Click (PPC) and affiliate marketing? Should an affiliate use PPC in tandem with affiliate marketing?

PPC is one of the methods to drive traffic to an affiliate program. I would suggest that affiliates use PPC to test conversion rates of both their Web sites/blogs and the affiliate program(s) that they are considering promoting.

INTERVIEW WITH JAMES NARDELL

Is it realistic for someone to make a living entirely on affiliate programs?

It is entirely possible. However, I would strongly advise anyone to build their business in their spare time in tandem with their day job, and then move to full-time once they can swap salaries. Otherwise, make sure you can live for at least a year without significant income coming in.

For a small business that has products to sell online, what advice can you give them before they deploy an affiliate program?

- Make sure the affiliate technology you choose has everything you will need for the long-term.

- Create compelling affiliate content.

- Employ a full-time affiliate manager.

- Learn best practices.

- Devote considerable time/expense to publicizing your affiliate program.

- Create a Terms of Use agreement and stick to it.

What is the best thing a small business or individual can do to increase online income?

If they want results quickly, paid search is the best way. Also, for those businesses/individuals in the testing phase of operations, paid search is the best method to drive targeted traffic, and make sure that conversion rates are on target.

How do you see affiliate marketing changing in the next five years?

I think that the model will remain intact. However, there will be stricter rules in place with regard to trademark bidding, and more transparency in general for the merchants/affiliates. The days of the wild west will be truly over in five years, and I suspect that the industry will become dominated by a relatively small number of players. While mom and pop operations will not become extinct, they will become more of a rarity.

INTERVIEW WITH JAMES NARDELL

What kind of Web sites does affiliate marketing work best for?

Affiliate marketing can have a place on any Web site. It is merely one of the monetization models available. There is also CPM, CPC, pay per lead, pay per download, etc.

Are there any types of products that are particularly well-suited for affiliate marketing?

Virtually any product or service can be pushed through the affiliate channel. There is no doubt that soft products — software and eBooks — fit the affiliate marketing model well.

What is the most important thing to remember when beginning or promoting an affiliate program?

Once you have established that the affiliate program fits your marketing plan, contact the affiliate manager and introduce yourself. If you get no response, the odds are that further down the line you will have issues with payment, tracking, and so forth. Make sure the affiliate program is proactively managed.

What is the relationship, if any, between blogging and affiliate marketing?

Blogging is one of the methods or platforms to create or host content in order to drive traffic to an affiliate program. There are also e-mail marketing, paid search, data feed utilization, and other methods of content marketing. Some bloggers, though not many, have no interest in affiliate marketing or monetization of their content, and simply want to voice their opinions.

What affiliate marketing or industry sites do you read regularly?

ABestWeb.com   WebProWorld.com

Revenews.com   RevenueToday.com

AffiliateTip.com   WebMasterWorld.com

amwso.com   ReturnOnAffiliate.com

INTERVIEW WITH JAMES NARDELL

Revenue Magazine   **AssociatePrograms.com**

Network Newsletters   **AffiliateBoards.com**

What is your favorite affiliate development tool or application?

WebVideoZone.com. This tool allows affiliates and merchants to add video to their Web sites that includes affiliate links. There is also the ability to totally customize the video player.

James Nardell is originally from Bristol, England. He has lived and worked in Bangkok, Thailand, for the past nine years. Prior to joining AMWSO, James was involved in corporate training, focusing on presentation skills, negotiation skills, and business writing. His clients have included ExxonMobil, Shell, Philips, Bank Thai, Carrefour, Hapag Lloyd, AIG, and many other well-known organizations. James is also a successful online publisher in his own right, and has successfully run multiple PPC campaigns. He has also designed, developed, and marketed two affiliate-focused Web sites. James has worked as an affiliate manager across all the major affiliate networks, with Panda Security, Gaiam, GT Media, Waterfront Media, Shopster, Jobs In Sports, and Prime Poker.

INTERVIEW WITH CHRIS SANDERSON

What is your experience with Affiliate Marketing?

Six years as an affiliate manager.

When just starting out as an affiliate, what advice can you give someone?

Do not overstretch yourself by trying to be all things to all people, or trying to use every kind of recommended technology. If you do, it will more likely lead to information overload rather than success. Work with what you know and are comfortable with, and grow from there.

For a small business that wants to start their own affiliate program, what words of wisdom can you give them?

INTERVIEW WITH CHRIS SANDERSON

Affiliate marketing is not free. It is a highly competitive industry. Trying to succeed on a shoestring budget will lead to shoestring results.

What advice would you give someone who is considering joining affiliate programs?

- Know what you want to sell.

- Start with well-known brands.

- Start with established affiliate programs.

- Perform a due diligence check for discussions about the affiliate program you wish to join.

- Have a live site set up that fits the program you wish to join.

- See how much contact information is available to the affiliate manager.

- See how much support material is available (content, data feeds, creatives, video, etc).

Can you suggest three things merchants could do to help drive more sales from their affiliates?

1) Provide timely personal support.

2) Ensure the landing pages are designed to drive a sale.

3) Ensure the checkout process is fluid and painless.

As a potential affiliate, what qualities should I look for in merchants, and how do I find them?

- Is there an assigned affiliate manager?

- Does the affiliate manager respond quickly, if at all?

- Is the site free of leaks and outbound links?

INTERVIEW WITH CHRIS SANDERSON

- Is the merchant's site focus on selling?

- Is a wide range of creatives available?

- If they have a data feed, is it updated frequently?

What is the relationship between Pay-Per-Click (PPC) and affiliate marketing? Should an affiliate use PPC in tandem with affiliate marketing?

A lot of affiliates do use PPC — some to drive traffic to their site, some to drive traffic to the merchant's site. An affiliate should contact the merchant and read the Terms and Conditions very carefully before doing any form of PPC. Many merchants have very strict rules governing the use of PPC in their affiliate programs.

Is it realistic for someone to make a living entirely on affiliate programs?

Yes, very possible, but even then do not get too comfortable. Make sure your revenue is from a diverse number of merchants and industries.

For a small business that has products to sell online, what advice can you give them before they deploy an affiliate program?

- Make sure your checkout process is perfect.

- Make sure your site is free of leaks.

- Ensure that your site is competitive. What will differentiate it from other merchants?

- Research competitors' affiliate programs.

- Affiliate marketing will not work for everyone. Make sure the ROI is going to make sense before you start.

- Hire an affiliate manager, either in-house or from a professional management firm.

- Ensure that affiliate marketing plans are going to work alongside your PPC and SEO marketing, not in competition to them.

INTERVIEW WITH CHRIS SANDERSON

What is the best thing a small business or individual can do to increase online income?

Right product, right time, right audience. If a site's traffic is not targeted and landing on the right page, then everything else is irrelevant.

How do you see affiliate marketing changing in the next five years?

On the surface, a lot of change might appear to be going on, with merchants getting stricter with their affiliates and what they do not allow their affiliates to do. However, this is not affecting the underlying strong affiliates who rely on their own loyal customer base, newsletters, and subscribers to market a merchant's products. The way affiliates add value has not changed; it has just been clouded of late by affiliates who do not add value.

What kind of Web sites does affiliate marketing work best for?

Any. It depends on the site users and the type of product being presented. There are types of sites that might make us cringe when we see them, but pretty much any site is going to appeal to someone who can be influenced by that site. However the more traffic a site can get, the more impact it can have, and that is the real battle. A one-page site can have more impact than a thousand-page site if it can get the traffic.

Are there any types of products that are particularly well-suited for affiliate marketing?

Instant gratification products such as software can do very well. So can products that are sold online cheaper than offline, or based on specifications rather than style. It all depends on the merchant's ability to build a site that will make a consumer comfortable with buying the product. When merchants first started selling diamonds online, everyone laughed and said it couldn't work. But it did, and people pay $4,000 to $20,000 online for diamonds every day through affiliate programs.

What is the most important thing to remember when beginning or promoting an affiliate program?

INTERVIEW WITH CHRIS SANDERSON

Once you have established that the affiliate program fits your marketing plan, contact the affiliate manager and introduce yourself. If you get no response, the odds are that further down the line you will have issues with payment, tracking, etc. Make sure that the affiliate program is proactively managed.

What is the relationship, if any, between blogging and affiliate marketing?

Blogging is just another type of publishing system for creating and managing content on a Web site. Blogging makes it easy for anyone to have a Web site and update it daily. Concept-wise, blogs became known for being personal and timely, although any Web site could be made personal and timely without using blog software. There is now an increase in marketing and revenue opportunities in the area of blogs.

What affiliate marketing or industry sites do you read regularly?

ABestWeb.com   **amwso.com**

Revenue Magazine   **e-consultancy.com**

affiliates4u.com

What is your favorite affiliate development tool or application?

SEOQuake, a plug-in for Firefox, can be a huge help in reviewing sites and getting all the information I need on a site in one place at one time, as well as digging deeper if I need to.

Chris started in the Internet industry in 1996 with Web Studio-1 (WSO), focusing on Web site design and applications for businesses worldwide. In 2002, WSO started providing affiliate management and marketing services for their clients.

In January 2004, AMWSO (a subdivision of WSO) was launched in order to provide improved support and focus for the affiliate marketing clients of WSO. In 2006 AMWSO formed into a separate firm dedicated to affiliate marketing. AMWSO is currently involved in the management of more than

INTERVIEW WITH CHRIS SANDERSON

25 affiliate marketing programs on a global basis. Chris is the managing director of AMWSO and oversees all the daily operations of the business.

Chris.Sanderson@amwso.com

Tel: UK 0161 408-6624

Tel: USA 904-350-0510

Fax: USA 604-608-5580

Skype: chrissanderson

INTERVIEW WITH CHRISTOPHER LOW

What is your experience with affiliate marketing?

Affiliate marketing is a great way to drive online sales through a cost-effective model. You pay only for performance which speaks for itself. To be truly effective in affiliate marketing, the marketer needs to be involved and to create a constant stream of campaigns to push affiliates.

When just starting out as an affiliate, what advice can you give someone?

Make sure to check the integrity of the merchant on forums or blogs in terms of payment issues. It would also be ideal if the merchant has a third party affiliate solution to manage the affiliate program, as this would ensure data integrity.

For a small business that wants to start their own affiliate program, what words of wisdom can you give them?

Be involved in creating compelling motivation or welcome packages for new affiliates. These packages typically decide if a new affiliate will start to promote a small business affiliate program. If your welcome package is not easy to understand or use, you can consider this affiliate lost.

INTERVIEW WITH CHRISTOPHER LOW

What advice would you give someone who is considering joining affiliate programs?

Join affiliate programs that are relevant to their Web site content. However, I often have seen affiliates joining high-paying programs that are totally irrelevant to their own Web site's content, believing that some money is better than no money.

Can you suggest three things merchants could do to help drive more sales from their affiliates?

1) Create an affiliate newsletter that constantly keeps your affiliates abreast of your latest promotions, incentives, products, etc.

2) Try to use dynamic data feed to ensure that content on an affiliate's site is constantly updated automatically. Make sure the affiliate software company, like AffiliateShop, has this feature.

3) Offer a Best Affiliate Award, and give additional prizes to the best-performing affiliates.

As a potential affiliate, what qualities should I look for in merchants, and how do I find them?

Go to affiliate networks like Commission Junction or AffiliateShop, which offer a comprehensive directory listing of affiliates. Make sure an affiliate program suits your Web site's content and the merchant has been consistent in paying.

What is the relationship between Pay-Per-Click (PPC) and affiliate marketing? Should an affiliate use PPC in tandem with affiliate marketing?

Many affiliates like PPC, as it guarantees a commission as soon as someone clicks on the link. How PPC works in tandem with a regular PPS (Pay-Per- Sale) would depend on the merchant's sales process.

Is it realistic for someone to make a living entirely on affiliate programs?

INTERVIEW WITH CHRISTOPHER LOW

Well, I have heard of super-affiliates earning obscene revenue from commissions.

For a small business that has products to sell online, what advice can you give them before they deploy an affiliate program?

Make sure to go with an affiliate solution that already offers a network service affordably. A service like AffiliateShop allows a new small business to start an affiliate program, and list their new affiliate program in the directory. This offers valuable visibility to the new business's affiliate program, and ultimately helps in recruiting new affiliates.

What is the best thing a small business or individual can do to increase online income?

Set up an affiliate marketing program.

How do you see affiliate marketing changing in the next five years?

It is here to stay. But, the traffic touchpoints may evolve with Web 2.0 and mobile technology. However, as with all things in business, technology always moves ahead first. So my advice to new businesses is: move with the market's rhythm.

What kind of Web sites does affiliate marketing work best for?

Almost all types of businesses are suitable. What works best is really a matter of execution.

Are there any types of products that are particularly well-suited for affiliate marketing?

Affiliate marketing is for everyone and for every business. It may just take on a different meaning. Even a typical Member Get Member program is a form of Affiliate Marketing.

What is the most important thing to remember when beginning or promoting an affiliate program?

Tune and retune your new affiliate welcome package.

INTERVIEW WITH CHRISTOPHER LOW

What is the relationship, if any, between blogging and affiliate marketing?

Blogging has a tremendous effect on affiliate marketing. It establishes a kind of intrinsic trust between the viewer and the blog site owner. This makes blog sites generate a higher click-through rate and eventually sales.

What affiliate marketing or industry sites do you read regularly?

Revenue.

What is your favorite affiliate development tool or application?

AffiliateShop and Commission Junction.

INTERVIEW WITH JEREMY JORDAN

What is your experience with Affiliate Marketing?

I work at an affiliate performance tracking software maker.

When just starting out as an affiliate, what advice can you give someone?

Find Web sites that interest you and join their affiliate program. If you are interested, then you will be knowledgeable about their products or services, and will be able to give an honest evaluation which can result in a better conversion rate.

For a small business that wants to start their own affiliate program, what words of wisdom can you give them?

It can take time to get an affiliate program going. After setting it up, people have to be able to find it to join. Also, it can help to offer incentives like having two tiers so your affiliates can also work to get you more affiliates.

What advice would you give someone who is considering joining affiliate programs?

INTERVIEW WITH JEREMY JORDAN

Try to find an affiliate program that relates to your Web site so visitors will find any links or banners useful.

Can you suggest three things merchants could do to help drive more sales from their affiliates?

- Stay in contact with your affiliates. Sending them a short e-mail every so often will help let them know what is going on, if you are planning on making any changes, and that you are involved.

- Offer some kind of incentive that they can work toward. For example, if they have a certain level of performance, they can earn extra commissions. This will help keep them involved to work toward earning more.

- Work with your affiliates. If they need a custom link or banner, work with them, as they may have a niche market segment that could provide good results.

As a potential affiliate, what qualities should I look for in merchants, and how do I find them?

When looking for a merchant to become an affiliate with, start by looking at Web sites you are interested in or know of, and look around on their site to see if they have an affiliate program. If you do not see anything on their site, you can e-mail them to see if they have one they may not be advertising.

You can also try looking at affiliate program directories to find one that is suitable for you. Keep in mind commission rates, payout periods, if they have a minimum payment amount, and the size of the target audience.

What is the relationship between Pay-Per-Click (PPC) and affiliate marketing? Should an affiliate use PPC in tandem with affiliate marketing?

PPC is really about getting traffic, whereas affiliate marketing is about getting conversions. Most of the time, affiliate marketing pays based on referred sales. However, if the affiliate program is meant to grow a company's brand, common with media-driven Web sites, PPC can be good

INTERVIEW WITH JEREMY JORDAN

as it ideally gets visitors who will remember the site and return on their own.

Is it realistic for someone to make a living entirely on affiliate programs?

While it can be possible, this is usually not the case. In order to attempt to make a living from affiliate marketing, the person will need to pay very close attention to his or her performance, and be able to tweak the program very carefully to get the best results.

For a small business that has products to sell online, what advice can you give them before they deploy an affiliate program?

Make sure you have a large enough market to be able to get both affiliates and customers. If the market is too small, you may have trouble getting either one of these, which can make the program struggle.

What is the best thing a small business or individual can do to increase online income?

Make sure people can use your site. If people do not like your site because it has problems or is badly designed, they may not stick around long enough for advertisements or products to matter.

How do you see affiliate marketing changing in the next five years?

In the next five years I believe that affiliate marketing will get much more tied into blogs or social network sites. As people realize they can make some extra money promoting things that they like, they may join a program and place some advertisements on their page.

What kind of Web sites does affiliate marketing work best for?

Affiliate marketing works best for a Web site that sells a certain type of product or service. If they have too many or very different products, then it becomes difficult to target your marketing efforts.

Are there any types of products that are particularly well-suited for affiliate marketing?

INTERVIEW WITH JEREMY JORDAN

Products where people can be repeat customers are good because if you can get their business, it can be easier to keep these customers than always trying to get new ones.

What is the most important thing to remember when beginning or promoting an affiliate program?

Affiliate programs take work and need to be maintained, especially when first starting. In the beginning, the program will be small and will require more monitoring to ensure that it is running efficiently. As the program grows, it can be monitored a little less, as there will be more people helping to market it, but it still requires attention to ensure that nothing is wrong.

What is the relationship, if any, between blogging and affiliate marketing?

Blogging can be used for affiliate marketing. This especially can be true if the blog is about a certain topic. When this is the case, anyone who is reading the blog regularly most likely will be interested in the topic, and so if the affiliate program relates to it, they also will be interested in the product or service.

What affiliate marketing or industry sites do you read regularly?

I do not read any sites specifically, but I always try to look around for relevant information.

What is your favorite affiliate development tool or application?

TrackingSoft's ROIAdvantage.

INTERVIEW WITH GEORGE COZMA

What is your experience with Affiliate Marketing?

I specialize in consulting online entrepreneurs about the efficiency of their affiliate programs. More precisely, I go through everything beginning with the copy promoting the affiliate program, the affiliate program structure,

INTERVIEW WITH GEORGE COZMA

and various other elements aimed at increasing the effectiveness of the program.

When just starting out as an affiliate, what advice can you give someone?

Start with what you know. The amount of affiliate programs out there is staggering. The best approach is to use those that sell products you are familiar with. Also try to judge the products you sell from the viewpoint of a prospective buyer rather than the commission you will win. What you need are products you know and that will sell.

For a small business that wants to start their own affiliate program, what words of wisdom can you give them?

A third-party affiliate platform such as CJ or ClickBank is the best choice for a company still fresh in the game. Also, I highly recommend promoting the affiliate program to the existing customer base. This is one of the most important opportunities that newcomers tend to neglect. Your customers know your product, are satisfied by it, and are active in niches you are targeting.

What advice would you give someone who is considering joining affiliate programs?

There are three things you must pay attention to when joining an affiliate program. The first is the integrity of the merchant. Do they pay their commissions? Do they have any special conditions? The second thing to look at is the product you are going to promote. Does it have a competitive price? Is the market saturated? Finally, you have to look at what commission they pay. Are there better offers on the affiliate market? Is the structure of their commission suitable to your business model?

Can you suggest three things merchants could do to help drive more sales from their affiliates?

The first thing would be to give your affiliates good marketing materials. This means more than banners and templates. Special deals with a sense of urgency to them, and creating brand awareness through conventional advertising can go a long way. The second thing you could do is teach your affiliates how to sell. Never make the assumption that your affiliates are marketing gurus. Some of them might be, but an important part of them are beginners. The third thing you could do, obviously, is attract more affiliates. There are many ways to achieve this, but your first priority must be to make your product look more sellable.

As a potential affiliate, what qualities should I look for in merchants, and how do I find them?

More than the size of the commission, what you should look at is the competitiveness of the product, and how well it fits the niche you are catering to. As for affiliate offers, places like CJ or ClickBank are a must-visit, but it also pays to search for the dominating merchants in your niche. Often, these merchants will have an affiliate program.

What is the relationship between Pay-Per-Click (PPC) and affiliate marketing? Should an affiliate use PPC in tandem with affiliate marketing?

Promotion is a crucial part of affiliate marketing, and PPC is one of the easiest methods to attract quality traffic quickly. What you must pay attention to is the bottom line. If the PPC campaign gives you a net profit, stick with it, even if you reach the first position on Google for your most competitive keyword.

Is it realistic for someone to make a living entirely on affiliate programs?

Of course it is realistic, but you must also be aware that you must work for it. Getting rich while doing nothing is only wishful thinking. It will take time and a lot of work, but it can be done.

For a small business that has products to sell online, what advice can you give them before they deploy an affiliate program?

Take a close look at what your competition is doing, especially if they are doing well. What is the structure of their affiliate program? Where do they promote it and how? Also, never assume that everything will go according to plan. It rarely does. Give yourself some breathing room, and always a contingency plan. Finally, get curious. Test everything you are doing and

INTERVIEW WITH GEORGE COZMA

become a habitual split tester. People and markets change. To be on top of things, you must know what works, and testing is the only way to know for sure.

What is the best thing a small business or individual can do to increase online income?

Diversify your streams of income. Use multiple affiliate offers, and sell advertising space and reviews. If a particular strategy works better than the average, try to duplicate it. Always be on the offensive, and on the move trying to find new streams of traffic and income. Also try to keep up to date with what is going on. Start frequenting Webmaster forums and specialized Web sites.

How do you see affiliate marketing changing in the next five years?

It is obvious that multimedia elements such as streaming video and disrupting innovations such as Bit Torrent will shape the Web of the future in general. Beyond this, however, what will mark the Internet of the future will be the increased number of people using it. The American market is the Goliath today, but in a few years there will be a multitude of important markets, which right now are only emerging, most notably India and Southeast Asia. It is hard to make any predictions regarding China, since the political background is not clear. As general advice I would recommend searching niches which cater to these markets. In a few years the pioneers in these emerging markets will be the leaders of some established ones.

What kind of Web sites does affiliate marketing work best for?

Every type of Web site has its use. Affiliate marketing is flexible enough to be used with almost any of them. The best Web site format is the one that fits with the line of products you are promoting and appeals to the niche you are catering to.

Are there any types of products that are particularly well-suited for affiliate marketing?

Informational products and software packages are considered to be the best suited for online marketing, but this does not mean you should restrict

INTERVIEW WITH GEORGE COZMA

yourself to them. What matters is the field you are familiar with. The online market has reached a phase when even products usually associated with brick-and-mortar stores have their place.

What is the most important thing to remember when beginning or promoting an affiliate program?

There is only one way to get it right and a thousand ways of getting it wrong. Setting and promoting an affiliate program requires, more than anything, patience and a proactive stance.

What is the relationship, if any, between blogging and affiliate marketing?

The problem with affiliate marketing is that you need a lot of traffic to make it work. Setting a blog is easy; setting a blog with decent traffic is incredibly difficult. I tend to consider affiliate marketing as a useful income stream for bloggers, but not as its main one. Paid posts, link selling, and (obviously) networking can be much more profitable, at least in the initial stage.

What affiliate marketing or industry sites do you read regularly?

My favorite Web site is the DP forum at **forums.digitalpoint.com**

INTERVIEW WITH STEFAN MISCHOOK

What is your experience with affiliate marketing?

I have used and offer affiliate programs, and I have found them to be a useful tool for developing a client base and revenue streams. As an affiliate user, I have been able to easily offer products to my site visitors without the expense and cost of creating that product or service myself. As an affiliate provider, it is an interesting way for me to drive traffic to my Web site, and to sell more products. I am happy to give my referrers their percentage.

When just starting out as an affiliate, what advice can you give someone?

INTERVIEW WITH STEFAN MISCHOOK

Be patient and build up your business slowly. Unless you get some hit best–selling item, it will take time to develop.

For a small business that wants to start their own affiliate program, what words of wisdom can you give them?

Again, patience is good. It takes time to attract people. With that in mind, you might want to start with an inexpensive affiliate software/script to see how things go before building your own custom solution. Turn-key software is always cheaper than building from scratch.

What advice would you give someone who is considering joining affiliate programs?

Again, be patient and take your time. I would look for competing programs to compare what you get.

Can you suggest some things merchants could do to help drive more sales from their affiliates?

Better branding and lots of samples, photos, demos, if possible. The Web is all about the soft-sell.

As a potential affiliate, what qualities should I look for in merchants, and how do I find them?

There are probably networks or Web sites with lists of affiliate programs.

What is the relationship between Pay-Per-Click (PPC) and affiliate marketing? Should an affiliate use PPC in tandem with affiliate marketing?

Like anything else, test and see what happens. PPC is just one way to drive traffic to your site.

Is it realistic for someone to make a living entirely on affiliate programs?

Yes. But it can take some time and effort. Passive income business models

INTERVIEW WITH STEFAN MISCHOOK

are time-consuming to build, but once moving, they are nice to have since upkeep is very small.

For a small business that has products to sell online, what advice can you give them before they deploy an affiliate program?

Build your brand as best you can. Have a great Web site with plenty of images, demos, and testimonials, if you have them.

What is the best thing a small business or individual can do to increase online income?

Develop your brand.

How do you see affiliate marketing changing in the next five years?

It will become more and more saturated.

What kind of Web sites does affiliate marketing work best for?

Hard to say; it depends on the industry. But, it is safe to say that basic Web design usability rules still apply.

Are there any types of products that are particularly well-suited for affiliate marketing?

Anything that people do not need to touch or feel to want to buy.

What is the most important thing to remember when beginning or promoting an affiliate program?

The brand and the trust associated with it are the most important. People must trust you.

What is the relationship, if any, between blogging and affiliate marketing?

The Web is about soft-selling. Blogging helps there.

What affiliate marketing or industry sites do you read regularly?

INTERVIEW WITH STEFAN MISCHOOK

None. I use Google a lot.

What is your favorite affiliate development tool or application?

I have no favorites. That being said, there are many to choose from.

Stefan Mischook has been designing Web pages since 1994. Over the past ten years he has worked on Web projects of all sizes and types, giving him a broad perspective on Web design.

Along with his Web design experience, Stefan is also knowledgeable in many programming languages and Web technologies including PHP, JAVA, ASP, ASP.net, SQL, Javascript, and VB Script, among others. His Web sites are **www.killersites.com** and **www.killerphp.com**.

INTERVIEW WITH ALEXANDAR GUTIN

What is your experience with affiliate marketing?

My company, Web Scribble Solutions, makes Web-based affiliate software that powers hundreds of online affiliate programs.

When just starting out as an affiliate, what advice can you give someone?

Give some sort of incentive to your affiliates to join your program. There are thousands of affiliate programs; find a way to distinguish yours.

For a small business that wants to start their own affiliate program, what words of wisdom can you give them?

Automate everything from the beginning. Find a software package that will handle sale tracking, commissions, payouts, and so on.

What advice would you give someone who is considering joining affiliate programs?

Research in advance, and try to get an idea of the conversions others are getting. Joining fewer well-converting programs is much better than joining many poor ones.

Can you suggest three things merchants could do to help drive more sales from their affiliates?

1) Keep your affiliates up to date with company news, products, features, or any other developments that may help them sell your software.

2) Give your affiliates a favorable commission rate so that they promote your program rather than your competitor's.

3) Always pay your affiliates promptly.

As a potential affiliate, what qualities should I look for in merchants, and how do I find them?

Many individual sites have affiliate programs, and there are also many affiliate directories. Look for reliable programs that pay out on time.

INTERVIEW WITH ALEXANDAR GUTIN

What is the relationship between Pay-Per-Click (PPC) and affiliate marketing? Should an affiliate use PPC in tandem with affiliate marketing?

Some affiliate marketers promote their affiliate links through PPC search engines. This works for some programs, but not all. The best way to find out if it works for you is to try it and see if your conversions are profitable.

Is it realistic for someone to make a living entirely on affiliate programs?

Yes. There are people out there who do just that.

For a small business that has products to sell online, what advice can you give them before they deploy an affiliate program?

Do your research and find the right affiliate software first. Once you have it running, see what your competitors offer their affiliates and try to beat it.

What is the best thing a small business or individual can do to increase online income?

An affiliate program is one of the most cost-effective ways to advertise online. Let others promote your products rather than experimenting with different advertising channels yourself.

How do you see affiliate marketing changing in the next five years?

With Google's presence increasing daily, we may see more and more affiliate marketers advertising through Google AdSense.

What kind of Web sites does affiliate marketing work best for?

If done right, affiliate marketing can work for just about any Web site. It is important to know what others in the market are doing and be competitive to make it work.

Are there any types of products that are particularly well-suited for affiliate marketing?

Affiliate marketing can work for many different products. Amazon sells

INTERVIEW WITH ALEXANDAR GUTIN

everything from books to electronics, and a considerable amount of their revenue comes from their affiliates. Electronically delivered products such as software, eBooks, and subscriptions are particularly well-suited for affiliate marketing.

What is the most important thing to remember when beginning or promoting an affiliate program?

Be patient and do not get discouraged. You probably will not have thousands of affiliates a week after launching your affiliate program, but if you actively promote, your chances of success increase.

What is the relationship, if any, between blogging and affiliate marketing?

Blogging and affiliate marketing are the perfect blend of content and advertising. Niche blogs can use affiliate programs to monetize their content.

What is your favorite affiliate development tool or application?

WebAffiliate.

Web Scribble Solutions is a privately owned company founded in 2001 to provide the best Web-based software to power Web sites. Their goal is to create the most feature-filled software to help customers do what they need. They are always hard at work listening to customer needs and constantly improving their existing products. They are the manufacturer of webAffiliate, a fully featured and customizable affiliate script. WebAffiliate™ is a unique affiliate tracking software package that allows you to easily set up and maintain an affiliate base for your site that will earn you commissions and make your sales skyrocket. This fully automated affiliate script allows you to pay your affiliates commissions for sales that they refer to your site. Features include 10-level-deep referrals, ad campaigns to track separate marketing methods, and statistics detailed down to the hour. For more information on webAffiliate, contact: **www.webscribble.com/products/webaffiliate/features.shtml.**

INTERVIEW WITH WEI YAU

What is your experience with affiliate marketing?

We do not do affiliate marketing. We provide software for small businesses to run an affiliate program so they can have their own affiliates market their products.

When just starting out as an affiliate, what advice can you give someone?

Same as above.

For a small business that wants to start their own affiliate program, what words of wisdom can you give them?

Go for it. Having an affiliate program means that you have people out there promoting your products or services at no extra cost to you. It is like having tons of salespeople out there without having to pay them. You only pay a commission when that sales person sells your product to a customer.

As a small business, though, you want to promote your affiliate program as much as possible and get as many people to register for the affiliate program as you can. The more people who register for the program, the more people are telling others about your products. It is a great viral marketing technique.

Be careful not to over promote your affiliate program, because you do have a product that you want to sell, and your Web site needs to cater to the potential customers who come in through your affiliates. After all, you still need the sales to be in business. There is no point in having so many potential customers coming to your site, only to leave as all they see is an affiliate program.

What advice would you give someone who is considering joining affiliate programs?

If you believe in the product, you will do well. Make sure you join a program where the payouts are reasonable so you can be adequately compensated for the time you intend to spend promoting their product.

INTERVIEW WITH WEI YAU

You should also browse their Web sites and judge for yourself to see if that site or their customer service is able to pull in sales. If their site is really bad, then chances are, they won't convert the leads that you bring them. If that's the case, find another program to join.

Can you suggest a few things merchants could do to help drive more sales from their affiliates?

• Adequately reward them with commissions.

• Turn a single-level affiliate program to multiple levels so affiliates can earn commissions from people they refer who end up being affiliates themselves.

• Keep in constant contact with your affiliates with ideas for how they can promote your site and earn a huge income.

• Give specials to affiliates, e.g. 50 percent commissions for the month of May.

As a potential affiliate, what qualities should I look for in merchants, and how do I find them?

You should browse their Web sites, and judge for yourself to see if that site or their customer service is able to pull in sales. If their site is really bad, then chances are they will not convert the leads you bring them. If that is the case, find another program to join.

What is the relationship between Pay-Per-Click (PPC) and affiliate marketing? Should an affiliate use PPC in tandem with affiliate marketing?

Yes. If you are a serious affiliate marketer, you should use PPC. Again, you need to do your research. Is the amount you spend advertising on PPC less than or greater than the rewards you get in terms of commissions?

If you are not sure about this, it might be a good idea to research the average PPC rate for relevant search terms for that particular merchant and then search various affiliate marketing discussion forums for advice on whether it is a good merchant to join.

INTERVIEW WITH WEI YAU

You never know — if someone has never heard of that merchant before, and that merchant has a multi-level affiliate structure, you just might be able to refer an affiliate and earn commissions on that affiliate's sales too.

Is it realistic for someone to make a living entirely on affiliate programs?

Yes. I have heard of people making tens of thousands of dollars a month purely from affiliate programs. First, they set up a single PPC account and test various keywords with a single merchant. As soon as they find that the merchant is profitable, after their own advertising costs, and after testing keywords, they automate it. They constantly tweak their PPC account to ensure that they keep referring potential customers to the site. Then, once they have the first one set up and profitable, they move on to the next merchant and repeat the process again. With experience, they are able to sign up with multiple merchants, and test multiple keywords with each merchant at the same time.

For a small business that has products to sell online, what advice can you give them before they deploy an affiliate program?

Know your affiliates, and know your competitors. What kind of affiliates are you looking to recruit? What are your competitors doing? Check the setup of their affiliate program. Can you afford to offer better rewards than them? Maybe you can use a multi-level program instead of a single-level program.

There is a bit of research to do for this. If you are not sure you can always use trial and error. Open an affiliate program and interview those who register. Ask them what they are after and how you can modify the program to suit their needs.

What is the best thing a small business or individual can do to increase online income?

Start an affiliate program.

How do you see affiliate marketing changing in the next five years?

Without a doubt, there will be a lot more merchants and a lot more affiliate

INTERVIEW WITH WEI YAU

programs popping up all over the place. So, competition will be intense. Amazon.com has an affiliate program and they started early, so the sooner you start an affiliate program, the better off you will be.

What kind of Web sites does affiliate marketing work best for?

Anything that involves selling products or services online.

Are there any types of products that are particularly well-suited for affiliate marketing?

As stated above, anything that can be sold online can benefit from affiliate marketing.

What is the most important thing to remember when beginning or promoting an affiliate program?

Research your market. Find a balance between promoting your product and promoting your affiliate program. I think it might be best to have a separate site for the affiliate program and have a link in your footer to that program. Affiliate marketers usually look at the footer for links to the merchant's affiliate programs, whereas customers would just look at the site.

What is the relationship, if any, between blogging and affiliate marketing?

It depends on what you are blogging about. If you are blogging about something that is relevant to the merchant's products, then you do not need to rely on PPC, just relevant search engine traffic to your blog.

What affiliate marketing or industry sites do you read regularly?

I do not read affiliate marketing sites, but I follow the latest news from **sitepoint.com**.

What is your favorite affiliate development tool or application?

I am not involved in affiliate marketing, so we do not use those tools. Again, we provide software to merchants to run their own affiliate program.

INTERVIEW WITH WEI YAU

Wei Yau is the founder of DH Softwares. He lives in Melbourne, Australia. **www.dhsoftwares.com**, enquiries@dhsoftwares.com.

INTERVIEW WITH EMILY ROBBINS

What is your experience with Affiliate marketing?

I've been doing affiliate marketing for over a decade, and have had many months where my affiliate earnings exceeded five figures.

When just starting out as an affiliate, what advice can you give someone?

Diversify, diversify, diversify. Many affiliates say it is important to stay focused on a particular niche, and try to dominate in that area. I partially disagree; it is better to choose about five different niches to start, and create five different affiliate sites promoting those niches. It is always hard to tell which niche will work well for you and which will not, which advertisers within those niches will convert, and how the search engines will rank each of your sites. Do not put all of your eggs in one basket — if Google decides it does not like one of your sites, at least you have others to fall back on.

For a small business that wants to start their own affiliate program, what words of wisdom can you give them?

Choose a program where your affiliates can choose their own landing pages, even if you decide to do an in-house affiliate program. For example, if an affiliate is promoting a specific product of yours on their site, it is better if their affiliate link enables them to send their visitors to that product's page within your Web site instead of to your homepage — you will get far more conversions. Both Linkshare and Commission Junction have features that allow for this, but my personal opinion is that Commission Junction has done a much better job of this. The benefits of going with Commission Junction or Linkshare are that they have a large network of affiliates to whom they will promote your program. If you are not already a well-known brand or site, then I believe that justifies the expense of the high fees those networks charge.

INTERVIEW WITH EMILY ROBBINS

What advice would you give someone who is considering joining affiliate programs?

First, evaluate the company or Web site. How easy is it to navigate, search for products, etc.? Do they require a customer to create an account before the customer can check out or even see their final cost including tax and shipping? If so, avoid that affiliate program — those types of sites lead to many abandoned shopping carts. Check out their customer service policies. How easy do they make it for a customer to return a product if they do not like it? Customers need to feel safe buying on the Internet, and a good return policy, especially with free return shipping, ends up generating more sales. Decide if this is a Web site you would feel comfortable buying from.

Can you suggest three things merchants could do to help drive more sales from their affiliates?

1) Offer realistic tiered commissions.

2) Run contests where the affiliate who improves their sales by the largest percent over the previous month's sales, or something similar, will win a cool prize.

3) Allow affiliates to directly link to any page within your Web site.

As a potential affiliate, what qualities should I look for in merchants, and how do I find them?

The easiest way to find merchants is through affiliate networks like **www. cj.com, www.linkshare.com, www.performics.com, www.clickbank. com**, etc. You can also look for a link on a specific merchant's site that says Webmasters or Affiliates to find their in-house affiliate programs. Get recommendations from other affiliates in forums such as **www.abestweb. com**. Check out the merchants' EPC values (earnings per 100 clicks) — the higher, the better.

What is the relationship between Pay-Per-Click (PPC) and affiliate marketing? Should an affiliate use PPC in tandem with affiliate marketing?

INTERVIEW WITH EMILY ROBBINS

While there are many people who use PPC marketing to promote affiliate programs, the competition in that arena has gotten pretty stiff, and costs have skyrocketed. It is a very dangerous game to play — for some, it pays off big-time, but you can also spend a lot of money without results in a very short period of time. I personally avoid PPC and instead rely on search engine optimization (SEO) tactics to get natural, free traffic from the search engines.

Is it realistic for someone to make a living entirely on affiliate programs?

Absolutely. I used to work for a well-known software company as a software quality assurance engineer, which meant I was responsible for finding the bugs in the software as the developers wrote the code, and before the program was released to market. I worked outrageous hours but made a pretty good salary. But, I worked way too many hours without taking breaks in a poor ergonomic setting, and ended up on disability for about a year due to repetitive strain injury, including multiple-level disc damage in my cervical spine. The doctors all said I could never work full-time with computers again — no more overtime, taking very frequent breaks, no working during flare-ups — basically making me unhireable in the software industry.

Being unwilling to give up my love for computers, I decided to try to make a go of it on my own … something I do not think I would have had the guts to do had I not gotten injured … who quits a high-paying job to wing it and work from home? It took a while before the income started rolling in, but if you keep building sites, eventually the money starts pouring in and even snowballs. Ultimately, I ended up working only part-time, and making three times what I used to make at my old job. Granted, affiliate marketing is only a portion of what I do … I am all over the place: domain investing, blogging, SEO, keyword research … but affiliate marketing, especially for the first five years or so, has usually resulted in the bulk of my income.

That being said, you need to have a strong stomach to be in this line of business. Your income will vary, sometimes greatly, from month to month. You must set aside savings to compensate for the slow months and know that your income will rebound. There are a lot of variables at play — some sales are seasonal, sometimes search engines make changes to their algorithms that result in less traffic to your site — and you cannot control them all. Make sure you are comfortable with this varying income stream before you take on affiliate marketing.

INTERVIEW WITH EMILY ROBBINS

For a small business that has products to sell online, what advice can you give them before they deploy an affiliate program?

Offer a high enough commission to make it worthwhile for affiliates to promote your program. Allow affiliates to directly link to any page on your site, especially individual product pages. Spend a lot of time figuring out your terms and conditions; questions like, "Will you allow an affiliate to use PPC to bid on your company name?" Consider going with an established affiliate network such as Commission Junction rather than using an in-house program. Ask for advice on affiliate forums.

What is the best thing a small business or individual can do to increase online income?

Use your affiliate Web site to pre-sell the customer on either the product or the merchant you are promoting. Use SEO tactics to try to get more traffic from the search engines. And, keep plugging away at it even when you are having a bad month.

How do you see affiliate marketing changing in the next five years?

The amount of competition may increase amongst affiliate marketers as more people enter the field. However, people are always giving up too soon and leaving the field, so who knows. Far more merchants will have affiliate programs. Hopefully the major affiliate networks will have even better user interfaces and reporting tools. I think affiliate marketing will grow significantly over the next five years, both for merchants and for affiliates.

What kind of Web sites does affiliate marketing work best for?

Given the wide variety of products available, as well as services one can promote, almost any niche should be able to find affiliate programs that work for them. Of course, the best types of Web sites are either those that promote or sell products or those that drive leads, such as requests for a health insurance quote, loans, and so on.

Are there any types of products that are particularly well-suited for affiliate marketing?

INTERVIEW WITH EMILY ROBBINS

Books, toys, electronics, and gifts all do well online. With electronics especially, people tend to do their research in brick-and-mortar stores to decide what to buy and then go online to find the best prices. Software or guides that are available for instant download online are particularly well-suited for affiliate marketing.

What is the most important thing to remember when beginning or promoting an affiliate program?

I cannot address beginning an affiliate program, as I have not done that. With regard to promoting an affiliate program, make sure you are in compliance with the Terms and Conditions of the merchant you are promoting so you get paid for all those commissions you generate.

What is the relationship, if any, between blogging and affiliate marketing?

Blogging is simply one of many ways to conduct affiliate marketing. It is best suited for affiliate sites that want interaction with their visitors, since they will have the ability to comment on your posts. It also provides an easy method for those without much experience in technical Web site development, without having to delve too much into the code.

What affiliate marketing or industry sites do you read regularly?

RevenueToday.com,   AbestWeb.com,   Webmasterworld.com,   blog. affiliatetip.com, http://affiliate-blogs.5staraffiliateprograms.com.

What is your favorite affiliate development tool or application?

GoldenCAN's affiliate data feed solution.

INTERVIEW WITH MERYL K. EVANS

What is your experience with affiliate marketing?

I have been an Amazon.com affiliate for years and have found success as a casual games affiliate.

When just starting out as an affiliate, what advice can you give someone?

Research and pick the topic that interests you. You can find affiliate products from every category and industry.

For a small business that wants to start their own affiliate program, what words of wisdom can you give them?

Take your time to do it right by reading, educating, and creating a useful Web site.

What advice would you give someone who is considering joining affiliate programs?

After you figure out the topic of interest, research affiliate programs, and pick a handful that fit your needs. Having more than one service ensures you can offer a broader selection than if you stick with just one.

Can you suggest three things merchants could do to help drive more sales from their affiliates?

1) Provide a Web site or blog with valuable content— not just selling your stuff.

2) Update the content on a regular basis.

3) Make sure you have an "About" page. No "About" page makes you lose credibility quickly.

As a potential affiliate, what qualities should I look for in merchants, and how do I find them?

INTERVIEW WITH MERYL K. EVANS

A good way to find merchants is to look at reputable sites using affiliates and see what merchants they use.

Is it realistic for someone to make a living entirely on affiliate programs?

Like all things in life, it takes time. People do make a living off affiliate programs, but not without effort. Do not quit your day job; start building your affiliate program on the side.

For a small business that has products to sell online, what advice can you give them before they deploy an affiliate program?

Make sure there is a need for your products. Is it an eBook or videos? If so, is the content compelling enough to sell if no one has heard of you?

What is the best thing a small business or individual can do to increase online income?

Read, read, read.

What kind of Web sites does affiliate marketing work best for?

Blog and content-based, meaning lots of articles and resources. Do not just create a directory pointing people to affiliate sites. This is an instant turnoff.

Are there any types of products that are particularly well-suited for affiliate marketing?

Products work well if they are affordable and tangible. I do not like to recommend eBooks or video because people do not know you. The ones that succeed have established a name for themselves.

What is the most important thing to remember when beginning or promoting an affiliate program?

Give the users something, and they will buy in return. Give them junk, and they will treat your stuff as junk.

INTERVIEW WITH MERYL K. EVANS

What is the relationship, if any, between blogging and affiliate marketing?

Blogging provides an easy way to add content and reference products. If you are selling skydiving-related stuff, then write articles about skydiving — how to do it, how to get started, where to go for lessons, etc., and then link to products and services within the entries and on the sidebar. Take care to balance your content with ads — 80/20 is always a good rule, with the 20 percent being ads.

Meryl K. Evans, content maven, is the author of *Brilliant Outlook Pocketbook* and coauthor of *Adapting to Web Standards: CSS and Ajax for Big Sites*. Meryl writes and edits content for businesses and publications. She helps businesses build and maintain relationships with clients and prospects through content. She has been blogging for more than eight years on her Web site at **www.meryl.net**. She is the original editor-in-chief of Shavlik's, *The Remediator Security Digest*, a popular newsletter on computer security that started with a few thousand subscribers, and climbed to more than 100,000 subscribers during her tenure. She is also the editor of *Professional Service Journal*, an e-mail newsletter for business-to-business (B2B) service providers, Intel Solution Services' **Connected Digest**, Attus' **The Compliance Advisor**, and TailoredMail's *E-mail Marketing Insider*.

INTERVIEW WITH COLIN TELFORD

What is your experience with Affiliate Marketing?

I have been involved in affiliate marketing since we set up the first affiliate management agency in October 2004. R.O.EYE was developed following a clear requirement from merchants for professionally managed affiliate programs on the UK's affiliate networks. It was apparent at this time that although affiliate marketing was the new buzzword, many programs were running unmanaged on the networks and were out of control.

When just starting out as an affiliate, what advice can you give someone?

INTERVIEW WITH COLIN TELFORD

Clearly identify the niche that you are a specialist within. Understand how that niche translates online, who your competitors are, and the scope for scalability.

For a small business that wants to start their own affiliate program, what words of wisdom can you give them?

Do not expect the world from the beginning. Affiliate programs take time to grow because you are promoting your program and brand to consumers as well as affiliates. Where the brand is relatively unknown, it will take time and resources to build an effective affiliate schedule. Remember, there are up-front costs, and you should be looking at a level of returns over a 6-12 month period. But, do not over-invest; not all affiliate programs are a success.

What advice would you give someone who is considering joining affiliate programs?

An affiliate who is joining an affiliate program should first look into the conversion rate of the existing traffic to that merchant's site. Combine this with the commission on offer, and you can calculate what the levels of return are likely to be for the amount of traffic you are going to send through. Furthermore, if you are going to buy that traffic and invest, then it must generate the required ROI for you to move forward. Also, it is essential that you clarify exactly what the commission parameters are, and know exactly where you stand. The last thing an affiliate needs is to misinterpret the Terms and Conditions and invalidate their commissions.

Can you suggest some things merchants could do to help drive more sales from their affiliates?

Apply resources to their affiliate programs by either staffing internally or outsourcing the management. Be transparent to your affiliate base, and tell them exactly what is going on. The last thing your affiliates need is an updated shopping cart with no warning, major items going out of stock without notice, or the Web site closing down for repairs without any advance communications.

INTERVIEW WITH COLIN TELFORD

As a potential affiliate, what qualities should I look for in merchants, and how do I find them?

- Attractive commissions

- On-time payments

- High conversion rate

- Secure validation policy

- Unique propositions

- Healthy volume of creatives

- Open communication channel

What is the relationship between Pay-Per-Click (PPC) and affiliate marketing? Should an affiliate use PPC in tandem with affiliate marketing?

PPC affiliates can add incremental sales to the client's total sales in tandem with the merchant's own search activity. This works by either sending traffic directly to the merchant's page using keywords that have not been utilized by themselves or building their own landing pages and sites for the same keywords. In the second example, the affiliate may experience a higher conversion rate on their site than the merchant, and deep-link the user through to the shopping cart with more success. However, PPC activity may cannibalize the merchant's PPC or even SEO activity, depending on the maturity of the existing search campaign. Every merchant's situation is different.

Is it realistic for someone to make a living entirely on affiliate programs?

This is possible, and affiliates do leave their day job to become affiliates. However, the sector is maturing, and there are significant affiliate companies with healthy-sized teams and huge budgets that are trying to cover the affiliate possibilities for most active UK merchants. Finding a niche can be very profitable, but many profitable affiliates only supplement

INTERVIEW WITH COLIN TELFORD

their existing part-time or full-time jobs, and many achieve an amount to pay for their annual holiday!

For a small business that has products to sell online, what advice can you give them before they deploy an affiliate program?

They need to be price-competitive in order to attract the affiliate's attention.

What is the best thing a small business or individual can do to increase online income?

Search marketing first, affiliates second.

How do you see affiliate marketing changing in the next five years?

Bigger super-affiliates who develop into companies. Content sites developing into traditional publishers. Agencies becoming more important due to the lack of skill-set.

What kind of Web sites does affiliate marketing work best for?

Retail and finance.

After earning a media degree at Manchester University, Colin has focused his media career within online advertising and marketing. Honing his skills within the financial services and retail sectors, he has more than six years of experience creating and deploying online marketing and affiliate strategies for some of the UK's biggest blue chip brands. Colin is seen as one of the leading strategic minds within the affiliate community.

Colin Telford, Affiliate Director - R.O.EYE Limited. 9th Floor, St. James' Building, 79 Oxford Street, Manchester, M1 6FQ. **www.ro-eye.co.uk.**

INTERVIEW WITH ASHLEY DEVAN

What is your experience with affiliate marketing?

I am the director of marketing for Commission Junction, the largest affiliate network. Prior to Commission Junction, I worked for Dell Computers and oversaw their consumer affiliate program, so I have experience as an advertiser as well as a network provider.

When just starting out as an affiliate, what advice can you give someone?

Find a niche and make the most of it. Seek out as much advice as possible before you get started. There is a ton of easily accessible information already written on the subject of affiliate marketing, and a little due diligence up front will provide much more positive results down the line.

For a small business that wants to start their own affiliate program, what words of wisdom can you give them?

Know your value proposition cold. As a small business you will compete with hundreds of already established businesses for the attention of top publishers. Put yourself in the mind of a publisher by asking what benefits you have to offer your affiliate partners. Remember that your affiliate partners are an extension of your team, so treat them accordingly.

While a CPA program is inherently less risky for an advertiser (when compared to their CPM and/or CPC cousins) it actually presents a much greater risk for a publisher. The publisher can come up short on otherwise profitable traffic if the consumer's Web site visits do not convert. You must have a healthy conversion rate within your vertical to run a successful affiliate program.

What advice would you give someone who is considering joining affiliate programs?

Establish a mission for what you are trying to accomplish, and stay focused. If you have a blog or content site, find the right advertiser for your audience. Do not talk about a shoe program when your site is about kitchen electronics, it will not make sense, and will look like an advertisement

INTERVIEW WITH ASHLEY DEVAN

instead of a recommendation. Know your demographics, know what you are trying to communicate, and be realistic. For additional insight, consider attending the Affiliate Summit or individual networks' sponsored events.

Can you suggest three things merchants could do to help drive more sales from their affiliates?

Advertisers should focus on three basic concepts: Communication, Compensation, and Conversion.

Communication: Have monthly newsletters to communicate your top offers, and cultivate strong relationships with your top publishers.

Compensation: Make your payout terms competitive and fair. Recognize the need to structure your payout to meet the needs of different types of publishers.

Conversion: Create tools that help your publishers succeed, such as custom coupon codes, deep linking availability, an optimized data feed, fresh creative, and a search policy that encourages publisher search.

As a potential affiliate, what should I look for in merchants, and how do I find them?

Look for advertiser programs that support your message and your goals. Consider factors including compensation, cookie duration/return days, occurrence rates, EPC (if available), and product selection. If you are in a niche field, the compensation is more of a factor than selection. You can locate advertisers through search functionalities on all major affiliate networks, including Commission Junction's "Get Links" area. You can also find out if an advertiser has an affiliate program by checking the "Affiliates" tab on their site (usually located at the bottom of the page's navigation). Ask yourself a simple question: "Would I shop at this advertiser's site?" It is such an easy question, but it makes all the difference in the world. Many advertisers do not realize that the customer experience on their site may be horrible. Count the number of clicks it takes to check out. Most consumers do not appreciate a lot of flash content or pop-ups, so think twice before promoting advertisers who are still stuck in the Web 1.0 era.

INTERVIEW WITH ASHLEY DEVAN

What is the relationship between Pay-Per-Click (PPC) and affiliate marketing?

Should an affiliate use PPC in tandem with affiliate marketing? Believe it or not, they can complement one another. There is an urban marketing legend that they cannibalize one another, but we have seen advertisers shut down affiliate search and not be able to pick it up with the PPC campaigns that they run in-house or with an agency. Be careful about the balance: It doesn't have to be all or nothing, and the balance varies by business.

Is it realistic for someone to make a living entirely on affiliate programs?

It is definitely possible. We see it every day, although it is the exception and not the rule. It takes a lot of work to build the business, and maintenance is key to continued success. Things change quickly in this market. Many people start in affiliate marketing thinking it is the easy way out, but ask any successful publishers, and they will tell you it took old-fashioned hard work to get where they are.

For a small business that has products to sell online, what advice can you give them before they deploy an affiliate program?

Many smaller advertisers do not realize the difficulty of scaling their own operations. If cash flow presents an issue, consider running a paid search campaign that you can turn on and off. Use PPC to test your site's conversion rate. If you are not able to convert sales with PPC, then you have a major red flag for the success of your affiliate marketing program. PPC marketing allows advertisers the ability to pause a campaign in order to make adjustments before moving forward.

What is the best thing a small business or individual can do to increase online income?

Drive word of mouth. Smaller businesses have less to spend, so be sure you treat every customer or prospect like a newscaster. It is amazing how relationships drive behavior in smaller businesses. If the product is good, the word will spread even if there is little or no marketing effort. Focus on making your product or service invaluable to your customers, and you will have made a huge lead toward success.

INTERVIEW WITH ASHLEY DEVAN

How do you see affiliate marketing changing in the next five years?

I think social networking is going to change the way we do everything, turning everyone into a publisher of sorts. Affiliate marketing has come a long way since its inception. However, as a marketing channel it still needs to become more accountable. In the next few years, I see the industry leaders rising to the top, and the rest getting flushed out.

What kind of Web sites does affiliate marketing work best for?

Although content was king in the early days of affiliate marketing, SEO-rich coupon/deal sites and blogs that are directly marketing to consumers have great metrics. Search marketing is still a growing and viable business model for publishers, but you must be a skilled professional in search, and have a clear understanding of what the advertiser will and will not allow. Cash-back or incentive Web sites can provide repeat customers but are closely monitored by advertisers. This should not come as any surprise. Competitively priced, multi-product Web sites with strong brand recognition perform best.

Are there any types of products that are particularly well-suited for affiliate marketing?

Items with lower price points in which consumers are more likely to make quick, spontaneous purchases (vs. longer considered purchases) are generally better-suited for affiliate marketing. However, any products that sell well online, and do not require an extended sales cycle can do well also.

What is the most important thing to remember when beginning or promoting an affiliate program?

Focus on building quality relationships with valued partners rather than spending a lot of time working with a large quantity of publishers.

What is the relationship, if any, between blogging and affiliate marketing?

Blogging has yet to tap into the power of affiliate marketers. The concept.

INTERVIEW WITH ASHLEY DEVAN

of blogging is to make the Web experience more personal. By giving out advice on products and services, a blogger can have a potential revenue stream by communicating these through an affiliate program. By understanding what the reader's purpose is (i.e., bodybuilding blogs can link to supplements that the writer uses), it can be a powerful direct selling tool. Today it is a slim connection, but I suspect that in the future the bond will be stronger. In fact, I bet that by the time someone reads this, I will have already been proven wrong

What affiliate marketing or industry sites do you read regularly?

Here is a short list, certainly not all-inclusive: **www.revenews.com, www. abestweb.com , www.revenuetoday.com , www.clickz.com , www. adotas.com , www.jangro.com , http://goyami.corante.com**

What is your favorite affiliate development tool or application?

The Commission Junction Network, of course! I could not resist.

INTERVIEW WITH JB MCKEE

What is your experience with Affiliate Marketing?

I became interested in affiliate marketing in the late 1990s. My wife was making and selling hair bows. I made a simple site for her to sell the bows online, and naturally wanted to utilize an affiliate program to promote the site. However, I quickly became disillusioned by the costs to start a program, running into the thousands of dollars, which was beyond our capacity at the time. So I decided to create my own affiliate tracking solution.

Once created, I decided to offer it to anyone. At the time, I offered it free of charge. It was called FreeFiliate and was intended to be supported by advertising pop-ups. FreeFiliate was launched in August 2000. The free idea did not pan out due to the nature of affiliate marketing, and the amount of support required to set up a program. So I changed the program to FusionQuest and instituted a reasonable fee .

INTERVIEW WITH JB MCKEE

When just starting out as an affiliate, what advice can you give someone?

Do what you love. Create niche sites about things you are interested in. Build communities. Niche sites are the best way to promote targeted affiliate offers.

For a small business that wants to start their own affiliate program, what words of wisdom can you give them?

Persevere. Manage your expectations. Do not expect to join a major network and magically start making sales. Successful affiliate programs are actively managed. Find good targeted affiliates and make them a sweet offer. A few good, active super-affiliates are far better than many inactive regular affiliates.

What advice would you give someone who is considering joining affiliate programs?

Use good judgment. Check references. Make sure they are legitimate and will pay commissions due. If it does not look professional and has not been around long, be careful.

Can you suggest several things merchants could do to help drive more sales from their affiliates?

Stay in contact. Keep in front of them. Call them if possible. Affiliates join multiple programs; keep yours at the top of their list. If they produce, be sure to sweeten their commissions and offer them perks. Listen to them and build a good relationship.

As a potential affiliate, what qualities should I look for in merchants, and how do I find them?

Networks are a good place. If the network is paying the affiliates, you have a much better chance of being paid commissions due. Watch out for PPC offers as they generally have the most fraud and the most trouble.

INTERVIEW WITH JB MCKEE

What is the relationship between Pay-Per-Click (PPC) and affiliate marketing? Should an affiliate use PPC in tandem with affiliate marketing?

The problem with PPC is fraud. It is nearly impossible to totally mitigate fraud in a PPC program. Do not believe anybody who tells you otherwise. CPA is the way to go. Even if the traffic is not outright fraudulent, it may be useless or incentivized. For these reasons, FusionQuest no longer offers PPC tracking.

If referring to CPC advertising, like Google AdWords, this can be an effective method for affiliates to use. However, it is generally frowned on to bid on trademarks and compete with the merchant. Each program has their own policy on this.

Is it realistic for someone to make a living entirely on affiliate programs?

Absolutely. Many people are doing just that.

For a small business that has products to sell online, what advice can you give them before they deploy an affiliate program?

Do not go bankrupt paying for your affiliate tracking solution. Some are very expensive, needlessly so. Look for direct linking technology where the affiliate links are direct links to your site with no query string or redirection. Click-throughs are much higher; the links brand your domain, and will count toward search engine link popularity. Go with an experienced, stable company known for providing good customer support.

What is the best thing a small business or individual can do to increase online income?

Revenue sharing through CPA affiliate programs.

How do you see affiliate marketing changing in the next five years?

We will see the emergence of niche networks. Instead of the current massive networks of all kinds of affiliates promoting all kinds of programs,

INTERVIEW WITH JB MCKEE

you will see networks begin to spring up that focus on specific niches and verticals. These will be much more effective by matching up the right affiliates with the right programs and getting the affiliates the tools they need for their niche.

What kind of Web sites does affiliate marketing work best for?

It can honestly work for any kind of site. It is in the management of the program, not the type of product. Of course, products with higher margins are much better in that they can offer a more lucrative commission structure.

Are there any types of products that are particularly well-suited for affiliate marketing?

Informational products, which generally have very high profit margins, are particularly popular and work well. CPA programs for things like lead generation are also great. However, tangible products using data feeds are also very successful.

What is the most important thing to remember when beginning or promoting an affiliate program?

If you have traffic and are not able to sell through your site prior to setting up an affiliate program, you will not be any more successful after setting up a program. You want to have a proven product and sales funnel that you can pitch to super affiliates. The more stats the better. Conversion ratios and things of that nature are important to sell the productive affiliates on your program. Also, do not expect instant results. It takes months of hard work and management to make an affiliate program pay off.

What is the relationship, if any, between blogging and affiliate marketing?

Blogs are great ways to communicate with affiliates. Affiliates can use blogs to build communities to pitch affiliate products to. It would be nice to have the ability for merchants to offer blogs that can be subscribed to through affiliate links highlighting products and advertising offers and have the affiliates receive credit (this is in the works).

INTERVIEW WITH JB MCKEE

What affiliate marketing or industry sites do you read regularly?

http://blog.affiliatetip.com

www.5staraffiliateprograms.com

What is your favorite affiliate development tool or application?

FusionQuest, of course! **www.fusionquest.com**

J. B. McKee is currently CEO of FusionQuest, Inc., a full-featured yet affordable affiliate tracking solution. An e-commerce specialist and Internet system developer, J. B. founded FusionQuest in the summer of 2000 to provide an affordable yet robust affiliate tracking system for merchants to promote their e-commerce site through affiliate marketing.

Expert Affiliate Advice, Tips and Hints

This chapter contains information, advice, tips, tricks, and suggestions from expert affiliate marketers. This information is straight from the masters of the trade, and will help you to succeed as you begin your journey into affiliate marketing.

TIPS FOR AFFILIATE MARKETING SUCCESS BY ALLAN GARDYNE

Can you name five tips for successful affiliate marketing?

To succeed as an affiliate, one of the most powerful things you can do is write case studies. Most affiliates are going to read this tip and decide it sounds too much like hard work. That is good news for you. If you do it, you will stand out from the pack, and achieve results which are likely to be hugely better than theirs.

Here is a highly profitable example.

Ken Evoy's Site Build It! (SBI) has been my top earner for years, partly because it is a very good product, and partly because of the way I have promoted it. I usually receive five-figure monthly commissions from Ken.

Here is one of the most effective things I did: I hired an assistant, gave him a copy of SBI, and told him to read the instructions and create an affiliate Web site. When he had done that successfully, I asked to him to write an article describing what he had done. Later, he used SBI to create another successful site, and wrote a second case study.

His articles are not brilliantly slick. They are not talking about earning

TIPS FOR AFFILIATE MARKETING SUCCESS BY ALLAN GARDYNE

millions. What they do is give honest, precise details in an entirely credible way. That is why they work.

Here are the case studies Rupert wrote:

www.AssociatePrograms.com/articles/135/1/Affiliate-marketing-case-study-using-SBI

www.AssociatePrograms.com/articles/138/1/Web-affiliate-programs-experiment-2

Successful affiliate marketing is all about forming connections between you and your reader. Do not create a bland, boring, safe site that is just like 10,000 other sites. Take a few risks, be a little different, show some personality. It will help you make a connection, and it will help you be remembered and make sales.

In my newsletter, the articles that are different strike a chord with my readers. For example, when someone stole parts of my Web site, I wrote "Open Letter to a Thief." For days, I received a heap of encouraging e-mails.

On another occasion, I reviewed an off-topic book that had nothing to do with affiliate marketing. It was called, *Why Men Don't Listen and Women Can't Read Maps*. I discussed it simply because it intrigued me and I thought my readers would be interested. Judging by the feedback I received, they were.

When I was in the hospital in 2004 suffering from a rare blood disorder, anemia, and had to have a bone marrow transplant, I wrote about it in my newsletter. Then I reported my progress on our affiliate forum. This attracted a lot of attention, and although I was working much less than usual, 2004 turned out to be an excellent year financially, much better than 2003. How is that for turning a lemon into lemonade?

One more example: When someone e-mailed me complaining rudely about one of my newsletters, I used his remarks as the basis for an item that attracted a lot of comments.

Seven ways to be your own BS detector

TIPS FOR AFFILIATE MARKETING SUCCESS BY ALLAN GARDYNE

www.AssociatePrograms.com/articles/493/1/Seven-ways-to-be-your-own-BS-detector

Note that the item was not written just for entertainment. It also provides useful information and builds my credibility.

Collect e-mail addresses. When you collect e-mail addresses and publish a newsletter, or at least have a list of e-mail addresses you keep in touch with, you are connecting with people. First you connect, then you make sales.

Experts love to tell you that one particular method is the best way to earn a living online. I think they are wrong. I believe the best way is to think about your skills and interests, and design a business that matches them.

For example, if you hate writing but appreciate the importance of owning a newsletter, you could hire someone to research and write articles for you.

As soon as you can afford it, hire help. Hire assistants to do the tasks you are not very good at, or tasks you do not enjoy doing. You get powerful leverage by employing people to help you, and doing so makes your life more enjoyable. Over the years I have tried many different ways to hire assistants. Here is what I've learned.

10 ways to find online assistants

www.AssociatePrograms.com/articles/631/1/10-ways-to-find-online-assistants

Can you name five common mistakes in affiliate marketing?

I can do better than that. Here is an article I wrote that describes 12 mistakes affiliates make. It was written some time ago, but I still see affiliates making the same mistakes over and over.

12 mistakes affiliates make

www.AssociatePrograms.com/articles/108/12/12-mistakes-affiliates-make

TIPS FOR AFFILIATE MARKETING SUCCESS BY ALLAN GARDYNE

What other expert advice would you give to someone considering starting or joining an affiliate program?

If you are new to affiliate programs and are not sure where to start, I strongly recommend you concentrate on learning the basics. A friend of mine once commented to me that I have built a whole business out of simply concentrating on the basics. I suppose that is true. I try to avoid overcomplicating things.

An excellent way to start is to choose a niche and then build a keyword-rich Web site around that niche, designed to attract targeted, free traffic from search engines, and earn revenue from affiliate links.

My free affiliate program tutorial describes how to do this:

www.AssociatePrograms.com/articles/188/1/Affiliate-Program-Tutorial

Start today. The hardest step is the first step.

TIPS FOR AFFILIATE MARKETING SUCCESS BY TONY TATEOSSIAN

Make sure you:

- Have all the standard banner sizes

- Have banners to mesh up with most Web sites or a variety of banner graphics

- Have different landing pages corresponding to each banner's marketing message

- Enable six-month cookies in order for affiliates to feel comfortable promoting your products

- Pay out on commission and leads for most effective promotions

TIPS FOR AFFILIATE MARKETING SUCCESS BY TONY TATEOSSIAN

- Consider promoting a new affiliate program, go with **ShareASale.com** or ClixGalore.com

- Consider affiliate management sites like CJ.com and LinkShare.com, as they are the best way to go

- Create an affiliate sign up page on your site leading them to your affiliate management URL

- Test different banners to see which ones are performing better

- Send monthly newsletters to your affiliate list promoting your affiliate program.

Good luck with your affiliate programs!

Tony Tateossian

Tony@cosmodex.com, **www.Cosmodex.com**

TIPS FOR AFFILIATE MARKETING SUCCESS BY FRANK SYLVESTRE

Five tips for successful affiliate marketing.

- Build your own Web site.

- Build your list of subscribers.

- Invest in your education.

- Test everything.

- Track your promotions.

Five common mistakes in affiliate marketing.

- Thinking that money will come overnight.

- Wanting everything for free.

TIPS FOR AFFILIATE MARKETING SUCCESS BY FRANK SYLVESTRE

- No consistency.

- Failure to keep up with the trends.

- Not treating affiliate marketing like a business.

Learn everything you can about affiliate marketing, and promote your affiliate products like they were your own. Promote quality products and deliver value to people's lives. This is the key to success.

TIPS FOR AFFILIATE MARKETING SUCCESS BY VLAD MARCHENKO

Can you name five tips for successful affiliate marketing?

- Maintain constant contact with your affiliates.

- Use well-known technology.

- Be on time with affiliates commissions.

- Update, optimize your creatives inventory regularly.

- Competitive commission rates.

Can you name five common mistakes in affiliate marketing?

Not doing what is listed above.

What other expert advice would you give to someone considering starting or joining an affiliate program?

You are new, so do your homework. Study online resources, technology providers, affiliate-related forums, etc.

TIPS FOR AFFILIATE MARKETING SUCCESS BY GEORGE COZMO

Can you name five tips for successful affiliate marketing?

- Know what you are selling.

- Always be on the lookout for new products.

- Do use link cloaking.

- Try to establish yourself as an expert.

- When a project fails, do not hesitate to move on.

Can you name five common mistakes in affiliate marketing?

- Getting blinded by a big commission and trying to sell an unsellable product.

- Creating backlash by overhyping the product.

- Buying cheap traffic that fails to convert.

- Advertising in the wrong places.

- Lowering the guard once a project starts rolling in money.

What other expert advice would you give to someone considering starting or joining an affiliate program?

Affiliate marketing is always a long-term commitment. It takes time to build a decent Web site, a mailing list, and trust, and thus you will not be making money quickly. However, affiliate marketing is the real deal. It is how business online is made and where the real money is.

TIPS FOR AFFILIATE MARKETING SUCCESS BY ALEXANDER GUTIN

Can you name five tips for successful affiliate marketing?

- Get the right software to automate all the tedious tasks involved in affiliate marketing from sales tracking to payouts.

- Actively promote your affiliate program to get marketers to join.

- Research your competitors, see what they're offering, and beat it.

- Pay your affiliates generously and timely.

- Stay in contact with your affiliates on a regular basis.

Can you name five common mistakes in affiliate marketing?

- The "if you build it, they will come" mentality. Putting up a program isn't enough if no one knows about it. Promote it through your Web site and others.

- Paying your affiliates late. This causes distrust and for them to move to a competitor.

- Using software that's inadequate.

- Not giving your affiliates the resources they need to help sell your product.

- Never keeping your affiliates updated.

What other "expert advice" would you give to someone considering starting or joining an affiliate program?

Do your research. If you're starting an affiliate program, research your competitors. If you're joining an affiliate program, research it to make sure it's right for you.

TIPS FOR AFFILIATE MARKETING SUCCESS BY MERYL K. EVANS

Can you name five tips for successful affiliate marketing?

- Write relevant and valuable articles or blog entries with links to the affiliate product or service.

- Choose a topic, product, or service you know and often cover.

- Use more than one affiliate.

- Study your Web and other related stats (an e-mail newsletter, for example) to make sure you are using the right affiliates.

- Add content on a regular basis. If you post content once and leave it alone, everyone else will leave it alone, too.

Can you name five common mistakes in affiliate marketing?

- Using "spammy" content with keywords all over the place.

- Supplying content that is not valuable to readers. They recognize spam a mile away and will not read the content or click affiliate links.

- Selecting products and services not related to your topic or industry.

- Using banners all over the place. Stuffing your site with banners and animated ads chases off potential customers (not to mention makes your site look ugly).

- Jumping into affiliate marketing without doing research. It takes work — no miracle pill here.

What other expert advice would you give to someone considering starting or joining an affiliate program?

- Do not quit your day job for the affiliate marketing life.

- Build your affiliate marketing business slowly and thoroughly to ensure greater success. Do it slowly and get it right the first time.

- Do not believe the claims that you can become an instant millionaire with little effort. It takes work.

TIPS FOR AFFILIATE MARKETING SUCCESS BY MICHELLE ANTHONY & COLIN TELFORD

Can you name five tips for successful affiliate marketing?

- **Give a little:** Listen to what your affiliates need to push your product. Treat them as an additional arm of your sales channel. Affiliates invest their own resource in your product; as such, they will require resources from you too. Consider the materials you can provide to help affiliates ensure that they are sending through the best quality and most targeted traffic. If you are a finance company, provide eligibility criteria. If you are a travel merchant, compile a product feed or develop a search box. Do they need copy? Press releases for a blog? Can you supply discount codes? Of course, what we are talking about here is above and beyond the standard reporting on clicks, sales, and conversions.

- **Listen a lot:** Communication is essential, as your program will be dynamic, especially since affiliates are often at the forefront of Web technologies. Listen and react to changing needs; it is not just what is communicated, but how. Does your affiliate only like e-mail communication? Can he or she only accept calls after four o' clock? Work within the comfort zone of your key partners.

- **Build great relationships:** A large part of affiliate marketing is the synergy gleaned from the relationships you build. Like any relationship, it is a partnership and a two-way street. Providing the right feedback is also paramount; share statistics and program performance, and work towards building strategic partnerships. You will find that the more personable you are, the more people are willing to go that extra mile for you. Affiliate marketing is also a very vocal industry. Past mistakes are well-publicized, but if you gain trust and deal with issues swiftly, you will get a good write-up and great results.

- **Set clear terms of engagement:** Clarify the conditions of your program and give affiliates a chance to read and agree to these before they commence delivery. There are a wide range of affiliate genres, so think carefully about what you do and do not want to allow. Brand bidding PPC affiliates can be great at adding incremental sales, but unmanaged brand bidding can increase costs. So think through the pros and cons, then clearly state your standpoint.

TIPS FOR AFFILIATE MARKETING SUCCESS BY MICHELLE ANTHONY & COLIN TELFORD

- **Pick the right network:** Affiliate opinions on networks vary; some are undoubtedly more popular than others, but popular opinion is not always consistent. Certain networks excel in particular areas, so get some advice on the best network for your product as well as the extras available for the affiliates and for you as a client. Perhaps it is best for you to run the program on a closed network or in-house. If the affiliates are not happy, they will leave your program, so it pays to do your research.

Can you name five common mistakes in affiliate marketing?

- **Flawed commission model:** Your commission model must be attractive to sales partners, and should reward them fairly for the business they generate for you. Having a long lead-time is customary in some verticals but will rule out certain genres of affiliates depending on the risk taken to secure sales. Take a look at what other companies are offering and make your deal attractive.

- **Poor validations/poorly converting site:** Great commissions mean nothing if affiliates are only paid for every one in a hundred sales. You are likely to be met with lethargy and low morale. Ensure that your validation process is robust and your site converts traffic as well as it possibly can. Scan your site for leakage points and either account for these or mask them. Comparatively low commissions can sometimes be countered by a stronger than average conversion rate, which is an important factor in calculating earning per click.

- **Choosing image over efficacy:** Affiliate marketing is a sales channel, not a branding exercise. It is great when you can combine the two, but selecting pretty placements over robust productive affiliates will leave you with empty zeros on your bottom line.

- **Using a marketing budget over a sales budget:** Think about what your commission is based on. If it is cost per sale, then treat your program as part of the internal sales budget. Treating your affiliate program as marketing spend often leads to controversial cap setting or even more controversial budget shortages. This type of operation does not suit retail programs. In some cases, for example, where an action is a lead

TIPS FOR AFFILIATE MARKETING SUCCESS BY MICHELLE ANTHONY & COLIN TELFORD

and not a sale, a closed program run to budget is perfectly manageable, but possibly not on an open network solution.

- **Unrealistic expectations:** Remember that affiliate marketing is only one of many online channels. You cannot expect your affiliate channel to convert as heartily as search and direct activity. You will often be one of many merchants on a site, and there will be a drop-off rate from transition to affiliate site to client site during the online buying journey.

What other expert advice would you give to someone considering starting or joining an affiliate program?

Tips for starting a program

- **Ensure a good balance of genres:** Do not be over-reliant on one type of affiliate. Search engines are constantly moving the goal posts, and a whole genre can be disenfranchised overnight. Besides, we often see certain products performing differently across different types of affiliates.

Therefore, an effective genre mix is especially important on multi-product programs.

- **Ensure that your program is well-managed:** A good affiliate manager will get the full potential from the program. An unmanaged program is often reliant on a small number of unpoliced affiliates and can be heavily skewed towards pay-per-click activity. A program that is not managed effectively will be underutilized.

- **Promote your program properly:** Get the word out there. Affiliates cannot push your products if they are not aware of the program or its potential. Remember that you are selling the program to sales partners and not end users, so target your USPs correctly.

Tips for joining a program

- **Find your niche, both in terms of products and promotion.** Although affiliate marketing is still new, and there are plenty of opportunities, some verticals are becoming increasingly saturated. Think about how you are going to get traffic to your site. How are you going to achieve quick wins, yet run a sustainable, monetized site?

TIPS FOR AFFILIATE MARKETING SUCCESS BY MICHELLE ANTHONY & COLIN TELFORD

- **Use your contacts and your affiliate mangers:** Use your affiliate managers as much as possible. Get your affiliate manager to provide you with copy, reporting, unique codes. Ask for ideas for keyword lists. Use your industry contacts to further your knowledge, and share technical queries; there are many great brains out there willing to share their wisdom with new affiliates. Read industry blogs, and join the forums to take full advantage of the information available.

- **Take advantage of new opportunities:** Test new programs. We always recommend that new affiliates run a three-month trial to get a feel for the program and clear evidence of its potential for them. During the early stages try and get as much feedback as you can to help you optimize your site.

Michelle Anthony

Program Executive

E-mail/MSN: michellea@ro-eye.co.uk

Tel: 0161 228 1228 | Fax: 0161 228 0448

R.O.EYE Ltd | St James Buildings | 79

Oxford Street | Manchester | M1 6FQ

Colin Telford

Affiliate Director

E-mail/MSN: colint@ro-eye.co.uk

Tel: 0161 228 1228 | Fax: 0161 228 0448

R.O.EYE Ltd | St James Buildings | 79 Oxford Street | Manchester

TIPS FOR AFFILIATE MARKETING SUCCESS BY MICHELLE ANTHONY & COLIN TELFORD

TIPS FOR AFFILIATE MARKETING SUCCESS BY KARA HOFFMAN

Can you name five tips for successful affiliate marketing?

- Look for established affiliate programs, but don't ignore new affiliate programs with good potential. Do research and check what people say, keeping in mind that what worked for the others may not work for you.

- When joining the affiliate program, think of original ways in which you can present this product or service to your customers. Try to be unique.

- Do not use more than three affiliate banners on your site. Make sure that the banners and links are closely related to your Web site content.

- Change the affiliate banners from time to time. People get used to the content they see, and a new banner will catch their attention. Use your affiliate link in a smart way; write an interesting article and add your affiliate link there.

TIPS FOR AFFILIATE MARKETING SUCCESS BY KARA HOFFMAN

- Learn how to optimize your Web site for search engines before joining any affiliate program. No traffic, no money.

Can you name five common mistakes in affiliate marketing?

- Expectations and excitement that are too high when starting something new. Do not expect to start selling the moment you join the program.

- Investing too much into the program without the proper knowledge. Do not spend hundreds of dollars per month if you do not see any return of investment. Change tactics.

- Choosing the wrong affiliate program. If you do not like the product, you cannot sell it.

- Do not expect other affiliates to share their secrets. Why should they?

- Do not leave the successful affiliate program if the competitor offers to pay you more. Products and services differ. Take some time to consider and study the company and the offer.

What other expert advice would you give to someone considering starting or joining an affiliate program?

Take a look at your Web site. Is it user-friendly? How long do people stay on your Web site? Is your content unique and interesting? What can you suggest to your Web site visitors as an option that will go well with the services you offer? Ask yourself all these questions and then start looking for the right affiliate program. Depending on the market and commission, determine whether this program works for you or if it is better to sell links and place for the ads.

Kara Hoffman is currently the Head of the MyTemplateStorage affiliate program. She joined the TemplateMonster company in the spring of 2006 as the sales manager at **www.templatetuning.com**. She can be contacted at **www.mytemplatestorage.com**, E-mail: kara@templatemonster.com, Phone: 518-312-4162.

TIPS FOR AFFILIATE MARKETING SUCCESS BY KARA HOFFMAN

Ad: an ad is a banner, a graphic image, or set of animated images. An ad for a campaign is often known as the "creative."

Ad impression: An ad impression occurs when a user opens a Web page through a browser and sees an ad that is served on that page.

Ad rotation: Ads that are rotated into Web site ad spaces.

Ad space: Ad space is a space on a Web page that is reserved for displaying ads.

Ad view: A single ad that appears on a Web page when the page arrives at the viewer's display.

Affiliate: The publisher or salesperson in an affiliate marketing relationship.

Affiliate agreement: Terms between a merchant and an affiliate that govern the relationship.

Affiliate directory: Categorized listing of affiliate programs.

Affiliate fraud: Activity generated by an affiliate in an attempt to generate illegitimate, unearned revenue.

Affiliate link: A URL tracking link that identifies the affiliate and sends traffic to the merchant's Web site. These may be displayed as either text links, images, products, or banner ads.

Affiliate manager: The individual who manages and runs the merchant's affiliate program.

Affiliate marketing: Revenue sharing agreement between merchants and online publishers/salespeople, in which compensation is based on performance measures typically as a percentage of the sale.

Affiliate merchant: The advertiser in an affiliate marketing relationship.

Affiliate network: An entity providing services for affiliate merchants and affiliates.

Affiliate program: Also known as an associate program. The merchant will reward an affiliate for Web traffic, sales, or leads on a pay-per-click, pay-per-sale, or pay-per-lead basis.

Affiliate program directory: A listing of merchants' affiliate programs.

Affiliate software: Software which provides tracking and reporting of commissions based on Web traffic, sales, or leads on a pay-per-click, pay-per-sale, or pay-per-lead basis.

Authentication: An automated process that verifies an e-mail sender's identity.

Banner: An advertisement in the form of a graphic image on a web page.

Blacklists: Lists of IP addresses that are being used by or belong to organizations or individuals who have been identified as sending spam. Blacklists are often used by organizations and Internet Service Providers as part of their filtering process to block all incoming mail from a particular IP address.

Blog: Short form for Weblog. A blog is a public Web site with posts or entries, most often ordered with the most recent first. Blogs generally represent the personality of the author or reflect the purpose of the Web site that hosts the blog. Blog can also be used as a verb, meaning to maintain a blog by posting text, links, images, or other content using blogging software.

Blogger: A person who creates and posts to a blog.

Blogosphere: The Internet blogging community. The collective content of all blogs worldwide.

Blogroll: A list of blogs, usually placed in the sidebar of a blog, that reads as a list of recommendations by the blogger of other blogs.

Brand, brand name, and branding: A product, service, or concept that is publicly distinguished and known from other products, services, or concepts so that it can be easily communicated and marketed.

Click: When a visitor interacts with an advertisement by clicking on it so that they are taken to the destination page of the advertisement at the destination, but just started going there.

Click stream: A record of the pages a user requested in going through one or more Web sites

Click-through: The result of an ad click.

Click rate: Percentage of ad views that resulted in click-throughs.

Cookies: Small text files stored on the visitor's computer, which record information that is of interest to the merchant site. In affiliate software cookies are utilized to track which affiliate the web visitor came from and which banner or link they clicked.

Conversion Rate: Percentage of clicks that result in a commissionable activity.

Commission: Income an affiliate earns for generating sales, leads, or clicks.

Cost-per-click (CPC): The amount of money an advertiser will pay to a site each time a user clicks on an ad or link.

Cost-per-lead: Cost-per-action in which a visitor provides enough information at the advertiser's to be used as a sales lead.

Conversion rate: The percentage of site visitors who respond to the desired goal of an ad campaign (i.e. clicking on the advertisement) compared with the total number of people who see the ad campaign.

Domains: Registered domain name (with name server record)

Dynamic Ad Placement: The process by which an ad is inserted into a page in response to a user's request.

HTML: The language in which Web pages and blogs are written and created.

IP address: An IP address is a unique identifier for a computer on the Internet. It is written as four numbers separated by periods. Each number can range from 0 to 255. Before connecting to a computer over the Internet, a Domain Name Server translates the domain name into its corresponding IP address.

Manual Approval: The process of manually validating an affiliate application and then approving them after validation.

Merchant: The person or business selling the goods services.

Page impressions: A measure of how many times a web page has been displayed to visitors.

Page requests: A measure of the number of pages that visitors have viewed in a day. Often used as a crude way of indicating the popularity of your Web site.

Pay-per-click: The advertiser pays a certain amount for each click-through to the advertiser's Web site.

ROI: ROI is how successful an ad or campaign was in terms of what the returns were for the money invested.

Search engine marketing (SEM): Promoting a Web site through a search engine.

Search engine optimization (SEO): Making a Web site more friendly to search engines, resulting in a higher page rank.

Super Affiliates: The highest performing affiliates.

Two-tier Affiliate marketing: A system which allows affiliates to sign up additional affiliates below themselves, so that when the second tier affiliates earn a commission, the affiliate above them also receives a commission. Two-tier affiliate marketing is also known as MLM (Multilevel Marketing).

Unique visitor: A unique visitor is someone with a unique address who is entering a Web site for the first time that day.

Wiki: A collaborative online environment which allows contributors and readers to add to subjects, as in to **en.wikipedia.org**.

Yield: The percentage of clicks versus impressions on an ad within a specific page.

Recommended Reference Library

I recommend you build a quality reference library to assist you with your overall Web design, marketing, advertisement and marketing portfolio, SEO, and general business planning. While there are plenty of excellent books on the market, I definitely recommend you add the following to your library. All are available through Atlantic Publishing Company at **www.atlantic-pub.com.**

How to Use the Internet to Advertise, Promote and Market Your Business or Web site—With Little or No Money

Interested in promoting your business and/or Web site, but do not have the big budget for traditional advertising? This new book will show you how to build, promote, and make money off of your Web site, or brick and mortar store using the Internet, with minimal costs. Let us arm you with the knowledge you need to make your business a success! Learn how to generate more traffic for your site or store with hundreds of Internet marketing methods, including many free and low-cost promotions.

This new book presents a comprehensive, hands-on, step-by-step guide for increasing Web site traffic and traditional store traffic by using hundreds of proven tips, tools, and techniques. Learn how to target more customers to your business and optimize your Web site from a marketing perspective. You will learn to target your campaign, use keywords, generate free advertising, search-engine strategies, learn the inside secrets of e-mail marketing, how to build Web communities, co-branding, auto-responders, Google advertising, banner advertising, eBay storefronts, Web-design information, search-engine registration, directories, and real-world examples of what strategies are succeeding and what strategies are failing.

ISBN-13: 978-0-910627-57-3 • $24.95

The Complete Guide to Google Advertising—Including Tips, Tricks, & Strategies to Create a Winning Advertising Plan

Are you one of the many who think Google is simply a search engine? Yes, it is true that Google is the most popular search engine on the Web today. More than 275 million times a day, people use Google and its related partner sites to find information on just about any subject. Many of those people are looking for your products and services. Consider this even if you do not have a Web site or product. There are tremendous opportunities on the Internet and money to be made using Google.

Google has created numerous marketing and advertising products that are fast and easy to implement in your business today including Adsense,

Adwords, and the Google APIs. This new book takes the confusion and mystery out of working with Google and its various advertising and marketing programs. You will learn the secrets of working with Google without making costly mistakes. This book is an absolute must-have for anyone who wants to succeed in advertising on Google. This book teaches you the ins and outs using all Google's advertising and marketing tools. You will instantly start producing results and profits.

In addition to the extensive research placed in the book, we spent thousands of hours interviewing, e-mailing, and communicating with hundreds of today's most successful Google advertising experts. This book contains their secrets and proven successful ideas, including actual case studies. If you are interested in learning hundreds of hints, tricks, and secrets on how to implement effective Google marketing campaigns and ultimately earn enormous profits, then this book is for you.

ISBN-13:978-1-60138-045-6 • $24.95

Online Marketing Success Stories: Insider Secrets from the Experts Who Are Making Millions on the Internet Today

Standing out in the turmoil of today's Internet marketplace is a major challenge. There are many books and courses on Internet marketing; this is the only book that will provide you with insider secrets. We asked the marketing experts who make their living on the Internet every day — and they talked. Online Marketing Success Stories will give you real-life examples of how successful businesses market their products online. The information is so useful that you can read a page, and put the idea into action — today.

With e-commerce expected to reach $40 billion, and online businesses anticipated to increase by 500 percent through 2010, your business needs guidance from today's successful Internet marketing veterans. Learn the most efficient ways to bring consumers to your site, get visitors to purchase, how to up-sell, oversights to avoid, and how to steer clear of years of disappointment.

We spent thousands of hours interviewing, e-mailing, and communicating with hundreds of today's most successful e-commerce marketers. This book not only chronicles their achievements but is a compilation of their secrets and proven successful ideas. If you are interested in learning hundreds of hints, tricks, and secrets on how to make money, or more money, with your Web site, then this book is for you.

Instruction is great, but advice from experts is even better, and the experts chronicled in this book are earning millions. This new exhaustively researched book will provide you with a jam-packed assortment of innovative ideas that you can put to use today. This book gives you the proven strategies, innovative ideas, and actual case studies to help you sell more with less time and effort.

ISBN-13: 978-0-910627-65-8 288 Pages • $21.95

The Ultimate Guide to Search Engine Marketing: Pay-Per-Click Advertising Secrets Revealed

Is your ultimate goal to have more customers come to your Web site? You can increase your Web site traffic by more than 1,000 percent through the expert execution of Pay-Per-Click Advertising. With PPC advertising you are only drawing highly qualified visitors to your Web site. PPC brings you fast results and you can reach your target audience with the most cost-effective method on the Internet today.

Pay-Per-Click, or PPC, is an advertising technique that uses search engines where you can display your text ads throughout the Internet keyed to the type of business you have or the type of products you are promoting. Successful PPC advertising ensures that your text ads reach the right audience while your business only pays for the clicks your ads receive.

Master the art and science behind Pay-Per-Click Advertising in a matter of hours. By investing a few dollars you can easily increase the number of visitors to your Web site, and significantly increase sales. If you are looking to drive high quality, targeted traffic to your site, there is no better way than to use cost per click advertising. Since you only pay when someone actually clicks on your ad, your marketing dollars are being used more effectively and efficiently compared to any other advertising method.

By 2010 online marketers will spend $7 billion dollars on PPC advertising (JupiterResearch). Thousands of companies will waste precious advertising dollars this year on ineffective or poorly organized PPC campaigns. There is an art form to this method of advertising, and that is what this new book is all about: the secrets of executing a successful, cost-effective campaign.

The key to success in PPC advertising is to know what you are doing, devise a comprehensive and well-crafted advertising plan, and know the relationships between your Web site, search engines, and PPC advertising campaign methodology. This groundbreaking and exhaustively researched new book will provide everything you need to know to get you started on generating high-volume, high quality leads to your Web site. This new book will teach you the six steps to a successful campaign: Keyword Research, Copy Editing, Setup and Implementation, Bid Management,

Performance Analysis, Return on Investment, and Reporting and Avoiding PPC Fraud.

In addition, we spent thousands of hours interviewing hundreds of today's most successful PPC masters. This book is a compilation of their secrets and proven successful ideas. Additionally, we give you hundreds of tips and tricks to ensure your Web site is optimized for maximum search engine effectiveness to drive business to your Web site, and increase sales and profits. In this book you will find actual case studies from companies who have used our techniques and achieved unprecedented success. If you are interested in learning hundreds of hints, tricks, and secrets on how to implement Pay-Per-Click advertising, optimize your Web site for maximum search engine effectiveness, develop a cost-effective marketing campaign, and ultimately earn enormous profits, then this book is for you.

ISBN-13:978-0-910627-99-3 • $ 24.95

The Complete Guide to E-mail Marketing: How to Create Successful, Spam-Free Campaigns to Reach Your Target Audience and Increase Sales

Researchers estimate that by 2008 e-mail marketing revenues will surpass $1.8 billion dollars annually. Are you getting your share? According to Jupiter Research, 93 percent of U.S. Internet users consider e-mail their top online activity. E-mail is a fast, inexpensive, and highly effective way to target and address your audience. Companies like Microsoft, **Amazon.**

2008
Eric Hoffer Award
WINNER
Excellence in
Independent
Publishing

com, Yahoo!, as well as most Fortune 1000 firms are using responsible e-mail marketing for one simple reason. It works — and it generates profits immediately and consistently!

In this new groundbreaking book you will learn how to create top-notch e-mail marketing campaigns, how to build stronger customer relationships, generate new qualified leads and sales, learn insider secrets to build your e-mail list quickly, deal with spam filters, and the optimum days and times to send your e-mails.

You will have step-by-step ways to:

- Build your business quickly using responsible, ethical e-mail marketing

- Leverage your current Web site using auto responders

- Write effective e-mail advertising copy

- Develop newsletters

- Write winning subject lines

- Get high click-through rates

- Format your messages

- Put the subscription form on your site

- Use pop ups

- Use single or double opt-in subscriptions

- Increase the response rate of your offer dramatically

- Format your e-mail so that it will be received and read

- Choose between text or HTML e-mail (and why)

- Reduce advertising expenses

- Have measurable marketing results with instant feedback

- Automate the whole e-mail marketing process.

In addition, we spent thousands of hours interviewing, e-mailing, and communicating with hundreds of today's most successful e-mail marketing experts. This book contains their secrets and proven successful ideas, including actual case studies. If you are interested in learning hundreds of hints, strategies, and secrets on how to implement effective e-mail marketing campaigns and ultimately earn enormous profits, then this book is for you.

ISBN-13:1-60138-042-9 • $24.95

How to Open and Operate a Financially Successful Web-Based Business (With Companion CD-ROM)

With e-commerce expected to reach $40 billion and online businesses anticipated to increase by 500 percent through the year 2010, you need to be a part of this exploding area of Internet sales. If you want to learn about starting a Web business, how to transform your brick and mortar business to a Web business, or even if you're simply interested in making money online, this is the book for you.

You can operate your Web-based business from home, and with very little start up money. The earning potential is limitless. This new book will teach you all you need to know about getting started in your own Web-based business in the minimum amount of time. This book is a comprehensive, detailed study of the business side of Internet retailing.

Anyone investigating the opportunities of opening a Web-based business should study this superb manual.

You will learn to:

- Build your Web-based business through keywords

- Generate free advertising

- Use search-engine strategies

- Market through e-mail

- Build Web communities

- Find products

- Drop ship

- Deal with zoning issues

- Create your Web site, HTML, graphics programs, domain names, and templates

- Use Web hosting, bandwidth, e-mail, shopping carts, and affiliate programs

- Develop merchant accounts

- Use PayPal, e-checks, search engine submissions, Pay-Per-Click ads, and co-branding

- Make more money through auto-responders, Google, and banner advertising

- Establish your own eBay storefront, Web design information, search-engine registration

- Be a part of directories

- Get real-world examples of successful strategies.

While providing detailed instruction and examples, the author teaches you how to draw up a winning business plan (The Companion CD-ROM has the actual business plan you can use in MS Word™, basic cost control systems, pricing issues, legal concerns, sales and marketing techniques, and pricing formulas. You will learn how to set up computer systems to save time and money, how to hire and keep a qualified professional staff, meet IRS reporting requirements, plan sales, provide customer service, track competitors, do your own bookkeeping, monthly profit and loss statements, media planning, pricing, and copywriting. You will develop the skill to hire and fire employees without incurring lawsuits, motivate workers, apply general management skills, manage and train employees, and generate high profile public relations and publicity. You will have the advantage of low cost internal marketing ideas and low and no cost ways to satisfy customers and build sales. Learn how to keep bringing customers back, accomplish accounting, do bookkeeping procedures and auditing, as well as successful budgeting and profit planning development.

This manual delivers literally hundreds of innovative ways demonstrated to streamline your business. Learn new ways to make your operation run smoother and increase performance, shut down waste, reduce costs, and increase profits. In addition, you will appreciate this valuable resource and reference in your daily activities and as a source of ready-to-use forms, Web sites, and operating and cost-cutting ideas that can be easily applied to your operation.

ISBN-13: 978-1-60138-118-7 • $39.95

The Secret Power of Blogging: How to Promote and Market Your Business, Organization, or Cause with Free Blogs

Blog is short for weblog. A weblog is a journal, or type of newsletter, that is updated often and intended for the general public. Blogs generally represent the personality of the author or the Web site. In July 2006 the Pew Internet & American Life Project estimated that the US "blog population has grown to about 12 million American adults," some eight percent of US adult internet users. The number of US blog readers was estimated at 57 million adults (39 percent of the US online population).

If you have a product, service, brand, or cause that you want to inexpensively market online to the world then

you need to look into starting a blog. Blogs are ideal marketing vehicles. You can use them to share your expertise, grow market share, spread your message, and establish yourself as an expert in your field for virtually no cost. A blog helps your site to rank higher in the search engines. This is because Google and the other search engines use blogs because of their constantly updated content.

Tiny one person part-time businesses use blogs as well as companies like Microsoft, Apple, Nike, General Motors, Amazon.com, and Yahoo!. Most Fortune 1000 firms are using responsible blogs and blog marketing as well as advertising on blogs for one simple reason: it works. And, it generates profits immediately and consistently. In addition, many blogs earn additional revenue by selling advertising space on their niche-targeted blog.

In this new groundbreaking book you will learn how to create top-notch blog marketing campaigns, how to build stronger customer relationships, generate new qualified leads and sales, learn insider secrets to build your readership list quickly.

You will have step-by-step ways to:

- Build your business quickly using responsible, ethical blog marketing

- Get your blog into search engines

- Learn blog marketing strategies

- Step-by-step guide for increasing Web site traffic with your blog

- Leverage your current Web site

- Write effective blog copy

- Write winning subject lines

- Get high click-through rates

- Format your messages

- Increase the response rate of your offer dramatically

- Attract Advertisers

- Have measurable marketing results with instant feedback.

In addition we spent thousands of hours interviewing, e-mailing, and communicating with hundreds of today's most successful blogging experts. This book contains their secrets and proven successful ideas, including actual case studies. If you are interested in learning hundreds of hints, strategies, and secrets on how to implement a highly effective blog marketing campaigns and ultimately earn enormous profits, this book is for you.

ISBN-13: 978-1-60138-009-8 • $24.95

Word Of Mouth Advertising Online & Off: How to Spark Buzz, Excitement, and Free Publicity for Your Business or Organization-With Little or No Money

Word-of-Mouth Marketing, WOMM as it is commonly known, is the least expensive form of advertising and often the most effective. People believe what their friends, neighbors, and online contacts say about you, your products, and services. And, they remember it for a long, long time.

Word-of-mouth promotion is highly valued. There is no more powerful form of marketing than an endorsement from one of your current customers. A satisfied customer's recommendation has much greater value than traditional advertising because it is coming from someone who is familiar with the quality of your work.

The best part is that initiating this form of advertising costs little or no money. For WOMM to increase your business, you need an active plan in place, and do what is necessary to create buzz. If your business is on the Web, there are myriads of possibilities for starting a highly successful viral marketing campaign using the Internet, software, blogs, online activists, press releases, discussion forums and boards, affiliate marketing, and product sampling. Technology has dramatically changed traditional marketing programs. This new up-to-date book covers it all.

This all sounds great, but what is the catch? There really is none except you must know what you are doing. This groundbreaking and exhaustively researched new book will provide everything you need to know to get you started creating the buzz; free publicity about your product or service whether online or off.

In this easy to read and comprehensive new book you will learn what WOMM is, how to get people talking about your product or service, how to get your customers to be your sales force, how to get WOMM to spread quickly, how to automate WOMM, how to create a blog, create awareness, and how to amplify it. The entire process is covered here: marketing, dealing with negative customer experience, writing online press releases, creating a customer reference program, bringing together a fan club/loyalist community, naming VIPs, using flogs/photos, and spurring evangelism among influential people. Included are tactics that pertain especially to non-profits, including reputation management.

In addition, we have gone the extra mile and spent an unprecedented amount of time researching, interviewing, e-mailing, and communicating with hundreds of today's most successful WOMM marketers. Aside from learning the basics, you will be privy to their secrets and proven ideas.

Instruction is great, but advice from experts is even better, and the experts chronicled in this book are earning millions. If you are interested in learning essentially everything there is to know about WOMM in addition to hundreds of hints, tricks, and secrets on how to put WOMM marketing techniques in place and start earning enormous profits, then this book is for you.

ISBN-13: 978-1-60138-011-1 • $24.95

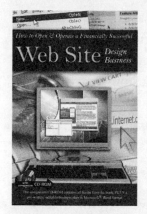

How to Open & Operate a Financially Successful Web site Design Business: With Companion CD-ROM

According to a 2007 survey by Netcraft, there are more than 108 million Web sites worldwide. Every Web site needs to be designed. The Pricing & Ethical Guidelines Handbook published by the Graphic Arts Guild reports that the average cost of designing a Web site for a small corporation can range from $7,750 to $15,000. It is incredibly easy to see the enormous profit potential.

Web design businesses can be run part- or full-time and can easily be started in your own home. It is one of the fastest growing segments of the Internet economy. This book will teach you all you need to know about launching a Web site design business in the minimum amount of time.

Here is the manual you need to cash in on this highly profitable segment of the industry. This new book is a comprehensive and detailed study of the business side of Web site design. This superb manual should be studied by anyone investigating the opportunities of opening a Web design business and will arm you with everything you need, including sample business forms, contracts, worksheets and checklists for planning, opening, and running day-to-day operations, plans and layouts, and dozens of other valuable, time-saving tools that no entrepreneur should be without.

While providing detailed instructions and examples, the author leads you through finding a location that will bring success, drawing up a winning business plan (the Companion CD-ROM has the actual business plan that can be used in MS Word), buying (and selling) a Web design store, pricing formulas, sales planning, tracking competitors, bookkeeping, media planning, pricing, copy writing, hiring and firing employees, motivating workers, managing and training employees, accounting procedures, successful budgeting, and profit planning development.

By reading this book you will become knowledgeable about basic cost control systems, retail math and pricing issues, Web site plans and diagrams, software and equipment layout and planning, legal concerns, sales and marketing techniques, IRS reporting requirements, customer service, direct sales, monthly profit and loss statements, tax preparation, public relations, general management skills, low and no cost ways to satisfy customers and build sales, and low cost internal marketing ideas, as well as thousands of great tips and useful guidelines.

The manual delivers literally hundreds of innovative ways to streamline your business. Learn new ways to make your operation run smoother and increase performance, shut down waste, reduce costs, and increase profits. Business owners will appreciate this valuable resource and reference it in their daily activities as a source for ready-to-use forms, Web sites, operating and cost cutting ideas, and mathematical formulas that can be easily applied. The Companion CD-ROM contains all the forms in the book, as well as a sample business plan you can adapt for your own use.

ISBN-13: 978-1-60138-143-9 • $39.95

The Complete Guide to Writing Web-Based Advertising Copy to Get the Sale: What You Need to Know Explained Simply

Since the advent of the Internet and since more and more people are making purchases online, writers have had to adapt to composing copy for the Web. Contrary to what many people think, writing for the Web and writing for print are not the same and involve very different skill sets. Instead of struggling to find the right words, copywriters should read this new book from cover to cover to discover how to write sales-generating copy.

The Complete Guide to Writing Web-Based Advertising Copy to Get the Sale
will teach you how to make your copy readable and compelling, how to
reach your target audience, how to structure the copy, how to visually
format the copy, how to forget everything you ever learned about writing,
how to pull in visitors, how to convince visitors to buy, how to outline and
achieve your goals, how to create a customer profile, how to create a unique
selling position, how to include searchable keywords in the copy, how to
convert prospects to paying customers, and how to compose eye-catching
headlines.

In addition you will learn about the trends in Web-based advertising;
the categories of advertising; the important information that needs to
be included in your copy, such as what you are selling, what sets your
product apart from the competition's, where you are located, what makes
your product affordable, and why you yourself would buy the product;
writing in the inverted pyramid style; the do's and don'ts of Web-based
advertising; and key phrases to incorporate in your copy. We will provide
you with some common mistakes to avoid, and tips for writing, revising,
and proofreading.

By incorporating the principles in this book, you will take your Web-based
advertising copy from boring to brilliant, while boosting your sales and
increasing your customer traffic.

ISBN-13: 978-1-60138-232-0 • $24.95

Internet Marketing Revealed: The Complete Guide to Becoming an Internet Marketing Expert

Internet Marketing Revealed is a carefully tested,
well-crafted, and complete tutorial on a subject
vital to Web developers and marketers. This book
teaches the fundamentals of online marketing

implementation, including Internet strategy planning, the secrets of search engine optimization (SEO), successful techniques to be first in Google and Yahoo!, vertical portals, effective online advertisement, and innovative e-commerce development. This book will help you understand the e-business revolution as it provides strong evidence and practical direction in a friendly and easy-to-use self-study guide.

Respected author and educator Miguel Todaro has created a complete introduction to Internet marketing that is instructive, clear, and insightful. This book is the result of several years of research and deep professional experience implementing online solutions for major corporations. Written in an instructive way, you will find fundamental concepts explained along with detailed diagrams. Many short examples illustrate just one or two concepts at a time, encouraging you to master new topics by immediately putting them to use.

Furthermore, you will find a variety of teaching techniques to enhance your learning, such as notes, illustrations, conceptual guidance, checklists of learned topics, diagrams, advanced tips, and real-world examples to organize and prioritize related concepts. This book is appropriate for marketing professionals as well as Web developers and programmers who have the desire to better understand the principles of this fresh and extraordinary activity that represents the foundation of modern e-commerce.

Finally, you will learn and understand why big and mid-size corporations in North America have redistributed more than $15 billion of their advertising budgets from traditional promotional activities to Internet marketing initiatives. Discover why online users spent more than $112 billion last year in the U.S. and Canada, and how you can be part of this successful business highway that is redefining the future of the world's digital economy.

ISBN-13: 978-1-60138-265-8 • $24.95

Bruce C. Brown is an award winning author of seven books, and an active duty Coast Guard Lieutenant Commander. He has served in a variety of assignments for nearly 24 years. Bruce is married to Vonda, and has three sons: Dalton, Jordan and Colton. His previous works include *How to Use the Internet to Advertise, Promote and Market Your Business or Website with Little or No Money*, winner of a 2007 Independent Publisher Award, as well as *The Ultimate Guide to Search Engine Marketing: Pay Per Click*

Advertising Secrets Revealed, winner in the USA Best Books 2007 Award program. He also wrote: *The Complete Guide to E-mail Marketing: How to Create Successful, Spam-free Campaigns to Reach Your Target Audience and Increase Sales; Complete Guide to Google Advertising: Including Tips, Tricks, & Strategies to Create a Winning Advertising Plan; The Secret Power of Blogging: How to Promote and Market Your Business, Organization, or Cause With Free Blogs,* and *Returning From the War on Terrorism: What Every Veteran Needs to Know to Receive Your Maximum Benefits.* His latest project, to be published in 2009, is entitled *The Complete Guide to Affiliate Marketing on the Web: How to Use and Profit from Affiliate Marketing Programs.* He holds degrees from Charter Oak State College and the University of Phoenix. He currently splits his time between Land O' Lakes, and Miami, Florida.

His books have been consistent best-sellers and have been recipient of prestigious awards such as the Best Book — USABookNews.com, Winner — Independent Book Publisher (Silver/Gold), INDIE Excellence Awards, and Book of the Year —— Foreword.

Index

D

E